ePro

ePro

Electronic Solutions for Patient-Reported Data

EDITED BY

BILL BYROM AND BRIAN TIPLADY

Routledge
Taylor & Francis Group

LONDON AND NEW YORK

First published in paperback 2024

First published 2010 by Gower Publishing

Published 2016 by Routledge
4 Park Square, Milton Park, Abingdon, Oxon OX14 4RN

and by Routledge
605 Third Avenue, New York, NY 10158

Routledge is an imprint of the Taylor & Francis Group, an informa business

British Library Cataloguing in Publication Data
ePro : electronic solutions for patient-reported data.
  1. Information storage and retrieval systems--Medical
  care. 2. Medical records--Data processing. 3. Self-report
  inventories--Data processing. 4. Clinical trials--Data
  processing.
  I. Byrom, Bill. II. Tiplady, Brian.
  362.1'0285-dc22

Library of Congress Cataloging-in-Publication Data
ePro : electronic solutions for patient-reported data / [edited by] Bill Byrom and Brian Tiplady.
    p. cm.
  Includes bibliographical references and index.
  ISBN 978-0-566-08771-4 (hardback)
  1. Clinical trials--Data processing. 2. Outcome assessment (Medical care)--Data
  processing. I. Byrom, Bill. II. Tiplady, Brian.
  [DNLM: 1. Electrical Equipment and Supplies. 2. Outcome Assessment (Health Care)--
  methods. 3. Clinical Trials as Topic. 4. Medical Informatics--instrumentation. W 84.41]
  R853.C55E67 2010
  610.285--dc22

                                                                            2010035548

ISBN: 978-0-566-08771-4 (hbk)
ISBN: 978-1-03-283791-8 (pbk)
ISBN: 978-1-315-58014-2 (ebk)

DOI: 10.4324/9781315580142

Contents

List of Figures

List of Tables

Foreword

The Patient's Viewpoint: Impact of ePRO Technologies on Clinical Research

Stephen A. Raymond

Orientation

What is the role of the patient in the discovery of new therapies? This foreword presents several main ideas intended to orient a newcomer to the context for the contributions in the book itself. It also introduces some concepts and vocabulary for the kind of research done with human beings as subjects. Such research is needed before regulatory authorities will allow companies to market new therapies. This background should help the reader understand what ePRO technologies are and how they have caused a major change in the conduct of such research by increasing the trustworthiness and reliability of reports coming directly from the subjects who consent to provide data in clinical investigations. During more than 50 years, the technology for capturing patient ratings and behavior consisted of pen and paper methods. Such methods were valuable to a point, but rarely overcame the skepticism of scientific reviewers. With ePRO methods, data provided directly by patients has better integrity and higher quality when compared with pen and paper methods. The result is that such data has crossed a threshold of scientific acceptance. There is now a growing attention to the viewpoint of the patient in medicine and research. In this book the reader will be informed about electronic methods and a variety of new technologies that are transforming clinical research. Such technologies merit study given the sea change in appreciation of the value of the patient's viewpoint at the councils where decisions are made about whether to deny or approve drugs, devices and medical procedures. Through ePRO, patients have a seat at that table.

Patient Reported Outcomes

When people report their personal opinions about a politician, restaurant or car, the reports may come directly from an individual but they are not 'outcomes'. In the context of clinical research outcomes are the results pertaining to the questions of interest in a clinical investigation. Some outcomes can be measured objectively. For example, tumor size can be tracked in area or volume; blood pressure in mm of Hg; body weight in Kg, lbs, stones; survival times in years, etc. This objective measuring of chemistry and process has been dominant in clinical research. No wonder the media so often call those who volunteer for clinical investigations Guinea pigs or lab rats. Here, we will call them subjects. Clinical evaluations (e.g. psychiatric functioning, improvement in arthritic joints, relative health of the subject, etc.) are another type of outcome usually supplied by clinical experts. For studies intended to provide evidence about how a therapy (drug, medical device or procedure) helps or hurts a patient, these *objective* measures and *clinical evaluations* are important outcomes. Ever since controlled clinical trials began in the late 1940s, these objective measures and medical assessments have been the main sources of scientific information for physicians deciding on a course of treatment. They have also been primary scientific resources for regulatory authorities deciding on whether to approve the marketing of a new drug or device.

For some outcomes, however, the patient knows best. Your doctor cannot measure how much pain you are experiencing except by asking you or by interpreting your behaviors. Your mother or caretaker cannot directly experience the level of nausea you feel. Exasperated parents guess at why their children cry, or wish that they could shoulder the debilitation of a childhood fever on behalf of a child. Although we might at times wish otherwise, we live inside ourselves and our direct experience is fundamentally personal. We can talk about it and share experience socially, but no matter how carefully others may observe us or listen to us, they do not become us. We are thus the direct best source for how we are feeling at any given time.

Given the findings of behavioral economics that show we make many decisions (what to buy, how much to pay) without knowing what has influenced us, one wonders when introspection may be true, or if it is merely interesting (Ariely, 2008). These answers still await us. There is work to be done to discover what we can learn by collecting self-assessments over time. These 'longitudinal' records of daily or even more frequent measures are just beginning to be explored scientifically and there is a lot left to learn.

This book is a compendium of work about how to obtain reliable information concerning three aspects of the experience of subjects engaged in clinical investigations: 1) how do they *feel* (pain, nausea, dizziness, anger, joy etc.); 2) how do they *behave* (I took a pill, I did my exercises, I urinated, etc.); and 3) how do they *function* (capacity to work, facility to integrate socially, ability to care for themselves). A patient in a clinical investigation is called a subject. For *feelings* (sensations and emotions) a subject is clearly *the* authority. Observers might have opinions but they do not have the direct experience of *feeling* or sensation. For *behaviors* subjects may also be the best authority, particularly when the behaviors occur where there are no observers who could undertake the responsibility of reporting them. Depending on the conditions of an investigation, observers can also provide reliable information about the behaviors of the subjects they observe. For assessing *function*, subjects have a viewpoint and probably should be part of the evaluation, but teachers, friends, work colleagues and professional evaluators are also legitimate sources for information about how well subjects perform.

In the world of clinical investigation, a patient reported outcome or PRO is 'any report of the status of a patient's health condition that comes directly from the patient' in other words a self-report, 'without the interpretation of the patient's response by a clinician or anyone else' (FDA, 2009). It is commonly understood, however, that the term Patient Reported Outcomes does not usually refer to objective measures made by devices such as blood pressure cuffs or thermometers. Furthermore, even though a *subject* in a clinical trial may in some cases NOT be a *patient* (i.e. not under the care of a physician for a disease or condition), these *subjects* nonetheless are said to provide PRO data when they use 'PRO instruments' to measure 'PRO concepts'. PROs are a class of measures made in a report coming directly from patients or subjects through interviews or self-completed questionnaires, or other data capture tools such as diaries, about their life, health condition(s) and treatment. Such measures are a logical cornerstone in establishing treatment benefit because they capture 'concepts related to patient symptoms, signs, or an aspect of functioning directly related to disease status' (FDA, 2009).

Pro Data and its Importance in Clinical Research Investigations

Over the last decade there has been a sea change in the investigations sponsored by the companies that develop new therapies. The viewpoint of the patient has begun to be included in the evidence gathered and evaluated in clinical investigations. In order for a drug to be approved for market, there must be 'substantial evidence' from 'adequate and well controlled investigations' of its safety and effectiveness in trials with human subjects. Such investigations are an industry of their own and billions of dollars are spent worldwide to be sure that patients will receive therapies that are proven and whose risks can be known in advance. The value of such testing became apparent in the US during the age of patent medicines and tonics where outlandish claims of benefits were made for substances of undisclosed composition. These had been offered directly to the general public with no controls on advertising or claims. Reforms followed episodes of contaminated food, the muckrakers' accounts of unsanitary practices in processing meat, and assessments that many patent medicines were either ineffective or dangerous. The Food and Drug Administration (FDA) was formed in the US to regulate these industries by instituting health standards and enforcing them by inspections. In approving medications, the FDA initially focused on 'safety', and while data on the effectiveness of therapies were considered, it was only safety data that the FDA required for their review panels to evaluate in approving drugs for market. In the 1960s there was a major regulatory change to require substantial evidence also for effectiveness. For the next 50 years, objective measures and medical expert evaluations have been the key elements in such substantial evidence. The direct viewpoint of the patient was rarely a component of decisions for market approvals, probably because the well-known deficiencies of PRO data on paper records made it difficult for review panels and scientists to trust such information (Raymond and Ross, 2000).

In the 1990's electronic technologies, now known as 'ePRO', were developed that have addressed many of the deficiencies of paper methods for obtaining reports directly from patients. Chapters in this book explain these deficiencies and how they have been overcome. Over the last decade sponsors (pharmaceutical and device companies conducting trials) and regulatory agencies (reviewing the results in the public interest) have become increasingly committed to considering PRO data obtained directly from the patient. Captain Laurie Burke of FDA has become a champion for the patient viewpoint as an important component of the evidence available, stating that 'Patients have a right to know how a treatment will affect them'. (Burke, 2006). The FDA has established criteria for PRO evidence that can be submitted by sponsors who seek to include claims of 'clinical benefit' in the formally approved product labels that are used by prescribing physicians (FDA, 2009). A therapeutic intervention may be said to confer 'clinical benefit' if it prolongs life, improves function, and/or improves the way a subject feels.

What the Subject Knows and Does Not Know

Subjects in clinical trials are not the best judges of whether the therapy being tested is working or not. In placebo controlled trials they may not even be recipients of the therapy under test. They might know how they feel at a given time but how can they be sure it is the therapy producing an improvement or perhaps causing a change for the worse? Maybe they would have gotten better anyway; maybe the chicken in yesterday's lunch was spoiled. Here's an illustrative story:

> *A year ago, a woman with diabetes visited her physician because she was having migraine headaches. The physician, a diabetologist, noted that the headache symptoms were not severe and elected not to prescribe treatment for the migraines. At the clinic he also noted that the patient had run out of her oral medication to control blood sugar and renewed her prescription. The patient filled the prescription and was pleased that her headaches went away. On her next appointment she thanked the physician for the wonderful pills and told him that they not only cured her headaches but when her husband had had a headache, with a moment's hesitation about sharing her prescribed medications, she gave some of her pills to him and he had been cured, too.*

The story shows how tempting it might be for subjects to believe strongly in the inferences they draw. The story should also help us to understand why FDA officials and clinical scientists are reluctant to take the opinions of subjects at face value concerning the effectiveness of therapies. The woman had not understood that in filling the prescription she had not obtained a new treatment for headaches but had renewed pills that she had been taking regularly for years. Instead, she inferred reasonably that the physician had intended to treat the headaches that had brought her to his office. Did the diabetes treatment cure headache? She had become convinced that the pills prevented her migraines. Her physician knew that preventing migraines was not a known clinical benefit of the diabetes medication he had prescribed. The story is a caution that will help us understand the need for clarity in writing questions to be used to obtain the viewpoint of a patient. Ideally, we should somehow distinguish facts or feelings patients should know directly and not confuse such reports with opinions that patients may merely believe.

What do patients experience when they are exposed to an experimental therapy in a clinical trial? They are not necessarily practiced in the art of introspective self-evaluation. Also, the scientists interested in the experience of patients may not know exactly how to guide the subject by selecting the right questions to ask. Not all investigators have the necessary skill or tools to prompt accurate and sensitive self-assessments from their patients. Furthermore, both parties, the subject and the scientist, have historically been limited by paper-based methods that have only recently changed to electronic. The exploration of what people can now discover and report about themselves is still near its beginning. We do not yet know how the increased use of ePRO technologies will extend the limits.

But we do know where to begin.

The first step in obtaining the viewpoint of the patient is obvious, and is suggested in the following maxim from an experienced expert researcher and wise man.

> *If you want to know what is happening to the patients, why not ask them?*
>
> *Dr Bengt-Erik Wiholm, MD, PhD, FRCP (London)*

If you had wanted to know what was happening to the diabetes patient in our story and had asked her opinion about the effectiveness of her recently prescribed medication, the resulting report, while fitting the definition of a PRO, would mislead because of the poor choice of question and because of the particular understanding she had of her own experience. So, how should we ask patients what is happening and how do clinical researchers obtain reliable and useful information from subjects?

A Branch of Science has Evolved to Ensure the Sensitivity and Reliability of Self Reports

Psychometrics is the study of measuring human psychological characteristics. Experts have learned how to avoid ambiguous questions of the sort that plague many surveys, e.g. Have you felt nauseated at any time during the morning today or have you been free of nausea? Yes/No. The discipline deals with the development of scales and measures and the methods for evaluating the accuracy, precision and reliability of self-reported assessments. As part of its interest in the patient's viewpoint, FDA has published guidance on the development and use of PRO measures that it would deem to be suitably valid and reliable for '*medical product* development', i.e. drugs, biologicals and devices. The document appeared in draft form in February of 2006, then as final guidance in December 2009 (FDA, 2009), and has captured the worldwide attention of the clinical scientists who design and carry out clinical investigations. The PRO Guidance notifies sponsors seeking to get approval for a medical product that the Agency considers the viewpoint of the patient to be useful and, if done properly, PRO findings concerning the patient's experience to be a legitimate and even welcome component of submissions for approval. Clinical teams worldwide are devoting increasing attention and effort to appraising the clarity, utility and validity of paper PRO questionnaires (PRO instruments) as well as to the task of properly developing electronic modes for gathering PRO data (ePRO). Chapter 2 concerns the psychometrics of ePRO and Chapter 3 presents evidence that ePRO instruments are more sensitive in measuring feelings and are as reliable as their paper counterparts.

We see that asking for subjects' opinions and conclusions can be misleading. What types of things can legitimately be asked of patients? It is generally agreed, even by militant logical positivists who philosophically discount variables that cannot be measured, that the most valid measure of pain is the patient's own report of it. And along with pain, the patient is the authority on other 'subjective' symptoms such as nausea, dizziness, fatigue, and moods such as irritability, anger and depression.

Psychometricians and 'outcomes researchers' have compiled evidence concerning what subjects do know and what they can gauge accurately. There are distinctions between a concept or construct such as 'flushing of the skin', which comprises several concepts that each have a degree of independence such as redness, warmth, tingling, and discomfort. Each concept might itself be graded by one or more 'items', which consist of a 'stem' and a 'scale' or 'response options'. For example, 'Rate the present intensity of your knee pain' might serve as a stem for an item pertaining to arthritic pain, and response options could be a set of descriptors ranging progressively from 'no pain', 'mild pain', 'moderate pain', 'severe pain'. As with measuring devices that sense and scale objective variables such as air pressure, PRO items differ in precision, accuracy, clarity, and reliability. Proving to a regulatory authority that a person's knee pain has, in fact, diminished by an important degree cannot be accomplished unless the items used in a self-report are ones that have been shown to be sensitive and reliable for assessing knee pain. One cannot rely on a seismometer to measure air pressure, and by analogy, asking a patient about distress; while distress might be important in its own right it would not be a suitable self- reported item if it was intended as a direct measure of pain.

Another factor to consider in reading the contributions in this book is the difference between a person's capability to make a rating based on remembered experience versus current experience. Immersed in live experience, people can use the flood of sensory input to make astonishingly resolved discriminations of the louder of two sounds, precisely match the colors of two objects, or perform other tasks that reveal the quantitative capabilities of human sensory physiological mechanisms (Rosenblith, 1961). Similarly, documenting contemporaneous behavior, e.g. 'tap here when you take your medication', is both simple and accurate in contrast to collecting similar information by asking a person to dredge it from memory: 'Did you take your medication today?, If yes, When?'. When it comes to subjective symptoms, evaluating a current symptom, e.g. 'rate your present pain', engages the full power of present consciousness for introspection concerning a perception or sensation. How much do I hurt *now*, I just took my pill; how well-rested do I feel *now*, how many times did I wake up last night, etc. Retrospective items, e.g. 'rate the average level of pain you experienced this week', engage the memory rather than the neural processes that support an active introspection for the intensity of present feelings. Memories fade and both scientists and regulatory bodies believe in the superiority of contemporaneous subjective assessments – a belief that is supported by the relative precision of timely PRO measures in comparison to recollected ones as presented in Chapter 1 of this book.

Value of Good Evidence About What Will Happen When Patients use a Medical Product

A MOGUL'S PERSPECTIVE

Imagine that you are in charge of a promising new cure for a prevalent disease such as ovarian cancer or Alzheimer's Disease. Take on the role of 'responsible person in charge' and think about the kind of evidence you would like to have in order to be sure that *you* would want to offer your cure to the public. Surely you would want to know that the therapy was an effective one, ideally more effective than other therapies available. Being a caring person you would also want to know about all the problems that the therapy could cause or aggravate. In these two objectives you would be aligned with regulatory authorities and past practice. In keeping with this tradition you might take guidance from medical experts who had observed subjects treated with your therapy in controlled clinical trials. After some thought you might also decide, especially if you were going to treat yourself, that you would like to know how it would be to undergo the treatment from beginning to end. How would you feel, what would happen, what would you experience, how well would you be able to function? As you came to understand how important such information would be to your own decision about using the therapy as a patient, you would certainly want to ask these subjects how they had felt during the clinical investigations. Even if you had no doubts about the truthfulness of the clinical experts, you would undoubtedly want information provided directly from patients. Equipped with such information, you would have a parallel means of assessing the efficacy and safety of the therapy by reviewing the self-reported symptoms and behaviors of subjects in these trials. Assuming that you proceeded to obtain direct evidence from subjects concerning subjective symptoms such as fatigue and nausea, symptoms that had also been evaluated by the medical experts caring for these subjects, you would likely be surprised at the poor level of agreement between the clinicians and their patients concerning how patients actually felt. Many studies show that what physicians or research associates glean from patients about symptom severity and symptom impact, for subjective symptoms ranging from fatigue to erectile dysfunction, does not match well with what patients report directly concerning the same symptoms. After reviewing such literature in an editorial urging that PROs be mandatory for toxicity reporting in clinical trials in cancer, Bruner noted that the more subjective the symptom, the lower the clinician-patient agreement (Bruner, 2007).

Think for a bit about what PRO evidence can reveal to patients, physicians and regulatory authorities and you will be able to appreciate how much more apparent such information is to the patient than to the physician. Such musings seem sensible and obvious when, as a therapy mogul, you arrange to administer your therapy in a trial and decide to capture timed self-assessments before and after the therapy. For each subject who volunteers to participate in your trial, you intend to learn:

- How severe were symptoms prior to the administration and how much were they changing?

- When was the administration done?

- How much did key subjective symptoms change at a certain time after the treatment?

- How long did it take for an effect to appear?

- How big was the effect?

- How long did the effect and any symptom change persist?

- How important was this degree of change to the subject?

- Given the variations in timing and dosing of the therapy, how important was close conformance to schedule and dose?

- Did other symptoms appear, and how strong were they?

- How much difference did they make in the way a subject who had such symptoms felt or functioned (symptom impact)?

Having played the role of the manager of a program and appreciated the economic, medical and ethical importance of what subjects can provide, you understand that properly executed PRO is a path to enlightenment. What you can explore in this book are examples of how *electronic* PRO methods (ePRO) provide such enlightenment. ePRO supplies documented evidence for regulatory authorities and other decision-makers. With such evidence you and they will know whether you should continue to pursue approval to market your medical product or devote resources to an alternative one.

A PATIENT PERSPECTIVE

Imagine now that you are a patient contemplating with your physician whether or not to undergo the therapy developed under the management of the Mogul. What would you like to have available for you to consider when deciding whether or not to try any prescribed therapy? No doubt you would appreciate the results of clinical research that had preceded market approval. You would learn what physicians and observers had concluded concerning efficacy and safety. You might also wish to have access to PRO results so you could forecast what your *personal* experience might be. The stories and personal experience of the subjects who were exposed to the medical product in the investigations would be of intense interest to you. Given that PRO methods had been used in the studies and that the findings from PRO instruments were part of the evidence available to practitioners and their patients, you could learn a lot.

You might want to know what is likely to happen during administration of the therapy; how much better you might get, and what will the treatments feel like; what were the varieties of personal history for patients who had used the medical product, both on average and in the extreme cases? Oliver Sacks writes, 'If we wish to know a man, we ask: What is his story – his real, inmost story? – for each of us is a biography, a story.' Our individual experience with a medical product is also a story and an essential way to learn about that product. FDA notes in its PRO Guidance (FDA, 2009) that patients are developing a sense of entitlement; they have a 'right' to know what to expect. To that end, claims supported by PRO evidence have been invited to be included in the Structured Product Label that accompanies all prescribed medications.

Personal Health Experiences in Clinical Research and Medical Care

How will PRO instruments ultimately affect clinical research and delivery of medical care? The following account of the introduction of a powerful medication gives us an exemplary story to show how such results might support a more participatory experience in both receiving and delivering medical care.

Many perceive a yearning for personal therapy and personal control of their own fate. To exercise such control it is almost an ethical matter that patients have access to the most trustworthy and accurate information available so they might decide how to balance risk and benefit.

In a conference in 2003, Dr Wiholm, whom I previously quoted, spoke about the Benefit/Risk ratio for drugs. He noted the need for valid information to 'share with patients' about the effectiveness and risk. He spoke about a 'dignified old lady' who had been angry that Merck had pulled a therapy for urinary incontinence because of a cardiac risk. Noting that the patient's 'risk acceptance' should be considered, he recalled the lady had asked him: 'Who are you to decide what I should die of?' Physicians generally do feel both justified and obligated to decide what therapies to administer on behalf of the patient because it is physicians who have access to medical literature about therapies and diseases as well as the expertise needed to make a 'good' decision. But can such information also become properly accessible to the patient? That is an agenda for the 21st century.

Dr. Wiholm also mentioned Lotronex, a Merck drug for irritable bowel syndrome that had been withdrawn because it caused ischemic colitis and constipation with reported deaths in a very few patients. But the drug was very powerful and effective for most others. To some public health officials, the risk of the drug was huge. The safety monitoring system for detecting and reporting adverse events showed that one in every 350 women who took it for six months suffered ischemic colitis as a result of blocked blood flow to the intestine. But to the people who had no other effective treatment, a 349-in-350 chance to lead nearly normal lives seemed a relatively small risk. For some who suffered from serious irritable bowel syndrome, Lotronex was the only drug on the market at the time that controlled their symptoms. There was concern by Dr Brian L. Strom of the University of Pennsylvania that AE monitoring was insensitive, resulting in 'vast' underreporting. After the recall, many people who had taken or prescribed Lotronex lobbied the FDA to restore market approval. The restriction lasted two years, but the FDA then permitted the drug to be prescribed under conditions of managed risk. So Merck designed a proactive risk management program to remarket the drug for severe cases, and trained prescribers to be part of the program. The program included a treatment contract specifying rigorous (and expensive) follow-up and close patient auditing as well as cessation of treatment within four weeks for any patient for whom the drug was 'not working'.

When there is an effective but risky medical product, what is the proper role for regulatory authorities, physicians, medical product developers and patients? The discussions and debates get heated, but such critical circumstances seem to cry out for better and more dependable evidence of symptom impact on individuals who clearly differ in susceptibility to side effects. Who is really at risk? During such extended treatment ePRO could provide timely information on the individual's degree of improvement, the occurrence of a sudden worsening, and other data that could prompt and guide timely intervention. Such careful monitoring for subjects based on ePRO data that patients furnish at visits has proven to be helpful; monitoring using ePRO data that patients provide daily or more frequently is just beginning to occur (Basch et al, 2007).

ePRO and 'Personalized Medicine'

Personalized medicine, where treatments would be tuned to individual differences, is a promising idea. Much work at present focuses on genetics, genomics or proteomics. Such work is rarely accompanied, however, by the collection of data about individual behavior, diet, attitude, mood or environment. Underlying this emphasis is technology that evaluates genes and gene expression in individuals with the idea that this evaluation will help predict *personal* response to tamoxifen, anti-depressants, or other prescription drugs metabolized by particular enzymes. The hope is that the prediction then will reliably indicate which drug and dose would maximize benefit and reduce side effects for an individual who is tested for gene activity and protein expression.

It is an appealing idea, particularly when the people exploring it are open to the importance of behavioral and environmental factors (Personalized Medicine Coalition, 2009). It is known, for example, that identical twins are not always allergic to the same things. Even if each has asthma, attacks will differ in severity and triggers for one may not match the stimuli that trigger attacks in the other. This knowledge establishes an important fact: individuals who begin life with the same genome will diverge in susceptibility to disease. It seems very likely that they will also differ in responsiveness to treatment. In an interesting study of identical twins living near San Francisco where 51 pairs differed on socio-economic status, the health measurements and self-reported level of health tended not to cluster with the genetic relationship but were linked to jobs. Health behaviors and measures tended to be better for the twin with the 'professional' job.

Pharmacogenomics explores the genetic basis of patient response to therapeutics, and it has had some successes. In October of 2006, for example, an FDA subcommittee agreed that the activity of a particular enzyme (CYP2D6) was a predictor of efficacy of tamoxifen treatment for breast cancer. But the text for the drug label recommended by FDA suggested that patients be notified that low CYP2D6 metabolizers who take tamoxifen have a higher risk for breast cancer recurrence. The mathematical description of risk and its quantification by 'frequentist' methods gives a person 'odds', but not necessarily a sense of the range of personal experiences that may occur. The stories of individuals, which could be gathered by ePRO reports, are today not laid out for review. From the kinds of data that are presently collected we cannot tell how people felt who were found to be improved nor if their experience differed from 'low CYP2D6 metabolizers' who did *not* suffer recurrence. The finding concerning group susceptibility is medically important, but in my opinion is not sufficiently personal because genomics data is too narrowly limited to encompass an individual story.

Technologies for Pro

The art of capturing data for human clinical trials is in flux. The underlying technology is changing from paper to electronic methods, and this book discusses the several electronic methods. See Chapter 5, for example, where the choice of solution is reviewed.

EVOLVING FROM PAPER TO ELECTRONIC METHODS OF PRO DATA CAPTURE

While we do not discuss in this book capturing PRO measures on paper, that 'paper technology' has strongly shaped the scientific approach to capturing data from patients. A paper questionnaire, for instance, usually has many questions because paper pages have space for a lot of text, and is intended to be completed relatively rarely – features that make sense when the interaction with the patient will occur at a visit to an investigative site. For electronic capture of PRO measures different constraints apply, and the tracking of PRO measures often includes frequent sampling with fewer items (ratings or responses). Two types of PRO measures are commonly implemented as ePRO today:

1.   Questionnaires, usually with several concepts, multiple domains and many items that have been validated for administration using paper forms;

2.   Diary type reports, usually with few concepts and items that are asked often (daily) and that are increasingly being directly developed for electronic administration.

EARLY ELECTRONIC PATIENT DIARIES (STORE AND PRESERVE)

MiniDoc AB was the first commercial organization to provide electronic patient diaries for use in sponsored clinical research for approvals of medical products. Using proprietary handheld devices as shown in Figure F1, the MiniDoc system stored data that patients entered from home and preserved it for later review and transmission from the site. The devices captured data long-term, and had a display screen, but lacked a touch screen and send capabilities. This meant that the data had to be off-loaded to a personal computer (PC) before being sent to a central server.

Figure F1   The MiniDoc proprietary handheld patient diary system
Source: Stephen Raymond.

In 1995, the architecture changed dramatically for such portable handheld units and systems were designed to support the daily sending of data captured and stored on each patient's handheld device to a central web server (Jamison et al (2001), Raymond et al (1998)). Automated telephone systems came into use to capture ratings to a central server (Interactive Voice Response Systems – IVR) at about the same time. As use of the Web, personal computers, cell phones, PDA's, wearable sensors, tablet computers, etc. has exploded, the universe of technical platforms for ePRO measures has also expanded.

PORTABLE EPRO/ESOURCE DATA CAPTURE TOOLS (STORE AND FORWARD, CENTRALIZED DATA)

Portable ePRO handheld devices, most commonly known for their electronic patient diary (EPD or eDiary) applications, are fully mobile and typically utilize touch-sensitive screens or telephone key pads for patient data entry. Front-end edit checks, data timestamps, programmed response time windows, alarms and alerts as will be described in chapters of this book correct or prevent many of the most common errors that patients make when completing paper forms. Electronic methods provide more and higher quality data than the traditional paper diary methods that ePRO is now replacing.

Modern eDiaries, see Figure F2 for an example, feature devices with store and forward capabilities or direct online connectivity that can transmit data to a secure central server complex for storage and review. This typically means that on completion of an eDiary report or item subjects transmit the data from their location to a server hosted by the ePRO provider. The data can then be made instantly available for permission-based review over the Web by investigative sites and sponsors.

eDiaries are translated, shipped and used by study subjects all over the world. Most providers are able to deploy updates and mid-study changes to devices in the field seamlessly from the central server. Physical logistical management of shipping and tracking devices through customs, etc., can provide a challenge, as can the reliability of telecommunications in some geographical areas. Most providers offer both analog and wireless handheld devices depending on the location of the subject and the ideal underlying telecommunications infrastructure of that geography. Some of these devices, wireless smartphones especially, feature smaller screen sizes that can be problematic for certain subject populations, such as geriatrics or the sight-impaired.

The Impact of ePRO

A principal impact of ePRO is that it supports reliable and accurate datastreams coming directly from the patient. Such reliable evidence of self-reported personal experience is new. We can now gather not just common experience but a personal, individualized view of therapeutic action. In the past you could

Figure F2   A contemporary handheld patient diary system based upon Palm technology

Source: Stephen Raymond.

introspect and observe. You might even introspect and write as a diarist like Proust or Samuel Pepys, but you did not have a structured assessment, validated scales, adaptive content. And you did not send the results incrementally where they could be analyzed longitudinally and compared to the results from other individuals across the world engaged in a common study using validated items. Thus, ePRO is like a psycho-behavioral two-way telescope that has the promise of telling us the truth of our experience. In terms of the scientific method, ePRO offers scientists the chance to collect and observe empirical measures and is a platform for discovery of individual stories, individual differences, and the detailed, high resolution description of change in individuals over time. A hallowed and proper role for such empirical evidence dawned in the Renaissance when Francis Bacon emphasized a scientific method as the way to free the mind from erroneous preconceptions. What sorts of erroneous beliefs and limited understandings might we have that ePRO may ultimately banish?

Bias is insidious. Our natural tendency is to require little evidence to support what we already believe and to reject evidence that contradicts our beliefs. We change our minds reluctantly. Irrational bias occurs when we hold a belief in the face of overwhelming evidence against it, when belief itself is the virtue, not the veracity of the belief. Scientists are not immune. For example, it is a widespread conviction among lay public and scientists alike that exercise assists in losing weight. Yet there is very little evidence of the sort that would be required of a therapy under trial to support this conviction. An important part of a scientific education is to learn and appreciate the rules that have been established over time to help us use evidence to arrive at truth. One practice that tends to surprise non-scientists is the discipline of devising experiments to provide evidence to *disprove* a hypothesis. When such experiments succeed, like the Michelson- Morley evidence that the speed of light did not depend on direction, they overcome entrenched beliefs that are erroneous. Such findings become important corrections for those who seek to find what is true. A trust in science remains bedrock for clinical researchers. But the challenge of discovering and preventing bias is daunting, requiring vigilance and honesty. At the beginning of the twenty-first century the findings of clinical trials are reported widely in public media and there is great interest in learning about ineffective or dangerous therapies.

The promise of ePRO is the emergence of veritas from the observed world. The importance and need to base policy on truth was eloquently stated by John F. Kennedy at the 1962 Yale University Commencement:

As every past generation has had to disenthrall itself from an inheritance of truisms and stereotypes, so in our own time we must move on from the reassuring repetition of stale phrases to a new, difficult, but essential confrontation with reality.

For the great enemy of truth is very often not the lie – deliberate, contrived and dishonest – but the myth – persistent, persuasive, and unrealistic. Too often we hold fast to the clichés of our forebears. We subject all facts to a prefabricated set of interpretations. We enjoy the comfort of opinion without the discomfort of thought.

Mythology distracts us everywhere...

John F. Kennedy (1962)

Concluding Comment: Clinical Research and Beyond

If ePRO offers the promise of measuring subjective experience and exposing our individual stories to study, then it is worth thinking again about the importance of measurement.

I often say that when you can measure what you are speaking about, and express it in numbers, you know something about it; but when you cannot measure it, when you cannot express it in numbers, your knowledge is of a meagre and unsatisfactory kind; it may be the beginning of knowledge, but you have scarcely in your thoughts advanced to the state of Science, whatever the matter may be.

William Thomson (1883)

While ePRO is a technology and infrastructure, it is interesting to think about the areas ePRO uniquely combines:

1. Introspection, observation, self-assessment – some of us spend a lot of our life looking inwards;

2. Self-reporting, notes, records – historically much of our self-observations have vanished in the haze of forgetfulness;

3.   Measurement, quantification over time, scaling – the precursor to analysis and discovery in science.

Could ePRO be a gateway to a better future?

Last night I felt disappointed with my day; I had worked hard but had accomplished less than I had hoped, and the undone tasks appeared mountainous. I was anxious and felt stress. This morning I awakened to a quiet city, covered with fresh snow. I feel calmer, more confident. My feelings *are* my experience, and they have changed without much observable alteration in my circumstances. I suggest you look no further than to your own experiences to see that your own feelings change, and some probably change quickly. All cultures have clichés about how powerful feelings, beliefs and ideas are in a world of imposing physicality. Faith moves mountains; there is nothing so powerful as an idea whose time has come, etc. Although weightless and without apparent substance or force, thoughts and feelings animate both individuals and cultures to act, and physical realities co-evolve with thought. In life, one's feelings, attitudes and thoughts are possibly the most important aspects of personal history, not just what happened. Recording and measuring subjective experience opens the door for psychological engineers who will use such measurements in conjunction with age-old yearnings to 'improve' experience. Could they manage the creation of a more joyful world, one being at a time, by developing a means to direct the simple ordinary miracle of changing one's mind? Through free choice informed by self assessments, one by one we might learn how to move the center of the psychological universe from where it is now to where we might wish to take it.

REFERENCES

Ariely, D. (2008). *Predictably Irrational: The Hidden Forces That Shape Our Decisions*. Harper Collins; NY: 304.

Basch, E., Lasonos, A. and Barz, A. et al. (2007). Long-term Toxicity Monitoring via Electronic Patient – Reported Outcomes in Patients Receiving Chemotherapy. *Journal of Clinical Oncology*; 25: 5274–5380.

Bruner D.W. (2007). Should Patient-Reported Outcomes Be Mandatory for Toxicity Reporting in Cancer Clinical Trials? *Journal of Clinical Oncology*; 25: 5345–5347.

Burke, L. DIA Webinar, April 5, 2006. Available http://www.dia.org

Clinical Data Interchange Consortium (CDISC). CDISC Clinical Research Glossary Version 6.0. Applied Clinical Trials 2007; 16: 12–50. http://www.cdisc.org/glossary/index.html

Food and Drug Administration. Guidance for Industry: Patient-Reported Outcome Measures: Use in Medical Product Development to Support Labeling Claims (Final), December 2009. Available at: http://www.fda.gov/downloads/Drugs/GuidanceComplianceRegulatoryInformation/Guidances/UCM193282.pdf, accessed 8 December, 2009.

Jamison, R.N., Raymond, S.A. and Levine, J.G. et al. (2001). Electronic diaries for monitoring chronic pain: One-year validation study. *PAIN*; 91: 277–287.

Kelvin, Lord. Electrical Units of Measurement. In (ed.) Thomson, William *Popular Lectures and Addresses* (1891–1894, 3 volumes), vol. 1, London. 1883, 73.

Kennedy, J.F. Commencement Address at Yale University. June 11, 1962. http://www.jfklibrary.org/Historical+Resources/Archives/Reference+Desk/Speeches/JFK/003POF03Yale06111962.htm, accessed 18 November, 2009.

Personalized Medicine Coalition. http://www.personalizedmedicinecoalition.org/sciencepolicy/personalmed-101_overview.php, accessed 18 November, 2009.

Raymond, S.A., Gordon, G.E. and Singer, D.B. (1998). 'Health Monitoring System'. United States Patent No. 5,778,882 July 14, 1998.

Raymond, S.A. and Ross, R.N. (2000). Electronic subject diaries in clinical trials. *Applied Clinical Trials*; 9: 48–58.

Rosenblith, W. (1961). *Sensory Communication*. MIT Press, Cambridge MA.

Sacks, O.W. (1998). *The Man Who Mistook His Wife for a Hat*. Simon & Schuster, NY: 110.

Wiholm, B-E. Worldwide Product Safety and Epidemiology, Merck Research Labs, DIA Conference on 'Quality of Life, Patient Reported Outcomes' March 17, 2003. – cited *Expediting Drug and Biologics Development, A Strategic Approach*, 3rd edn p. 200, Linberg, S. (ed.) Barnett © 2006.

About the Editors

Bill Byrom, PhD completed his PhD in disease control simulation at Strathclyde University in 1990 and this work took him to Africa to study the effects and spread of cattle diseases. This interest led him to join the pharmaceutical industry in 1991 where he began as a clinical trial statistician. Bill transitioned to clinical development where he became a trial director working in a number of early phase therapy areas. Before joining ClinPhone in 2000, Bill took on responsibility for the scientific content of the European market launch of a new antipsychotic agent. Throughout his clinical trials experience Bill maintained an active interest in how new technologies and methodologies could be leveraged in clinical development programmes, and so his move to Perceptive Informatics (formerly ClinPhone) in 2000 was an ideal fit. In his role as Senior Director of Product Strategy he has helped to shape a number of the company's products and services including ePRO solutions, patient recruitment technologies and RTSM (Randomization and Trial Supply Management) solutions. Bill is currently responsible for the company's eClinical strategy. Bill has authored over 60 articles in international and trade journals and is a regular speaker on the conference circuit. Outside the office, he enjoys time with his family and regularly spends cold evenings and wet weekends coaching his daughters' football teams.

Brian Tiplady started in the pharmaceutical industry in 1976 as a neuroscientist with Astra, carrying out clinical research in depression. His first involvement with computers in clinical research was with cognitive testing, comparing the sedative effects of new and old antidepressants, as well as their interactions, particularly with alcohol. For most of his career, academic and commercial interests have developed in parallel, and he worked on the mechanisms of these effects as well as the practical implications, using alcohol as a model compound.

Clinical research in depression naturally involves collecting data from patients, sometimes indirectly with clinician ratings, sometimes directly with self-rating scales. Brian was active in this area, not yet called patient reported outcomes (PRO), looking at the effect of clinician training on reliability of assessments and at approaches to scale development. When the first pen-based digital assistants (PDA) appeared in 1993, Brian initiated studies to evaluate their usefulness as patient diaries and questionnaires in respiratory and gastrointestinal conditions. Having helped to show that this approach is practicable and well-liked by patients, Brian continued to support the use of ePRO technology both with devices and interactive voice response (IVR) within Astra/AstraZeneca.

In 2004 he moved to invivodata Inc®, a vendor of electronic diary solutions, initially providing scientific support for ePRO. With the establishment of PRO Consulting he has been working more broadly on patient-based data collection methodology, and issues around the documentation and support of assessment strategies in clinical research. He continues to be active in cognitive testing, having developed both the first pen-based and the first mobile-phone-based applications in this area. He is an Honorary Research Fellow at Edinburgh University (Anaesthesia, Critical Care and Pain Medicine) and holds a Visiting Chair at Northumbria University (Psychology). He has published extensively in the areas of psychopharmacology and patient-reported outcomes.

List of Contributors

Paul Beatty has been a survey researcher for over 20 years, working for much of that time at the Questionnaire Design Research Laboratory at the U.S. National Center for Health Statistics (NCHS). He has contributed to the design and evaluation of dozens of major surveys, in addition to conducting research on question testing methodology, the design of complex questions, and cognitive aspects of survey response. Currently he is Chief of the Ambulatory and Hospital Care Statistics Branch at NCHS. He has a PhD in Sociology and an MA in Applied Social Research, both from the University of Michigan.

Sonya L. Eremenco, MA, has more than 14 years of experience in the field of patient-reported outcomes research and instrument development. She is currently ePRO Program Manager for United BioSource Corporation's (UBC) Center for Health Outcomes Research. Prior to joining UBC in 2008, she served as Director of Translation and Formatting Services at the Center on Outcomes, Research and Education (CORE) at the Evanston Northwestern Healthcare Research Institute. Ms. Eremenco received her MA in Multicultural Communication from DePaul University in Chicago and she received her BA in Cultural Anthropology with a concentration in linguistics from Duke University.

Dr Allen Ganser has a PhD in Physiology, UC, Berkeley (1974, BS in Biochemistry University of Wisconsin). He and associates currently provide clinical trial analytical and design services, particularly in the area of patient reported outcomes. In collaboration with Dr Stephen Raymond he discovered that the myelin sheath and Schwann cell modulate nerve conduction in single axons. Ganser Associates began as toxicology consultants (1990) with emphasis on neurotoxicity. Dr Ganser was Vice President of Biological Operations at MicroVesicularSystems (1989–90) developing liposomal-based vaccines and drug delivery systems. He did academic research at Harvard Medical School in Neuropathology/Neuroscience (1978–89) following post-doctoral research at McGill University in Cell Biology (1974–76). He discovered the enzyme that secretes gastric acid, anticipating the 'blockbuster' drug, Omeprazole, that inhibits it.

Breffni Martin, who took his BSc in Biochemistry at University College Dublin in 1983, spent the subsequent 25 years working in the pharmaceuticals industry, mainly in various aspects of late stage drug development. He currently runs Regintel, a life sciences consultancy based in Ireland. His chapter is based on several years involvement with the development of an ePRO-type solution aimed at resolving some of the issues associated with obesity.

Damian McEntegart studied Statistics at Bristol, Southampton and York Universities. After working as a statistician in the pharmaceutical industry for 20 years, Damian joined Perceptive Informatics (formerly ClinPhone) in 2002 where he is responsible for managing a group of 18 specialists. The areas his group supports are implementation of ePRO, randomisation and medication management algorithms. Damian has published over 40 articles on the areas that he supports.

Mikael Palmblad is a business analyst at AstraZeneca with a special interest in value management. He has been involved in developing and applying information technology in clinical research for many years, running his first ePRO trial in 1994 and building and deploying a pen-based eCRF system in 1995. Starting in 1996, he was part of the team that developed the first web-based data capture system used in regulatory clinical trials. In later years he has been developing and applying methodology for valuing investments in business improvement in pharmaceutical research.

Jay D. Pearson received a PhD in Human Population Biology from Pennsylvania State University in 1989 with a specialization in gerontology. His dissertation research used electronic data collection of behavioral observations to study the relationship between stress and health in traditional, modernizing, and migrant Samoans. From 1989 to 1995, he conducted longitudinal studies of age-associated diseases at the National Institutes of Health. Since 1995, Jay has been an epidemiologist at Merck Research Laboratories and holds an adjunct faculty position in the Urology Department at Johns Hopkins Hospital. Since 1999, he has been project leader of a Merck initiative to use ePRO technology to collect diary and questionnaire data in clinical trials and epidemiologic studies.

James Miguel Pierce has more than 10 years of experience in the pharmaceutical industry and is currently Principal Partner and Scientific Advisor at a boutique consulting firm providing a range of business development and commercialization services to the pharmaceutical industry. He has held positions ranging from Medical Science Liaison to Scientific Advisor. Skilled in both science and commercialization activities, including global medical marketing strategy, Dr Pierce was most recently a scientific consultant to the pharmaceutical and biotech industry on how best to incorporate patient reported outcomes (PROs) measures into clinical trials programs to support product labeling claims. He also has substantial direct industry experience having spent most of his career in a variety of medical affairs functions – managed care strategy, regional and global medical marketing brand management, key opinion leader strategy, investigator initiated study strategy, and medical communications strategy across multiple phases of drug discovery. In addition to his scientific responsibilities, he has deep expertise in global alliance management and development.

Stephen A. Raymond's interest in tracking individuals emerged from measuring the effects of impulse activity on firing thresholds of nerve axons. Longitudinal measurement was a common thread throughout his career: physiology (BS, Stanford University & Ames Research Center), neurophysiology (PhD, MIT 1969), electrical engineering and computer science (Asst. Professor at MIT, 1970–2001) and Anesthesia and Neurophysiology (Faculty, Harvard Medical School, Brigham & Women's Hospital, 1981–2002). He developed several electronic instruments and invented the personal health tracker in 1995. He co-founded PHT in 1994 to track trial subjects as they undergo experimental therapies, joining PHT as Chief Scientific Officer in June of 1997.

Dennis A. Revicki, PhD is Senior Vice President, Health Outcomes Research, at United BioSource Corporation in Bethesda, MD, with over 25 years experience in designing and conducting studies involving health-related quality of life assessments and instrument development. Dr Revicki's primary research interest is in studying health outcomes including applications of health-status assessment and health-utility measures in clinical trials and outcomes research, and mental health services research. Dr Revicki holds faculty appointments in the Department of Health Policy and Administration, University of North Carolina at Chapel Hill, Department of Epidemiology and Health Policy Research, University of Florida, and the Department of Psychiatry, Georgetown University Medical Center.

Alan Shields, PhD is trained as a clinical psychologist with emphasis in study design and instrument development. As a Senior Scientist for PRO Consulting®, the scientific division of invivodata Inc®, he works with industry groups developing and implementing PRO and ePRO instruments for use in clinical trials across a wide variety of therapeutic areas. Dr Shields is published in the areas of PRO instrument development and evaluation, regulations guiding development and implementation of PRO tools and the use of ePRO in real world settings. Dr. Shields has a BA in Psychology from the University of Dayton and a PhD in Clinical Psychology from the University of Montana.

Saul Shiffman, PhD is Research Professor of Clinical and Health Psychology, Psychiatry, Pharmaceutical Sciences and Clinical Translational Research at the University of Pittsburgh, and co-founder and Chief Science Officer of invivodata Inc®, which provides electronic diary services for clinical research. He was among the first to develop and use palm-top computers for real world, real time data collection. With Arthur Stone, he developed the fundamental concepts of Ecological Momentary Assessment, systematizing the methodological framework of diary and ambulatory assessment. Professor Shiffman has published over 300 scientific papers, and has been awarded the Good Clinical Practices Lifetime Achievement Award, among other honors.

Arthur A. Stone is Distinguished Professor and Vice-Chair of the Department of Psychiatry and Behavioral Science at Stony Brook University. He received his PhD in Clinical Psychology in 1978 from Stony Brook University and has been there since then. His research interests are primarily in the fields of behavioral medicine, self-reporting of patient symptoms and the measurement of well-being and emotions, and he has published widely in those fields. Professor Stone has served in various national and internal positions, including as editor-in-chief of both the *Annals of Behavioral Medicine* and *Health Psychology* and as the president of the Academy of Behavioral Medicine Research.

Keith W. Wenzel received his Bachelor of Science in Computer Information Systems from Northern Arizona University in 1987. He presently holds the position of eClinical Product Director with Perceptive Informatics, a clinical trial technology provider. Mr. Wenzel is a member of the core committee for the DIA's Study Endpoints SIAC. He is also a member of the leadership council of ISPOR's ePRO special interest group. He is author or co-author of several PRO-related articles and software systems including ACT, a database management system for clinical trials; CAID, a computer administered interview driver designed to eliminate the need for programming when automating Likert-type scales; and PDID®, an interview driver for interactive voice response systems.

Introduction

Bill Byrom and Brian Tiplady

As this book goes to press the FDA final guidance on Patient Reported Outcome (PRO) measures has just been published (Food and Drug Administration, 2009), three years since the draft guidance appeared in 2006. Produced by Captain Laurie Burke (Director, Study Endpoints and Label Development, Office of New Drugs, CDER, FDA) and colleagues this guidance is essential reading for anyone who wishes to use data from PRO measures to support product claims. PRO measures are increasingly being used as primary or key secondary endpoints for regulatory submissions (Willke et al. 2004), and a number of successful submissions have been made with electronic (ePRO) methods in recent years (see, e.g. Byrom and Mundt, 2005; Clauw et al., 2008). Sonya Eremenco and Dennis Revicki review regulatory issues, including the FDA guidance, in Chapter 4 of this book.

The guidance states that '...*an instrument will not be a credible measure without evidence of its usefulness from the target population of patients'*. Clearly the patient's perspective is central when assessing symptoms of an illness, or the impact on a person's everyday life. But the guidance goes beyond this, emphasising the importance of patient input in *constructing* the instruments used for PRO assessments, and the need to show that the instrument is relevant and valid in the specific patient group being studied. This is a welcome perspective. Using a generic instrument that asks subjects to assess their ability to walk a block or ascend a flight of stairs, for example, will be inappropriate to use with patients whose mobility is compromised, making such routine tasks difficult or irrelevant. Several chapters of this book consider aspects important to demonstrating the validity of an instrument in the target group, including Paul Beatty's Chapter 2 on cognitive interviewing, Mikael Palmblad's Chapter 5 on selection of an appropriate ePRO solution and Brian Tiplady's Chapter 8 that deals with the optimal design of electronic patient diaries.

One of the driving reasons behind the increased adoption of ePRO over paper diary methods is data quality. A long-standing anecdotal concern about paper diaries is 'parking lot compliance', which refers to a patient completing a month's worth of diary entries just before a clinic visit. In their seminal article in the *British Medical Journal*, Stone et al. (2002) showed conclusively that this was a real and a major factor in data quality. In their study, using an embedded light sensor to record when a paper diary was opened and closed, they found that few subjects recorded data on schedule and some even completed their diary ahead of time! Researchers using paper diaries often report high diary completion rates, and assume that this represents good data. As the Stone et al. article demonstrates, this is not necessarily the case. Importantly the FDA guidance picks up on this theme and states: *'If a patient diary or some other form of unsupervised data entry is used, we plan to review the clinical trial protocol to determine what steps are taken to ensure that patients make entries according to the clinical trial design and not, for example, just before a clinic visit when their reports will be collected.'* This is a compelling reason to consider an electronic solution which can be designed to incorporate fixed data entry windows to prevent or limit retrospective entries, and time and date stamping to provide evidence of exactly when entries were made. Alan Shields, Saul Shiffman and Arthur Stone consider the topic of recall as it applies to the design of studies incorporating patient reported outcomes in Chapter 1 of this book.

A second interest driving increased adoption of ePRO is the apparent promise of not just more valid data but cleaner, less noisy data — leading to the potential to reduce the sample size for equivalent statistical power. This topic is explored in Chapter 3 by Allen Ganser, Steven Raymond and Jay Pearson , who present previously unpublished study data comparing the quality and power of PRO data collected electronically and with paper. Their study supported this hypothesis. To capitalise on such potential benefits, researchers should plan to identify/develop and study ePRO in learning phase studies to enable accurate sample size calculation for confirmatory trials, a conclusion also proposed by the FDA guidance.

This book brings together the essential themes and topics that researchers should consider when developing and implementing patient reported outcome measures electronically in clinical research or healthcare. In their second chapter, Chapter 6, Alan Shields, Saul Shiffman and Arthur Stone discuss methods to improve and measure diary compliance. In Chapter 7 Bill Byrom, Keith Wenzel and James Pierce review data on instruments designed to replace or compliment subjective clinician assessed scales, such as those used in CNS studies. Case study data in this chapter provides a strong case for the use of electronic assessment methods to reduce bias in baseline assessments when these also form part of study inclusion criteria. Damian McEntegart in his chapter on equivalence designs, Chapter 9, provides a valuable and comprehensive reference for the statistical methodology appropriate to demonstrating equivalence between paper and electronic PRO modalities when migrating existing diaries from original paper versions.

To complete the book we look back into the history of ePRO (Steven Raymond, another of the industry's early ePRO pioneers, presents his view of this in the foreword) and then beyond clinical trials into the wider utility of electronic patient reported outcomes. As more and more of the population become connected to various communication devices such as the internet, mobile phones and smart phones, the potential to utilise ePRO concepts and components in the provision of routine medical care or self-help disease management programmes is now a reality. In Chapter 10, Breffni Martin considers this with an example of a mobile phone solution developed for disease management of patients suffering from obesity. We (Bill Byrom and Brian Tiplady) develop this theme and other future directions in our final Chapter 11.

We are very grateful to all the contributors to this book, all of whom represent experts and thought leaders in the ePRO industry. We believe that it will provide a valuable reference for all involved in collection of patient reported outcomes, both within clinical research and more widely within healthcare.

References

Byrom, B. and Mundt, J.C. (2005). The value of computer-administered self-report data in central nervous system clinical trials, *Current Opinions in Drug Discovery and Development*, 8:374–383.

Clauw, D.J., Mease, P. and Palmer, R.H. et al. (2008). Milnacipran for the treatment of fibromyalgia in adults: A 15-week, multicenter, randomized, double-blind, placebo-controlled, multiple-dose clinical trial, *Clinical Therapeutics*, 30:1988–2004.

Food and Drug Administration (2009). Guidance for Industry. Patient Reported Outcome Measures: Use in Medical Product Development to Support Labelling Claims. US Department of Health and Human Services, FDA. December 2009. Downloaded 17th December 2009 from http://www.fda.gov/downloads/Drugs/GuidanceComplianceRegulatoryInformation/Guidances/UCM193282.pdf

Stone A.A., Shiffman S. and Schwartz J.E. et al. (2002). Patient non-compliance
    with paper diaries. *British Medical Journal*, 324:1193–1194.

Willke, R.J., Burke, L.B. and Erickson, P. (2004). Measuring treatment impact:
    a review of patient-reported outcomes and other efficacy endpoints in
    approved product labels, *Controlled Clinical Trials*, 25:535–552.

1

Recall Bias: Understanding and Reducing Bias in PRO Data Collection

Alan L. Shields, Saul Shiffman and Arthur Stone

Introduction

Patient Reported Outcomes (PROs) are reports coming directly from patients without interpretation from an outside evaluator such as a physician or research assistant, and are central in the evaluation of clinical treatment effectiveness (Wilke et al., 2004). PROs are uniquely important in clinical research because some end-points are inherently known only to the patient e.g. pain; can most conveniently be tracked by the patient, e.g. bowel movements; and because the patient is the ultimate 'customer' for therapeutic products. Due to advances in computer technology and the advantages of electronic PRO assessment, see Shiffman, 2000, the use of electronic or ePRO methods are increasingly common in behavioral and medical sciences (Hufford and Shields, 2002).

Collecting PRO data invokes unique measurement processes and the US Food and Drug Agency (FDA) released guidance on the appropriate development, use, and evaluation of PRO instruments (FDA, 2009). Though the use of PRO data in clinical research has always been standard practice, this document, 'Patient Reported Outcome (PRO) Measures: Use in Medical Product Development to Support Labeling Claims,' referred to as the PRO Guidance, has implicitly given credibility to PROs as the basis for evaluating drugs and biologics. This increased regulatory focus on PROs has created a need within the pharmaceutical industry for accessible and practical resources to better understand the nature of PROs and the best practices that facilitate the effective collection and use of PRO data within a clinical trial environment.

An important first step toward understanding PRO data is a clear understanding of the impact that recall has on the obtained data. The FDA PRO guidance (FDA, 2009) states that it is important to consider the patients' ability to accurately recall the information requested and to understand the recall period under evaluation. Understanding recall is important because PRO data are almost always based on autobiographical memory, i.e. recall of events in one's life, and, are therefore vulnerable to biases and inaccuracies inherent in human memory processes. The imperative to overcome these biases and limitations is one of the drivers behind the development of ePRO methods and technologies that capture data closer to real time. These advances fall under the rubric of Ecological Momentary Assessment or EMA – the capture of real time data in patents' natural environments (Stone and Shiffman, 1994). As will be shown, planning to capture real time, real world data invokes questions about how to sample and assess patient experience. Most of the chapter will be devoted to describing these sampling strategies, ending with two real-world examples of how EMA and ePRO can be implemented successfully and yield important results in terms of estimating treatment effects efficiently and effectively.

PRO Data and Recall

PRO assessments typically rely on recall. We ask patients to recall, for example, how severe their pain has been in the past week, how many cigarettes a day they have smoked, on average, in the past two weeks, or how many asthma attacks they have had in the past month. Inherent in these methods is the assumption that patients are capable of estimating such quantities in a roughly accurate and unbiased way, even if the information is somewhat degraded by forgetfulness.

Autobiographical recall is subject not just to forgetfulness and random error, but to biases that systematically undermine the validity of the information gathered and its utility for assessing treatment effects. Random errors in reporting introduce noise into clinical data; this, in itself, is not trivial; it can, for instance, escalate sample size requirements, but it still allows for balanced and valid evaluation of treatment effects, which can rise above the noise. Systematic bias, on the other hand, actually influences the direction of the data and can systematically distort the outcome, making valid evaluation of treatment effects difficult. These biases are introduced by the natural and involuntary processes that operate in autobiographical memory, particularly our implicit reliance on heuristic strategies to reconstruct experience (Bradburn et al., 1987; Hufford, 2007; Tourangeau, 2000), see Table 1.1. For example, patients are more likely to recall greater average pain intensity over the past week than they actually experienced if they are experiencing or have recently experienced pain at the time of recall (Eich et al., 1985). An important implication is that these biases are inherent in recall, even when the patients are doing their best and are confident in their recall and this makes these biases very hard to overcome. Of course, there is a continuum of recall, ranging from recall over a few minutes to recall over periods of weeks or months. Although some recall bias can appear even over very short intervals (Redelmeier and Kahneman, 1996), the risk of bias

Table 1.1   Memory heuristics that can bias PRO data

Heuristic	Definition/Description	Example of bias in PRO Data Collection
Availability	Significant (e.g., severe symptoms), unusual (e.g., exacerbation of pain), or more personally salient or meaningful experiences are more 'available' to memory processes and more likely to influence recall than other events.	Despite no differences in the total number of life events or measures of stress and distress, patients with bipolar disorder recalled more uncontrolled and unanticipated life events in the year prior preceding a manic episode than those bipolar patients who did not experience a manic episode (Joffe et al., 1989).
Recency	Recent events are more accessible to memory than distant ones and will disproportionately influence recalled experiences.	Patients are more likely to recall greater average pain intensity over the past week than they actually experienced if they are experiencing or recently experienced pain at the time of recall (Eich et al., 1985).
State Biases	Internal states (e.g., mood) can bias recalled experiences by making certain content more accessible than others.	Patients are more likely to retrieve negatively valenced information when they are in a negative mood (Clark and Teasdale, 1982, 1985).
Effort After Meaning	Tendency to reconstruct past events so as to make them consistent with subsequent events.	When recalling pretreatment fatigue, patients would over- or underestimate it relative to their treatment response (Sprangers et al., 1999).
Instruction Set	Patients can systematically misunderstand PRO instrument instructions, especially those that require them to aggregate and summarize their experiences.	Patients may not interpret the specified recall period consistently. For example, Bailey and Martin (2000) showed that if participants were asked on the 15th of a month to recall the 'past month', only 64 per cent correctly interpreted 'past month' to refer to the period from the 15th of the current month to the 15th of the previous month. 36 per cent of participants considered 'past month' to mean, for example, the past 2 weeks only, the entire month previous to the current month, or a 6-week period as the basis for their recall.
Aggregation	Akin to the availability heuristic, patients can incorrectly aggregate their experiences prior to recall based on their past experience of the concept being assessed.	Patient recall of 'average' pain is heavily influenced by a combination of peak pain and recent pain during the recall interval as opposed to an actual average of momentary pain reports (Stone et al., 2000).

likely grows as the recall period increases. Table 1.1 summarizes a variety of memory heuristics known to bias the recall of PRO data.

Concern about recall biases and their impact on the validity of PRO data has led to a focus on methods for collecting data closer to the point of experience. This is a scientifically supported approach, based on the fact that reports of our present states are quite reliable (Robinson and Clore, 2002a, 2002b). Clinical trial regulators, too, are recognizing the negative consequences of recall bias. For example, the US FDA's PRO Guidance urges sponsors to carefully evaluate the recall period for PRO instruments and states, 'items with short recall periods or items that ask patients to describe their current or recent state are usually preferable' (FDA, 2009, p. 14).

As will be discussed later in greater detail, field-based collection of PRO data broadly falls under the umbrella of Ecological Momentary Assessment (EMA) – a set of methods and design principles for collection of data closer to real time in patients' natural real-world environments. Originally articulated by Stone and Shiffman (1994), EMA methods are becoming increasingly important in clinical trials. EMA covers a variety of methods, including patient diaries and many forms of ambulatory recording.

Overcoming Recall Bias in Clinical Research

HISTORICAL PERSPECTIVE: PAPER-BASED PRO ASSESSMENT

The importance of PRO data to clinical research has historically not been matched by methodologies capable of collecting this data in a reliable and valid way. The limitations inherent in retrospective reporting have long led researchers to gather data closer to real-time, using a broad array of diary methods. For example, protocols may ask patients to complete daily diaries recording their pain, make a record each time they experience an asthma attack, or with end of day reports to characterize the intensity of their fatigue (Verbrugge, 1980). These methods attempt to overcome the problems of recall by minimizing the period to be recalled, sometimes eliminating recall altogether. Besides minimizing recall bias, the repeated assessments implemented in diary protocols are expected to provide more reliable and statistically powerful data, and to be capable of revealing treatment effects as they emerge over time. Thus, the rationale for collecting real time data repeatedly from patients in their natural environment is the possibility of obtaining a richer, more reliable, ecologically valid, and statistically powerful assessment of the phenomenon of interest.

The success of such methods in minimizing or eliminating recall bias varies with the technology used. To date, the most common type of diary used in clinical research is a paper diary (PD) – a technology that has remained unchanged for centuries. Paper diaries have a number of documented limitations (e.g. Bolger et al., 2003; Raymond and Ross, 2000; Shiffman et al., 2001). First, PDs often produce poor quality data due to missing responses, multiple responses, unreadable data, and/or out of range data. In addition, data derived from PDs have to be keyed into a computer – a lengthy and error-prone process. The net effect of this poor data quality has been to slow the completion of clinical research projects employing PDs and to cast doubt on the utility of collecting this type of data.

Another critical limitation of PDs is that the PDs can often be completed after-the-fact instead of in-the-moment, and the investigator has no way of verifying that they were completed in compliance with the diary protocol. Compliance rates in PD studies have historically been reported as quite high (Norman, McFarlane, Streiner, and Neale, 1982 ; Sherliker and Steptoe, 2000). But these optimistic statistics are based on what the patient records at the time of completion, a source that is not subject to verification. Indeed, many researchers using PDs report observing 'parking lot compliance' – that is, patients hoarding diary cards and completing them en masse before a research or clinic visit. This concern was brought to a head in a study by Stone et al (2002), which used an electronically instrumented PD to objectively assess compliance. This study found that only 11 per cent of PDs were completed close to the protocol-specified time. Most were back-filled, and some were actually forward-filled, that is, completed well in advance of the protocol-designated time. When patients fail to make their diary entries in real-time and instead back-fill diary cards after the fact, then the rationale for deploying diaries in the first place is subverted, as the retrospectively completed records become subject to the very inaccuracies and biases that motivated the use of diaries in the first place. This is why the FDA (FDA, 2009, p. 14) has signaled that they will evaluate diary data to assess whether reports could be made after the fact.

THE PROMISE AND DELIVERY OF ELECTRONIC PRO (EPRO) ASSESSMENT

To overcome the data quality and compliance problems associated with paper-based PRO data capture, scientists have developed electronic methods of gathering PRO data – ePROs. While the term ePRO has been variously described and can encompass a variety of data collection devices, it is most commonly collected via telephones, such as Interactive Voice Response Systems or IVR, and via pre-programmed, handheld or palmtop computers functioning as eDiaries. These modalities have come into common use in clinical trials as well as in academic research and can overcome the limitations of PDs. For example, they provide for structured responses, ensuring usable and avoiding out of range or invalid responses, and can even apply consistency checks at the time of entry. Further, these solutions can manage complex skip patterns and thus avoid missing data and confusion that plague PDs. Beyond just recording the patient's responses, most eDiaries are able to actively prompt patients for data, which is often important as we will see below. Finally, ePRO solutions can verify the time of entry and, therefore, document patient compliance. This critical advantage can eliminate the back-filling and forward-filling that also plague PDs. And finally, eDiaries can be used not only to measure compliance but to enhance it.

ECOLOGICAL MOMENTARY ASSESSMENT: A METHODOLOGICAL FRAMEWORK FOR EPRO

While diaries have been used for centuries, and used in clinical research for decades, and while technology has advanced to make diaries more capable, diary research also needs a conceptual framework. We (Stone and Shiffman, 1994) have developed a conceptual framework to cover a diverse set of methods, including diaries, that aim to characterize real-world patient behavior and in real time, under the rubric of Ecological Momentary Assessment or EMA. Ecological Momentary Assessment has four defining characteristics:

1. Ecologically valid assessment: Ecologically valid data apply or generalize to the real world, which is obviously the goal of clinical trials. As has been discussed, there is good reason to question the ecological validity of global self-ratings and of data collected through recall and summary (Bradburn et al., 1987; Hammersley, 1994; Schwarz, 2007). EMA avoids the problems of global summaries and recall bias by collecting data in the real world, ensuring that the data represent the full range of real life experience.

2. Momentary assessment: Momentary assessment gathers the patient's report of experience close to the time the experience occurs in order to minimize problems of retrospective recall. While there is evidence that their recall of past states is subject to bias, there is ample evidence that people are able to validly report their current or very recent state (Robinson and Clore, 2002a, 2002b; Ross, 1989).

3. Careful timing of assessments: Given the focus on real world and momentary data capture, and the realization that the patients' state at the time of reporting can affect their reports, EMA methods are concerned with appropriate timing of patient assessments. In other words, EMA researchers seriously consider the question, 'when should patients complete their assessments?' For example, if patients avoid completing their diaries when they are in pain, and complete them only when they are feeling well, this can bias their reports. Similarly, if being in pain serves as a reminder to complete a pain diary, so that diaries are disproportionately completed when the patient is in pain, the assessment may again be biased and unrepresentative. EMA methods aim to minimize such bias by collecting, as far as is possible, an unbiased and representative sample of patient experience. A key concept is that the assessments are conceptualized as a sample, thus requiring considerations of representative sampling and avoidance of sampling bias.

4. Repeated observations: When an investigator solicits global, retrospective reports of experience, there is an implied assumption that the patient will provide full and representative coverage of his or her experience. Therefore, single observations or widely-spaced say, once a month, assessments are sometimes considered adequate. In contrast, the EMA researcher relies on momentary 'snapshots' of real world experience. To provide a complete and precise picture of patient experience then requires multiple assessments or snapshots. The use of multiple repeated assessments also enables EMA methods to document in detail how patient experience changes over time, a core concern in many clinical trials.

While a complete discussion of EMA is well beyond the scope of this chapter, the interested reader is directed to a number of books and review papers that address EMA more completely and from a number of perspectives. For example, books on EMA methods and findings have been published by Stone et al. (2007), Hektner et al (2007), and Fahrenberg and Myrtek (2001). Schwartz and Stone (2007) provides an excellent resource for understanding the data analytic strategies to consider within EMA designs.

Methodological and Measurement Considerations

EMA DESIGNS: A DESCRIPTION OF SAMPLING STRATEGIES

One of the major advantages of using ePROs in clinical research is the variety of sampling strategies available to the researcher. Below is a description of each of the assessment procedures and examples of each.

Event-based assessment

In event-based sampling, assessments are triggered by the occurrence of a pre-defined event of interest to the investigator. In many clinical trials, the research interest is often a particular event or symptom episode. For example, patients might be asked to complete an assessment when they experience a hot-flash, have an exacerbation of pain, or take a medication. Typically, the patients themselves determine when the event has occurred and initiate an assessment, though some medical events can be automatically detected by devices, see Kop et al., 2001. Therefore, defining the rules for what actually constitutes an 'event', e.g. a hot-flash, is particularly important in these cases.

In some cases, the end-point of interest is simply a count of relevant events, e.g. the number of headaches or bowel movements, in which case the patient need only indicate the event has occurred. Often, though, the protocol includes collection of data to characterize each event, such as headache severity or completeness of evacuation. Ideally, event data are captured in real-time, as an event occurs. Frequent and routine events are easily forgotten, so a retrospective count of events can sometimes be suspect. Almost half, 47 per cent, of all eDiary studies include event-based assessments in their protocol (Hufford and Shields, 2002) and the interested reader is directed to Shiffman (2007) and Shiffman et al (2008) for discussion of other considerations in assessing events.

Time-based assessment

While event-based assessment strategies are initiated by the study patient, time-based assessments are triggered by a schedule. Several important variations of these designs can be identified. One of the most common schedules requests diary completions at socially-defined and imprecise intervals. The most common example is the daily diary, which patients are instructed to complete daily, often 'in the evening,' to summarize the entire day. For more intensive assessment, patients may be asked to complete diaries 'morning', 'afternoon', and 'evening'. Besides involving some recall, this assessment strategy leaves the patient considerable discretion about when to complete the diary. Accordingly, investigators need to be sensitive to the potential for bias that may thus be introduced. In such instances, however, the potential for bias can be balanced against tactical considerations. For example, in some circumstances, assessment of nocturnal symptoms may only practically be measured in the morning once a patient has awakened, such as night-time symptoms among severe asthmatics, and so implicitly must rely upon a degree of recall by the patient.

Another variation arranges for assessment at more quantitatively precise intervals – say, hourly. Ideally, such protocols use eDiary facilities to prompt the patient that it is time to complete an assessment via a signaling device such as a software driven 'beeper'; see Shiffman (2007) for discussion of devices. By narrowing the role of the patient in selecting the time of assessment, such protocols reduce the potential for 'selection bias'.

Finally, an approach increasingly used is to use the programming facilities of eDiaries to schedule assessments at random (Shiffman et al., 2002). As in sampling individuals to represent a population, random time sampling assures the representativeness of patient experience thus assessed. In such instances when designing a study, the potential benefits of increased representativeness of the patient experience may need to be balanced with the perceived intrusion or inconvenience for the patient.

When making decisions regarding the actual frequency of assessments, investigators are encouraged to consider patient burden as well as how rapidly the target phenomenon is expected to vary. Assessing subjects one time per day is common, but some studies have succeeded with as many as 20 or more assessments per day (Goldstein et al., 1992; Kamarck et al., 2007).

Combination designs

Event-and time-based assessment each represent singular assessment methods. But multiple or combined assessment strategies within EMA and ePRO methods are also possible. That is, protocols can implement more than one of the defined strategies simultaneously. For example, Van Gerven et al. (1996) combined event- and time-based assessments in an evaluation of self-medication to headache pain. Patients were instructed to turn on the ePRO device during a tension-type headache at which time the program assessed pain severity and instructed the patient to take the trial medication, i.e., event-based assessment. The eDiary then prompted the patient at 15, 30, 45, 60, 90, 120, 180, and 240 minutes after initial assessment in order to evaluate the onset of headache relief.

Another measurement circumstance that would benefit from a combination design is when the events targeted for assessment do not or may not occur very frequently, for example, as is the case with migraine onset symptoms. In this instance, researchers are faced with considering whether the absence of a record on a specific day represents no event occurring, or missing data. To address this issue, researchers may build an ePRO solution that asks subjects to make a record that no events have occurred. Supplementary questions can accompany the 'no event occurred' response to improve the apparent value of the diary to the patient and to facilitate compliance. For example, an end-of-day record, a time-based assessment, might accompany a symptom assessment design, an event based assessment, to capture information that ensures no events have been missed during the day.

Design considerations

We have only covered the basic building blocks of EMA and ePRO solution design. A key message is that investigators planning a trial using these methods need to carefully consider the appropriate design and implementation in the light of study objectives, knowledge about the underlying disorder and its natural history, the hypothesized mechanism of action of the treatment under study, the limits of the patient population, the psychometric properties of the measures used, and the statistical plan. In other words, EMA design requires careful consideration and planning, much as study design itself does (see Shiffman, 2007).

Methods in Action

To illustrate the application of EMA and ePRO methods, and their advantages, we present examples of application in clinical trials.

McKenzie et al. (2004) evaluated the impact of using eDiaries to collect PRO data in a large and pivotal Phase III trial for overactive bladder (OAB) treatment. The end-points in OAB trials are typically the number of micturitions per day, as reported by the patients. Patients with OAB may often record, on average, as many as 12–15 micturitions per day or more. Diaries have long been used to collect such outcome data, in order to minimize recall bias. This study compared the results obtained using eDiaries to results obtained from similar OAB Phase II trials that employed paper diary methods. McKenzie et al. compared two diary studies with similar design and patient populations. In one, using time-based sampling, patients were to complete a paper diary three times per day, reporting how many micturitions they had had since the last diary report. In the other, using event-based sampling, they used eDiaries to record micturitions as they happened. The event-based recording was back-stopped by intelligent prompting by the eDiary: If, and only if, the patient did not make a micturition entry for an 8 hour period during the day, the eDiary 'beeped' them to ask whether some micturitions had occurred, and, if they had, to capture data about them. In fact, though, 91 per cent of micturition reports were based on real time patient-initiated event entries.

A statistical analysis and comparison of the two studies revealed a striking result. Even though the two studies had similar populations, the study using eDiaries with the enhanced design yielded 33 per cent less within-treatment variability than the study using paper diaries and a traditional design. In other words, the end-point was assessed with less noise, thereby increasing the study's sensitivity or statistical power. Statistical power for the 800-patient study increased from 80 per cent based on the paper diary data to 98 per cent based on variance estimates from the eDiary study. The practical consequence of these findings is that future OAB clinical trials, when using these eDiary methods, can be run with 50 per cent fewer patients, which, in turn, results in 45 per cent lower cost and 60 per cent less time. Results from this study show how EMA, combined with electronic technology, can improve the quality of PRO data capture and yield important practical consequences for clinical research, including drug development economics and timelines. These ideas are discussed in more detail in Chapter 3 of this book.

The assessment of patient reported pain provides another good example of how EMA and ePRO methods have been successfully merged in a clinical trial environment to advance drug development. As part of an initiative to develop new treatments for Fibromyalgia Syndrome (FMS), Gendreau et al. (2003) identified a number of methodological issues in measuring clinical pain in patients with chronic widespread pain. First, because pain is a concept that can best be assessed directly from patients, it was natural that pain was to be measured as a PRO. Next, citing literature showing that retrospective reports of pain can magnify placebo effects up to 5 times relative to real time reports of pain (Feine et al., 1998), it was concluded that memory biases would prevent a clear understanding of treatment effects among patients with FMS. In other words, single, average estimates of pain over a period of time would not provide an adequate or powerful enough picture of pain to evaluate treatments of FMS. Alternatively, the use of EMA methods could be used to gather multiple assessments of current pain, in real time and in the patients' natural environment. Furthermore, because the advantages of EMA data necessarily rely on patient compliance with the assessment strategy (see Chapter 7 of this text) and the use of paper diaries has become suspect in this regard (Stone et al., 2002), the decision to use electronic data capture was made.

Based on the above logic and decision making process, EMA methods supported by eDiary technology have been used to capture pain data as the primary endpoint in a Phase 2 trial and several pivotal Phase 3 trials (Gendreau et al., 2007). These studies employed an assessment strategy which asks patients to record their daily pain at several random times each day as well as each morning and evening (the Phase 3 trials also include a weekly pain assessment on the eDiary). Compliance rates in excess of 90 per cent were reported for each of the Phase 2 (n = 125 FMS patients) and Phase 3 (n = 888 FMS patients), studies which provide strong evidence for the timeliness of these reports. Clinical efficacy data from the Phase 2 study showed that 37 per cent of treated patients reported that their pain was half as intense as it was at study baseline, versus only 14 per cent of placebo control patients, and this was interpreted as both statistically and clinically significant. Efficacy data from Phase 3 study is reported as consistent with this Phase 2 data but is not yet available.

Managing and overcoming the recall bias inherent in retrospective reports of pain motivated the need for EMA methods supported by ePRO technology in the studies of FMS discussed above. With verified compliance rates over 90 per cent, investigators can be confident that obtained results more accurately reflect the pain that FMS patients actually experience and are not influenced by the assessment inaccuracies that would have been present in averaged or aggregated reports of pain recalled over a period of time. Additionally, these investigators now have a PRO assessment approach and measurement strategy that the FDA agrees would be appropriate for the evaluation of FMS and, ultimately, the approval of treatments (Gendreau et al., 2007).

Other Approaches to Improve Recall

As illustrated above, EMA methods provide a valuable approach in limiting recall bias in PRO measurement. Although not as commonplace or well developed, some researchers have employed other methodologies in an attempt to enhance patient recall. One example is the Memory Enhanced Recognition of the Effects of Treatment (MERET) instrument (Mundt et al., 2005). With this approach, patients describe their feelings and experiences related to their condition in their own voice and words at baseline or pre-treatment. This is normally captured using an IVR system but could be achieved using an eDiary. At further time points, this baseline recording can be played back to the patient enabling them to more accurately recall their pre-treatment condition and rate their current state relative to it using a global improvement scale. Preliminary studies using this approach have yielded promising results (see Chapter 8) although more work is required to fully validate this methodology.

Summary

Patient Reported Outcomes or PROs have been an important component of clinical trial research for as long as clinical trials have been performed. Nevertheless, challenges exist that can interfere with gathering PRO data in reliable and valid ways. One particularly pernicious problem is the impact of recall on obtained PRO reports. Broadly, what patients remember about their past behavior or experience may not be a good reflection of their actual behavior or experience. The practical implication of this is that PRO data, especially those associated with long recall periods, may lack the validity necessary to make them useful as treatment effectiveness indicators.

Improved methods for collection of PRO data – namely the development of ePRO methods – are making PRO data more useful as well as more efficient. EMA and ePRO methods enable collection of ecologically valid, statistically robust data in patients' real world settings. EMA methods can reduce or eliminate recall problems and can increase power to detect treatment effects in clinical trials. Clinical investigators have successfully used EMA-based assessment procedures using a variety of electronic platforms. While the methods, technologies, and content of these examples differ, they all highlight the characteristics of EMA methods by focusing on assessing real world experience or behavior more or less 'live' in participants' typical environments and do so repeatedly over time. The FDA's Guidance on PRO data emphasizes the need for documented methodological rigor in PRO assessments. ePRO, EMA, and eDiary methods make essential contributions toward this goal.

References

Bailey, A.S. and Martin, M.L. (2000). In Quality of Life Questionnaires, What Do Subjects Understand 'Past Month' to Mean? Poster presented at the International Society for Quality of Life Research conference, Vancouver, Canada.

Bolger, N., Davis, A. and Rafaeli, E. (2003). Diary methods: Capturing life as it is lived. *Annual Review of Psychology*, 54: 579–616.

Bradburn, N., Rips, L. and Shevell, S. (1987). Answering autobiographical questions: The impact of memory and inference on surveys. *Science*, 236: 157–61.

Clark, D.M. and Teasdale, J.D. (1982). Diurnal variation in clinical depression and accessibility of memories of positive and negative experiences. *Journal of Abnormal Psychology*, 91: 87–95.

Clark, D.M. and Teasdale, J.D. (1985). Constraints on effects of mood on memory. *Journal of Personality and Social Psychology*, 48: 1595–1608.

Eich, E., Reeves, J., Jaeger, B. and Graff-Radford, S. (1985). Memory for pain: Relation between past and present pain intensity. *Pain*, 223: 375–79.

Fahrenberg, J. and Myrtek, M. (2001). Progress in Ambulatory Assessment: Computer-Assisted Psychological and Psychophysiological Methods in *Monitoring and Field Studies*. Seattle: Hogrefe & Huber.

Food and Drug Administration. Guidance for Industry: Patient-Reported Outcome Measures: Use in Medical Product Development to Support Labeling Claims (Final), December 2009. Available at: http://www.fda.gov/downloads/Drugs/GuidanceComplianceRegulatoryInformation/Guidances/UCM193282.pdf [Accessed December 8, 2009].

Feine, J.S., Lavigne, G.J., Dao, T.T. et al. (1998). Memories of chronic pain and perceptions of relief. *Pain*, 77: 137–141.

Gendreau, M., Gendreau, J.F. and Batten Navis, D. et al. (2007). Fibromyalgia trials successfully measure subjects' pain. *BioExecutive International*, January: 38–41.

Gendreau, M., Hufford, M.R. and Stone, A.A. (2003). Measuring clinical pain in chronic widespread pain: Selected methodological issues. Best practice and research. *Clinical Rheumatology*, 17: 575–592.

Goldstein, I., Jamner, L. and Shapiro, D. (1992). Ambulatory blood pressure and heart rate in healthy male paramedics during a workday and a non-workday. *Health Psychology*, 11: 48–54.

Hammersley, R. (1994). A digest of memory phenomena for addiction research. *Addiction*, 89: 283–293.

Hektner, J.M., Schmidt, J.A. and Csikszentmihalyi, M. (2007). *Experience Sampling Method: Measuring the Quality of Everyday Life*. Thousand Oaks, California: Sage Publications.

Hufford M.R. (2007). Special methodological challenges and opportunities in Ecological Momentary Assessment. In *Science of Real-Time Data Capture: Self-Reports in Health Research* (eds) A.A. Stone, S. Shiffman, A. Atienza, and L. Nebeling, pp. 54–75. New York: Oxford University Press.

Hufford, M.R. and Shields, A.L. (2002). Electronic diaries: An examination of applications and what works in the field. *Applied Clinical Trials*, 11: 46–56.

Joffe, R.T., MacDonald, C. and Kutcher, S.P. (1989). Life events and mania: a case-controlled study. *Psychiatry Research*, 30: 213–216.

Kamarck, T., Muldoon, M. and Shiffman, S. et al. (2007). Experiences of demand and control during daily life are predictors of carotid atherosclerotic progression among healthy men. *Health Psychology*, 26: 324–332.

Kop, W., Verdino, R. and Gottdiener, J. et al. (2001). Changes in heart rate and heart rate variability before ambulatory ischemic events. *Journal of the American College of Cardiology*, 38: 742–49.

McKenzie, S., Paty, J. and Grogan, D. et al. (2004). Trial power: How eDiary data can enhance the power and reduce the sample size in clinical trials. *Applied Clinical Trials*, 13: 54–68.

Mundt, J.C., DeBrota, D.J. and Moore, H.K. et al. (2005). Memory Enhanced Retrospective Evaluation of Treatment (MERET): Anchoring patients' perceptions of clinical change in the past. 45th Annual Meeting of the New Clinical Drug Evaluation Unit Program, Boca Raton, FL USA. Abstract I-30.

Norman, G.R., McFarlane, A.H. and Streiner, D.L. et al. (1982). Health Diaries: Strategies for compliance and relation to other measures. *Medical Care*, 20: 623–629

Raymond, S.A. and Ross, R.N. (2000). Electronic subject diaries in clinical trials. *Applied Clinical Trials*, March: 48–58.

Redelmeier, D. and Kahneman, D. (1996). Patients' memories of painful medical treatments: Real-time and retrospective evaluations of two minimally invasive procedures. *Pain*, 116: 3–8.

Robinson, M.D. and Clore, G.L. (2002a). Belief and feeling: Evidence for an accessibility model of emotional self-report. *Psychological Bulletin*, 128: 934–960.

Robinson, M.D. and Clore, G.L. (2002b). Episodic and semantic knowledge in emotional self-report: Evidence for two judgment process. *Journal of Personality and Social Psychology*, 83: 198–215.

Ross, M. (1989). Relation of implicit theories to the construction of personal histories. *Psychological Review*, 96: 341–357.

Schwartz, J.E. and Stone, A.A. (2007). Analysis of real-time momentary data: A practical guide. In *The Science of Real-Time Data Capture: Self-Reports in Health Research*, (eds) A.A. Stone, S. Shiffman, A. Atienza, and L. Nebeling, pp. 76–113. New York: Oxford University Press.

Schwarz, N. (2007). Retrospective and concurrent self-reports: The rationale for real-time data capture. In *The Science of Real-Time Data Capture: Self-Reports in Health Research*, (eds) A.A. Stone, S. Shiffman, A. Atienza, and L. Nebeling, pp. 11–26. New York: Oxford University Press.

Sherliker, L. and Steptoe, A. (2000). Coping with new treatments for cancer: A feasibility study of daily diary measures. *Patient Education and Counseling*, 40: 11–19.

Shiffman, S. (2000). Real-time self-report of momentary states in the natural environment: Computerized ecological momentary assessment. In *The Science of Self-report: Implications for Research and Practice*, (eds) A.A. Stone, J.S. Turkkan, C.A. Bachrach, J.B. Jobe, H.S. Kurtzman, and V.S. Cain, pp. 277–296. Mahwah, NJ, US: Lawrence Erlbaum Associates Publishers.

Shiffman, S. (2007). Designing protocols for Ecological Momentary Assessment. In *The Science of Real-Time Data Capture: Self-Reports in Health Research*, (ed.) A.A. Stone, S. Shiffman, A. Atienza, and L. Nebeling, pp. 27–53. New York: Oxford University Press.

Shiffman, S., Gwaltney, C.J. and Balabanis, M. et al. (2002). Immediate antecedents of cigarette smoking: an analysis from Ecological Momentary Assessment. *Journal of Abnormal Psychology*, 111: 531–45.

Shiffman, S., Hufford, M.R. and Paty, J. (2001). Subject experience diaries in Clinical research (part 1): The patient experience movement. *Applied Clinical Trials*, February and March: 3–8.

Shiffman, S., Stone, A.A. and Hufford, M.R. (2008). Ecological momentary assessment. *Annual Review of Psychology*, 4: 1–32.

Sprangers, M.A.G., Van Dam, F.S. and Broersen, J. et al. (1999). Revealing response shift in longitudinal research on fatigue: The use of the the n test approach. *Acta Oncology*, 38: 709–718.

Stone, A.A., Broderick, J.B. and Kaell, A.T. et al. (2000). Does the peak end phenomenon observed in laboratory pain studies apply to real-world pain in rheumatoid arthritics? *Journal of Pain*, 1: 203–218.

Stone, A.A. and Shiffman, S. (1994). Ecological momentary assessment: Measuring real world processes in behavioral medicine. *Annals of Behavioral Medicine*, 16: 199–202.

Stone, A.A., Shiffman, S. and Atienza, A. et al. (eds) (2007). *The Science of Real-Time Data Capture: Self-Reports in Health Research*. New York: Oxford University Press.

Stone, A.A., Shiffman S. and Schwartz, J.E. et al. (2002). Patient non-compliance with paper diaries. *British Medical Journal*, 324: 1193–94.

Tourangeau, R. (2000). Remembering what happened: memory errors and survey reports. In *The Science of Self Report: Implications for Research and Practice*, (eds) A.A. Stone, C.A. Bachrach, J.B. Jobe, H.S. Kurtzman and V.S. Cain, pp. 29–48. Mahwah, NJ: Lawrence Erlbaum Associates.

Verbrugge, L.M. (1980). Health diaries. *Medical Care*, 18: 73–95.

Van Gerven, J.M.A., Schoemaker, R.C. and Jacobs, L-D. et al. (1996). Self-medication of a single headache episode with ketopforen, ibuprofen or placebo, home-monitored with an electronic patient diary. *British Journal of Clinical Pharmacology*, 42: 475–481.

Wilke, R.J., Burke, L.B. and Erickson, P. (2004). Measuring treatment impact: A review of patient reported outcomes and other efficacy endpoints in approved product labels. *Controlled Clinical Trials*, 25: 535–552.

2

Cognitive Interviewing: The use of Cognitive Interviews to Evaluate ePRO Instruments

Paul C. Beatty

Introduction

Questionnaires are commonly used to collect data about individuals for a simple reason: they offer the most practical approach for obtaining information about many behaviors or characteristics of respondents. Indeed, asking questions is the only viable approach for obtaining inherently subjective data such as assessments of personal well-being. Fortunately, questioning and answering is part of the normal daily discourse for most people, and the communication processes involved are generally quite straightforward (Schuman and Kalton, 1985).

Considerable complexity is added when the goal of asking questions is to *systematically collect data across individuals*. Doing this requires standardized measurement – meaning that we not only need to ask the same questions to everyone, but the questions also need to mean the same thing to all respondents. This is difficult to achieve. At first glance, a question such as 'How many cars do you own?', appears to be quite clear – but when you look closer there is ambiguity around the definition of 'car'; should trucks or sport-utility vehicles count?; 'own'; what about vehicles leased or still being paid for?; and even 'you,' which can apply to the individual respondent or to other family members (DeMaio, 1983). Questionnaire designers face a constant tension between *simplicity* and *specificity*. We can reduce ambiguity by additional clarifications and instructions, but doing so makes questions more complicated, burdensome, and potentially confusing.

Other problems arise when standardized questions employ response categories that do not allow respondents to relay their experiences adequately. In one study, some older respondents had trouble answering the question 'For how many days during the past 30 days was your physical health not good?' Those respondents with symptoms that varied throughout the day, for instance generally good health but arthritis pain at night, had difficulty counting days as good or not good (Schechter, Beatty and Willis, 1998). Other questions place strong demands on respondent memory, asking for information that might not have been encoded in memory, such as 'for how many years have you had episodes of severe cough?', or in some cases, not known at all,' at what age did you first experience symptoms of asthma?' In addition to these challenges, such questions may be difficult when respondents' experiences vary over time.

The inherent ambiguity of language, complexity of experience and frailty of human memory make it difficult to design effective standardized questions. Doing so is time and labor intensive, although it is clearly in researchers' best interests to identify question flaws in advance of large-scale data collection. While quantitative data from questionnaires may appear to be in good order, questionnaire problems may manifest themselves in various forms of error, whether systematic, resulting in biased data, or random, resulting in imprecise or 'noisy' data.

Cognitive interviewing has emerged in the last twenty years or so as one of the predominant methods for identifying and correcting problems with draft survey questions. Although the term actually encompasses a variety of practices, Beatty and Willis (2007) define cognitive interviewing as 'the administration of draft survey questions while collecting additional verbal information about the survey responses, which is used to evaluate the quality of the response or to help determine whether the question is generating the information that its author intends.' Ideally, an iterative approach is used. After conducting a 'round' perhaps involving between ten and twenty interviews, researchers take stock of some initial results, revise the questionnaire, and test it again. It is a versatile method that can be applied to many different types of questionnaire, and indeed, it can be adapted to evaluate the effectiveness of other materials such as maps or informational brochures (Willis, 2005). Cognitive interviewing can make important contributions to the development of electronic self-report or ePRO instruments as well.

This chapter will explain how. It will begin with a general explanation of what cognitive interviewing is and how it fits within the overall toolbox of questionnaire evaluation methods. From there, the chapter will cover some general issues that apply to the design of any cognitive interviewing study and then it will address issues and decisions specific to the testing of a questionnaire that has migrated from paper and pencil to an ePRO format.

The Emergence of Cognitive Interviewing

For decades, questionnaire designers relied primarily upon general principles and illustrations to evaluate the quality of their instruments. One of the earliest sets of guidelines was provided by Cantril and Fried (1944), who developed a taxonomy of questionnaire problems including such pitfalls as 'technical or unfamiliar words' and 'questions obscure in meaning,' among others. Payne's classic *The Art of Asking Questions* (1951) provided more comprehensive advice, culminating with a 'concise' checklist of 100 questionnaire design considerations. Their suggestions are generally driven by observation of ambiguities or anecdotal evidence of respondent difficulties. Later guides, such as those by Sudman and Bradburn (1982), Converse and Presser (1986), Fowler (1995), and Dillman (2007) bolstered such common-sense suggestions with results from questionnaire design experiments. All of these resources remain available and their insights are often valuable. Yet there are no foolproof questionnaire design formulas, and it is not always clear how to use such principles to evaluate specific survey questions. Empirical evaluation – actually trying out the questions on real respondents – serves as an important reality check.

Most commonly, that empirical evaluation has taken the form of a field pretest. This has typically entailed administering a questionnaire to a small sample of respondents, usually around 50 or more representative of the target population, as a sort of dress rehearsal. The questionnaire is administered under realistic field conditions, replicating the content, mode, layout, sequencing and interviewing procedures. If the survey is administered by interviewers, the quality of survey questions is most commonly assessed through an interviewer debriefing session. For self-administered surveys, questionnaires may be inspected for completion and any obvious signs of respondent difficulty (DeMaio, 1983; Converse and Presser, 1986; Oksenberg, Cannell, and Kalton, 1991, and Fowler, 1995). In both cases, the insights gleaned are fairly limited; the data are not particularly detailed, and there is no clear information as to *why* problems occurred. Interviewers are generally not trained to notice or articulate the nature of problems they observe (Fowler, 1995), and sometimes there is no clear way to assess the quality of self-administered responses.

Cognitive interviewing emerged as part of a subsequent movement to improve questionnaire evaluation through more elaborate self-report data. The basic premise of such activities is that it can be useful to ask respondents directly about comprehension and thought processes related to responding. Before such development activities were referred to as 'cognitive interviewing,' researchers such as Belson (1981) and DeMaio (1983) had proposed activities that were quite similar in practice – for example, using various probing strategies to uncover respondent misunderstandings, incorrect reports, and also to shed light on frames of reference used in constructing answers. However, such approaches only achieved widespread application following an interdisciplinary seminar that directed new attention to the cognitive aspects of survey methodology, or 'CASM' (Jabine, Straf, Tanur and Tourangeau, 1984). In addition to producing an upsurge in scholarship related to the psychology of survey response (see Jobe and Mingay, 1991), developments following the seminar led directly to the establishment of 'cognitive laboratories' for applied questionnaire evaluation. These initially appeared in U.S. statistical agencies, later spreading into academic and commercial institutions (Fienberg and Tanur, 1996; Sirken and Schechter, 1999). Currently, the practice of cognitive interviewing is quite widespread across all types of survey organizations, and there is general agreement about its usefulness for questionnaire development – although there also continues to be significant debate regarding the most effective approaches for carrying it out (Presser, Couper et al., 2004; Beatty and Willis, 2007).

Preparing to Implement Cognitive Interviews

As noted earlier, the term 'cognitive interviewing' describes a variety of questionnaire development activities. In the next few sections, I will outline some of the key variations, as well as some considerations for making decisions about which approaches are likely to yield useful information given particular objectives or types of questionnaires.

BEFORE COGNITIVE TESTING

Some ePRO instruments will be new questionnaires that have never been administered in any form, while others will be electronic implementations of paper questionnaires that have already been through considerable development activity. In the former case, it is worth noting that cognitive interviewing does not replace the development activities mentioned earlier. Rather, the role of cognitive interviewing is to fill the considerable gap between completion of a first draft and the field testing of a nearly final instrument. Creating a well-constructed initial questionnaire is itself an intensive process, with the basic content hopefully driven by discussions with subject matter experts and with the ultimate data users. Some researchers also rely upon *focus groups* to learn about key experiences of relevant respondents and the words they actually use. For example, if designing a questionnaire about the quality of life of long-term care patients, focus groups of such individuals could be used to identify what they consider to be the most important components of 'quality of life,' thereby ensuring that the questionnaire covers relevant factors (Morgan, 1997). Concepts and domains to be measured by PRO instruments are generally developed from a combination of patient interviews along with reviews of the literature and expert opinion. After these sorts of activities have helped to determine the basic content, questionnaire design principles can be used to mould ideas into specific questions. It is beyond the scope of this chapter to systematically review these principles – they are outlined in a number of excellent books, including but not limited to the works already mentioned. It should be noted that Dillman (2007) focuses entirely on self-administered instruments, and his guidelines may be especially useful to ePRO questionnaire designers for that reason.

Practitioners generally accept that cognitive interviewing provides the most useful feedback *after* these initial development activities have been completed. In fact, Willis (2005) suggests that cognitive interviewing ideally falls as the seventh step in a ten step process, and that it is inefficient to use it as a substitute for earlier development activities. Once these activities are complete and a draft questionnaire is in hand, we are ready to determine the specific parameters of cognitive testing. Two of the earliest decisions to be made are (1) how will the questionnaire be administered to the participant,[1] and (2) what sort of additional verbal data will we collect to evaluate its effectiveness.

DECIDING HOW TO ADMINISTER THE QUESTIONNAIRE

Cognitive interviewing methods were initially developed to test questionnaires that were to be administered in the field face-to-face, by interviewers (for example,, see Lessler, Tourangeau, and Salter, 1989). Consequently, it was a natural development that the earliest cognitive interviews were also conducted by interviewers face-to-face. As cognitive interviewing gained increasing

---

1   The term participant applies to someone who takes part in a cognitive interview, as opposed to a respondent who takes part in a fielded survey.

acceptance, it was applied to surveys conducted in other modes, such as over the telephone or through self-administration. However, cognitive interview practitioners generally did not adjust the mode of testing to match the eventual mode of administration (Schechter, Blair and Vande Hey, 1996). A key consideration here was that face-to-face cognitive interviewing provides optimal 'communicative flexibility,' which can be important if practitioners use a range of verbal and non-verbal cues to judge participant difficulties with questions (Beatty and Schechter, 1994). But over time, the case became stronger that the mode of testing should mimic the mode of survey administration. Consider a self-administered instrument. In the field, respondents would process the questions *visually* at a pace of their choosing. In traditional cognitive testing, respondents would process the questions *aurally*, at a pace of the interviewer's choosing. The cognitive processes involved could be quite different. More generally, the presence of the interviewer changes the nature of communication and the flow of the interaction. For all of these reasons, the cognitive testing could produce an incomplete evaluation of how the questionnaire would actually perform.

Therefore, when testing ePRO instruments through cognitive interviewing, it is highly desirable to perform at least some of the evaluation with a self-administered, electronic instrument that closely resembles what will be used in the field. This is especially important when time pressure or other constraints allow only limited testing. Also, if a questionnaire has been well-tested in paper form, the primary concern is how well it performs when *switched* to electronic form. Obviously, in that case it is necessary to test the electronic version.

Keep in mind, though, that cognitive interviewing is ideally an iterative process, conducted in rounds. A broader approach, when feasible, would be to aim for maximum *insight* in early rounds and maximum *realism* in later rounds. Although face-to-face cognitive interviewing sacrifices some realism, it can facilitate detailed discussions about interpretations and thought processes, which makes it a reasonable choice for the earliest phases of testing – especially for questionnaires that have never been tested. As problems are identified and, hopefully, resolved, it might be reasonable to relinquish some of this flexibility in favor of more realistic self-administration.

DECIDING WHAT VERBAL DATA WILL BE USED TO EVALUATE THE QUESTIONNAIRE

As noted earlier, all forms of cognitive interviewing entail both the administration of a questionnaire and the collection of additional verbal reports about participants' responses. These verbal reports take two primary forms, 'think-aloud' reports and responses to follow-up probes. Cognitive interviewing can be based upon one or both, but the decision on which to use should take into account the strengths and weaknesses of each.

Initially, cognitive interviewing relied almost completely upon think-aloud reports. In practice, this means that interviewers ask participants to verbalize everything that they think while answering questions, in real time. Although interviewers prompt participants to continue verbalizing, they generally do very little to guide the content of what participants say. Advocates of the approach suggest that it has several advantages. Data collection is relatively standardized, with little opportunity for interviewers to bias the proceedings, and interviewers do not need much specialized knowledge (Bolton and Bronkhorst, 1996). On the other hand, Willis (2005) notes that some participants have difficulty performing the task, while others frequently veer onto tangents, providing information of little relevance. Perhaps more importantly for self-administered questionnaires, a think-aloud protocol might encourage participants to pay detailed attention to words or instructions that they would ordinarily have skimmed or passed over (Dillman and Redline, 2004).

Some consider probing to be an attractive alternative because interviewers ask directly about interpretations of questions, thought processes, the ease or difficulty of responding, and so forth. Many researchers note the usefulness of responses to direct probes (Groves, Fultz and Martin, 1992; Willis, 1994; Beatty, 2004), and interviewers have more control over the interaction than in a think-aloud interview. It has arguably become the basis of recent cognitive interviewing practice (Gerber and Wellens, 1997; O'Muircheartaigh, 1999). But it too has some downsides: probing clearly disrupts the normal flow of the questionnaire and introduces considerable content that would not otherwise be present. These changes could be especially profound in the case of responding to self-administered questionnaires.

Fortunately, it is not necessary to make all-or-nothing decisions here. From a pragmatic standpoint, the real decision is how much emphasis to place upon one or the other (Beatty and Willis, 2007), hopefully in a manner that minimizes the potential liabilities of each. A reasonable choice for ePRO evaluation is to ask participants to fill out the questionnaire as if they were doing so in the place they would usually complete it. Encourage participants to think out loud if possible, but do not insist upon it or spend much effort prompting them. The rationale for this approach is to maximize realism and minimize the effect of testing on participants' normal behavior. Some participants may be quite skilled at thinking out loud and elaborating upon their thought processes; if so, they should be encouraged to verbalize. On the other hand, some would ordinarily skip around and pay little attention to details. If this is their preference, it would be undesirable for the testing procedure to alter these tendencies. Observing what participants actually do and making note of whatever they verbalize is a useful component of the evaluation.

However, it also seems reasonable to use probes to obtain the lion's share of the evaluation data, following the general tendencies of current practice.[2] Quite simply, the benefit of asking directly about design issues of interest is too strong to ignore. This decision raises a number of important questions, including the appropriate time to probe, what probes should be asked and how should we select them, and how scripted should the probes be? These decisions are related to others about the ideal characteristics of interviewers.

Probing and Other Data Collection Decisions

CONCURRENT AND RETROSPECTIVE PROBING

Given that probes will be used in some form, one remaining decision is when to administer them. At one extreme, we could probe immediately after each question. At the other, we could delay all probing until the end of the questionnaire, allowing it to be administered without interruption. Willis (2005) refers to these approaches respectively as *concurrent* and *retrospective* probing. The key advantage of concurrent probing is the response process will have just been completed. This is the ideal time to ask about interpretations, computations, and how response decisions were made. Of course, as noted earlier, exploiting this freshness comes at a cost: we must interrupt the flow of the questionnaire, and we risk introducing ideas that participants would

---

2   It is worth noting that other recommendations are available regarding cognitive testing procedures for self-administered questionnaires – for example Hak, van der Veer and Jansen (2004) – propose a Three-Step hybrid approach that puts more emphasis on thinking-aloud and indirect requests for clarification. Ultimately, evaluators need to decide upon the balance between approaches that they feel most comfortable with.

not normally have had while answering. Retrospective probing avoids those problems, but has costs of its own: participants will be providing information about responses that have taken place at some point in the past. Presumably, such information will be less accurate than if it had been solicited immediately after the response. Also, when probing retrospectively it is possible that the interpretation of a question or item may be affected by the nature and content of questions delivered afterwards.

As with the choice between thinking-aloud and probing, compromises are possible. One option is to conduct retrospective probing at intervals throughout the questionnaire – for example, at the end of a section or short series of questions. Doing so allows participants to complete parts of the questionnaire in a relatively natural manner, while obtaining recent, if not quite concurrent, probe responses as well. As noted earlier, it is also possible to change data-collection strategies over the course of testing. Especially if testing a new questionnaire, it might make sense to interrupt with probes more often in earlier phases, sacrificing some realism in order to probe in depth immediately following responses, and less often in later phases, which more closely mimics what respondents will actually experience.

SELECTING PROBES

By this point, we have made general data collection decisions regarding how to administer the questionnaire, and how to solicit additional verbal responses within that process. As a next step, we need to think about what specifically we will ask participants about their responses. As with other aspects of cognitive interviewing methodology, there is no clear consensus regarding how to select probes or which probes are most effective (Beatty and Willis, 2007). However, practitioners do share certain assumptions about the response process that can be helpful in selecting probes.

One key product of the first 'CASM' seminar was a model of the stages that respondents go through while answering questions (Tourangeau, 1984). These stages are:

- Comprehension: understanding the meaning of the question

- Retrieval: searching memory for relevant information

- Judgment: assessing completeness of memories; estimating and integrating this material

- Response: providing the information in the format requested.

Parsing the response process in this manner is useful, as it provides us with ideas regarding specific components to probe about.

For example, consider this question: 'In the past week, on how many days did pain make it difficult for you to do everyday activities?' In assessing potential problems with *comprehension*, we might probe about interpretations of the key terms and concepts within it. Examples could include 'When I said *everyday activities*, what sorts of things came to mind?' and 'What particular time period were you thinking about while answering?'

Similarly, probes can be selected to assess difficulties with other phases of the response process. For *retrieval*, we can ask respondents 'was it easy or difficult to remember how much pain you experienced on a given day?' or 'what sorts of things came to mind while you were answering the question?' For *judgment*, we can probe 'how did you figure out how much pain you have experienced?' and 'was it easy or difficult for you to figure out how much pain has interfered with what you were doing?' For *response*, we can probe 'did you have any difficulty providing an answer in terms of days?' Of course, these are only suggestions; other probes could be selected based upon whatever issues a designer was interested in exploring.

The probes suggested above are fairly direct, focusing on particular components of the question or aspects of the response process. Such probes are appealing because they address specific issues that are likely to be of interest. However, it is difficult to assess whether responses to such probes are always valid, and participants may vary in their ability to answer them (Ericsson, 1998). An alternative approach is to ask more general probes, especially narrative ones (such as 'can you describe for me how much pain you tend to experience?') Narrative responses that seem out of line with questionnaire responses can highlight misinterpretations, for example when a participant answers 'none' to the question above, but then goes on to describe a series of seemingly painful conditions. Narrative probes may require follow-up; it may not be initially clear whether the participant misunderstood the question, or thought that her pain was of a different sort than the question was getting at, or whether there was some other difficulty. Direct questioning may be required to explain the apparent mismatch, although non-directive follow-ups such as 'can you tell me more about that?' may be effective as well.

In short, general probing often generates useful information, and is appealing because it is non-directive. Specific probes can be more efficient and precise when they work, but not all participants can answer them. Selecting these probes can be driven by an initial review of the questionnaire, guided by an understanding of the cognitive processes that respondents go through while answering questions. There is no comprehensive algorithm for producing probes, and different researchers would probably make different selections based on their particular backgrounds. To some degree, selection of probes is an art, although it is guided by certain principles. For a more detailed discussion of these principles and some additional considerations in probe selection, see Willis (2005).

SCRIPTED VS. FLEXIBLE INTERVIEWING

The value of determining a probing strategy and selecting particular probes in advance of conducting cognitive interviews is hopefully now clear. This leaves open the question as to whether our goal should be to produce a complete script for cognitive interviewers to follow, or whether it is desirable to allow them to improvise, at least to some degree.

Scripted interaction may seem preferable to survey researchers who view interviewing as a means for standardized measurement. Tucker (1997) suggests that a lack of standardization in cognitive interviewing threatens its scientific validity; providing cognitive interviewers with a set of procedures to be applied consistently across interviews would provide more objective data. However, it should also be clear that flexibility brings certain advantages as well. It is extremely difficult to predict all potential problems in advance – for example, both Beatty (2004) and Willis (2005) provide examples of interpretation problems that were identified only through 'emergent' probes, that is, unscripted probes selected by interviewers to explore issues that emerged in the interview such as seemingly contradictory responses. Both authors suggest that a significant proportion of insights gleaned from cognitive interviewing are derived from such unscripted probes.

Of course, there are numerous advantages to creating an interviewing protocol that, at a minimum, *suggests* particular probes. Not only does this practice encourage investigators to think systematically about potential questionnaire problems in advance, it also promotes at least some degree of consistency across interviews. Such consistency can be useful when analyzing results. At the same time, rigidly constraining interviewers against deviation arguably robs the method of its potential for insight and diminishes its exploratory character. Carefully watching for signs of confusion, contradiction, or subtle misunderstandings can be useful, and capitalizing on such observations requires at least some interviewer flexibility.

Reliance upon such probing of course places considerable trust in interviewers' knowledge and abilities. Beatty and Willis (2007) distinguish between interviewers who serve as *investigators* as opposed to those who are simply *data collectors*. Both may require certain communication skills, but investigators require more sophisticated qualitative interviewing skills; they also benefit from specialized knowledge, possibly including social science background, questionnaire design experience, and subject matter expertise (Willis, 2005). It might not always be possible to find interviewers with an 'ideal' set of skills, but at a minimum there is likely to be value in using interviewers who will actually analyze cognitive interviewing data and be involved in the subsequent modification of questions. Many institutions, including some federal agencies, operate in that manner on the grounds that stronger insights emerge from cognitive interviews when the interviewers have a broad investigative role in the process (Beatty and Willis, 2007).

SELECTION OF PARTICIPANTS

Obviously, data collection cannot move forward until we have identified and recruited the individuals who will actually be interviewed. We have already noted that cognitive interviewing typically entails small rounds of interviews, often with twenty participants or fewer per round. There are several reasons for the small numbers. First, cognitive interviewing produces an enormous amount of data; fully exploiting the content of even a small number of interviews can be quite labor-intensive. In addition, a round is often significant to identify a number of questionnaire design problems. Once problems are identified, it seems reasonable to move forward, revising the questionnaire in a manner that addresses these problems, and devoting energy toward testing the revisions.

But given that we are working with small numbers, how do we determine the optimal characteristics of our sample? Clearly, it is not possible to create a sample that is representative of the larger population in a statistical sense. Instead, the sample should be designed for *subject matter relevance*, and for variety within those constraints. For example, a questionnaire about quality of life for asthma patients should include individuals with different severity levels of asthma, different lengths of time that they have had asthma, or other important differences that might be meaningful in terms of their experiences with asthma. If questionnaires include skip patterns (branching), the sample should be diverse enough to ensure that the various permutations of response paths are covered. Within these constraints, some demographic variety is desirable – again, not for the sake of creating a representative sample, but to maximize the variety of experiences that are likely to be captured (Beatty and Willis, 2007).

Participants are commonly recruited through several mechanisms, including newspaper advertisements, strategically-placed flyers, contacts within organizations with relevant participants, and word-of-mouth. Written advertisements generally specify the nature of the research activity (testing questions), the general subject matter of the questions, criteria for selection, time required to participate, payment for participation (if any), and contact information for whoever schedules appointments (Willis, 2005). The content and overall approach can vary significantly depending upon the project.

One constraint worth considering is to avoid using key questions on the instrument as part of recruitment. For example, suppose we plan to recruit patients with hypertension, and one of the key questions on the instrument is whether or not the respondent has hypertension. If we specifically advertise for people who 'have hypertension,' we have deprived ourselves of the ability to evaluate their comprehension of the term and their certainty that they have the condition. Clearly, they must understand it and know they have it in order to respond to the advertisement. A more artful approach is required – perhaps recruiting people with certain characteristics that might be coincidental with hypertension, such as people of a certain age who are overweight. Such an approach does not yield a perfect rate of success, but it does allow us to test the questions without in effect having asked them in advance.

Analysis of Data from Cognitive Interviewing

Literature on cognitive interviewing has focused primarily on how to conduct cognitive interviews, paying relatively little attention to matters of analysis. On the one hand, this might not be troubling. Cognitive interviewing primarily produces qualitative data, and guides for qualitative analysis (for example, Miles and Huberman, 1994) are readily available; many of the insights from such guides should apply. At the same time, cognitive interviewing is conducted for a very specific purpose – to inform the design of standardized questions – and is often constrained by time pressures that are far from ideal for qualitative research. In that sense, cognitive interviewing is a unique activity and, given its uniqueness, the attention devoted to establishing clear analytic guidelines seems quite inadequate.

It is beyond the scope of this chapter to rectify that situation, or even to address the topic in the depth that it deserves. However, a few guidelines may be useful. The first consideration is *what* exactly will be analyzed. It is common for cognitive interviewers to take notes during interviews, and it is certainly possible to use such notes as the basis for analysis. Recording interviews either on audio or video is also highly recommended. Obviously such recordings are much more complete than any notes could be, and serve as a very useful reference when reviewing interview content. Transcriptions are also useful references, although producing them can be expensive and time-consuming and they do not replace recordings, since transcriptions cannot capture tone of voice and other important subtleties.

Using whatever notes, recordings, or transcripts are at hand, interviewers should compile observations on a question-by-question basis. It is useful to summarize each participant's actual response to the question; any details or insight regarding how the participant interpreted the question, computed a response, or performed any cognitive task and any observations about difficulties, misinterpretations, or errors. Analysts, who should preferably be the interviewers themselves, should then review the compiled information on each question and make assessments about how they are performing. Such analysis is primarily qualitative. This does not preclude quantitative assessment, such as counting the number of times that certain problems were experienced – but the focus should be on understanding thought processes and the meaning of responses.

Using the approach outlined previously, it is fairly easy to spot misinterpretations of questions, problems answering, and various response errors. It takes somewhat more skill to determine whether such errors reflect serious problems or are simply the product of unusual participants. An approach recommended by Beatty and Willis (2007) is to look for characteristics of the question that are responsible for the problem. For example, at the beginning of this chapter we considered the question 'For how many days during the past 30 days was your physical health not good?' When participants had difficulty answering, probing revealed that their health problems did not readily correspond to 'days', in other words it was difficult to categorize a day as completely 'good' or 'bad' because symptoms were not consistent throughout a day. The problem can be linked to a particular question characteristic –the use of 'days' as a response option – and it seems reasonable that this problem could recur for people with similar health situations. We conclude that that the response metric is causing a problem worthy of further consideration by the design team.

Other times, problems cannot be clearly linked to characteristics of the question, or the case that there is a problem is not particularly convincing, such as an unusual interpretation of a term that seems to be commonly understood otherwise. In such situations, the case for modifying questions may be relatively weak. It is also necessary to weigh the evidence of a problem against the viability of alternatives. Even if we decide that the 'days' metric cited above has problems, we might find that the flawed metric is more acceptable than alternatives, such as a more subjective rating scale. Ultimately, questionnaire design decisions involve tradeoffs – for example when we must choose between a simple question that might be ambiguous in a few cases, and an alternative that reduces that ambiguity but is more burdensome for all.

Questions that are re-written should of course be tested in their own right. Ideally, small rounds of interviews are repeated until it becomes clear that few new insights are emerging. Realistically, production time pressures may put a stop to testing before that point is reached. Even when that happens, researchers are generally equipped with rich data that can inform questionnaire design decisions in a number of useful ways.

In their PRO guidance (FDA, 2009), FDA state they plan to review instrument development to determine whether an instrument used in clinical trials is appropriate to measure the concepts required. Their recommendations regarding how to present such evidence are appended to their guidance document and discussed in more detail by Eremenco and Revicki in Chapter 4 of this book. Needless to say, the results of cognitive interviewing, including the interview schedule, transcripts and analysis findings, form an important part of this supporting submission.

Testing ePRO Instruments Converted from Paper Questionnaires

Many ePRO instruments will not be designed from scratch, but rather adapted from instruments that have already been evaluated and fielded in nonelectronic form. In such cases, designers might have considerable confidence in the quality of the questions. However, as noted earlier, changing the mode of administration can change the cognitive processes involved in responding. It is therefore useful to test such instruments with a particular eye toward evaluating the specific attributes that have changed in the transition to the new mode.

Figure 2.1 shows a multi-part question as it appears on a paper instrument. The question asks respondents to assess their limitations in performing a series of activities. Figure 2.2 shows the same question adapted to an ePRO instrument. Note that this version uses identical wording to the paper questionnaire, although the appearance is different.

The Seattle Angina Questionnaire

1. The following is a list of activities that people often do during the week. Although for some people with several medical problems it is difficult to determine what it is that limits them, please go over the activities listed below and indicate how much limitation you have had **due to chest pain, chest tightness, or angina <u>over the past 4 weeks:</u>**

Place an X in one box on each line

Activity	Extremely Limited	Quite a bit Limited	Moderately Limited	Slightly Limited	Not at all Limited	Limited for other reasons or did not do the activity
Dressing yourself	☐	☐	☐	☐	☐	☐
Walking indoors on level ground	☐	☐	☐	☐	☐	☐
Showering	☐	☐	☐	☐	☐	☐
Climbing a hill or flight of stairs without stopping	☐	☐	☐	☐	☐	☐
Gardening, vacuuming, or carrying groceries	☐	☐	☐	☐	☐	☐
Walking more than a block at a brisk pace	☐	☐	☐	☐	☐	☐
Running or jogging	☐	☐	☐	☐	☐	☐
Lifting or moving heavy objects (e.g. furniture, children)	☐	☐	☐	☐	☐	☐
Participating in strenuous sports (e.g. swimming, tennis)	☐	☐	☐	☐	☐	☐

© Copyright 1992–2000, John Spertus, MD, MPH International US English Version.

Figure 2.1   Example of a multi-part question on a paper PRO instrument – The Seattle Angina Questionnaire[3]

---

3   See www.cvoutcomes.org for technical and licensing information on the Seattle Angina Questionnaire.

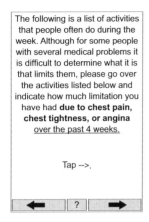

Figure 2.2   ePRO adaptation of a multi-part question from the Seattle Angina Questionnaire

As a first step, we should consider what exactly has changed across the two versions.

The most obvious change is that what originally appeared in a single page is now spread across several screens, only one of which will be visible to respondents at any particular moment. In the paper version, the introductory text is readily available as respondents answer for each activity. This material includes a prompt to specifically consider limitations *due to chest pain, chest tightness, and angina,* and an acknowledgment of potential difficulty in attributing limitations to a particular cause. In the electronic version, these instructions are only visible during the initial reading. Respondents may return to them, but by default they will respond to each item without visual reference to this text. These differences suggest a few lines of inquiry in cognitive testing.

First, do participants express any judgment difficulties that could reasonably be attributed to the reduced accessibility of these instructions; and, do participants remember to answer specifically with regard to chest pain, tightness and angina? These could be addressed through relatively simple probes such as:

- When you said that you had [difficulty] with [activity], what was it that made this difficult? [If necessary, add:] were you thinking about limitations caused specifically by chest pains, or were they because of something else?

- Tell me about how you decided on the level of limitation that you experienced for [activity]. Did you have any uncertainty regarding how to answer? [If yes, continue:] How did you figure out which answer applied best to your situation?

Another difference is that all of the limitations are visible at the same time on the paper questionnaire, whereas the electronic version asks about each condition in isolation. This difference is significant, because respondents use overall context to make inferences about intended meaning (see Sudman, Bradburn and Schwarz, 1996, Chapter 3). As an example, consider the second item on the list, 'walking indoors on level ground.' On the paper questionnaire, respondents can see related items such as 'walking more than a block at a brisk pace', at the same time. They may use these other activities to infer that the earlier one refers to walking at pace *slower* than brisk. Such judgments are not likely to take place in the electronic version, since respondents will generally only view items one at a time. This suggests another issue to explore in cognitive testing: how do participants interpret the individual items? Is there any evidence that they fail to make intended distinctions of meaning across items? Here, some general probes about meaning are likely to be helpful, such as:

- This question asked about [activity] – what sorts of things were you thinking about?

Here, contrary to earlier advice, it might be useful to probe immediately after each activity screen, so participants can provide fresh information about their interpretations untainted by any other activities.

In addition, there is the response scale itself. In the paper questionnaire, successive response categories are presented horizontally. In the electronic version, the categories are presented vertically. Respondents use visual cues as well as verbal ones to understand the meanings of categories (Schwarz, 1999; Dillman, 2007). Changing the presentation may alter interpretations of the scale, perhaps making it more,or less, intuitive that the most severe limitations are presented first at the left, or top, moving on to lesser degrees of limitation. This is another issue to explore through cognitive interviewing: do participants understand the descending nature of the scale? Are they able to explain the meanings of categories in a manner consistent with the designers' intent? Direct probes about the interpretation and usability of the scale might be useful, such as:

- Did you have any trouble finding an answer category that reflected what you wanted to say?

- What does [category] mean to you?

- [Refer to the screen with response categories.] Based on these answer categories, do you think 'moderately limited' is supposed be *more* or *less* limited than 'somewhat limited'?

As discussed earlier, the choice of probes follows from our assessment of which issues are worth exploring. These are not the only probes that could be used to explore them – there are many possibilities. Also, if participants provide us with the information we are looking for spontaneously, or with less probing than suggested here, that is perfectly acceptable. New issues to explore may also become apparent during the course of interviews.

Many other questionnaires are altered considerably when converted from paper to electronic instruments. Consider for example the EQ-5D Visual Analogue Scale – basically a 'feeling thermometer' asking respondents to rate aspects of their health by marking a point somewhere between zero and 100 (Euroqol Group, 1990). In traditional form, the scale is presented vertically and nearly fills a page. Duplicating it exactly on a handheld electronic device would not be feasible, but one alternative version considered by Ramachandran, Taber, Craig, and Coons (2005) flips the scale on its side, compresses it somewhat, and asks respondents to select a point on a touch screen. Several issues come to mind: first, when modified, do respondents still understand the basic nature of the scale; that it requires the selection of a single point between zero and 100, with 100 being 'best'? Second, do respondents tend to interpret scale points on the electronic scale differently from how they do on paper? As noted earlier, seemingly trivial changes in presentation, such as labeling of scale points, can affect responses. It is possible that the choice of axis, physical length of the scale or similar attributes could affect respondent perceptions of what qualifies for a particular threshold of health – for example, '90' might appear to be an extreme value on the vertical scale, but not so far from the middle on a compressed horizontal one. Ramachandran et al (2005) also noted that respondents to the electronic version were less likely to round their answers to the nearest five or ten, indicating that the format does affect decision processes to at least some degree.

Cognitive probing can complement the validation activities proposed by Ramachandran et al. (2005), by providing insight into participant perceptions and whether they vary across instruments. Probes such as 'can you explain to me how you are interpreting the response scale – for example, which end is better in terms of health' could be informative regarding overall interpretations. Probes that more directly assess participant thought processes might also be informative, such as 'how did you select your response? Did you have any uncertainty or indecision regarding which point to select on the scale?'

In a slight variation, it is worth noting that electronic *diaries*, which are designed to capture respondent experiences in approximately real time, pose somewhat different cognitive tasks than retrospective questionnaires. For example, respondents might be asked to provide more reports about current behaviors and symptoms, and fewer that cover a broad time range or that require dating of events further in the past. Still, many of the same probing strategies would apply, with an emphasis on probes regarding how participants figured answers, and additional prompts to identify any behaviors that were forgotten. Much of this probing would be appropriate within or immediately following completion of the diary. Debriefing questions could also be helpful for identifying reporting patterns for example, whether data were recorded according to instructions. Also, given that electronic diaries can be delivered in various modes – through handheld devices with key entry, pen entry, or through home computers (see Tiplady, Jamieson and Crompton, 2000) – debriefing can be used to learn about participant preferences, and whether alternative modes created any barriers to accurate or timely completion.

The objective of these studies is not to tell us whether the electronic version is 'better' or 'worse' than the paper version. Such an evaluation would require an experimental design, and the results of such a study might be useful. Using this method, we work to obtain an overall qualitative assessment of whether or not the ePRO instrument performs as we expect it to, and to identify any changes that might bring its performance closer to our objectives. If conducted thoughtfully, it would be likely to yield a great deal of information about the performance of questionnaires.

Other Testing Approaches

Several other evaluation approaches may be applicable to the design of ePRO instruments. The sister field of *usability testing* has some important similarities to cognitive interviewing, in that it also explores the interaction of a participant and a data collection system. They differ in that usability testing focuses on attributes of the hardware and software – for example, the navigability of applications; whether users are able to obtain additional information when needed; appropriateness of the data collection device for required tasks; and so on – rather than issues such as question interpretation (Hansen and Couper, 2004). These are important issues to be sure, and usability testing is especially appropriate for computerized self-administered data collection because the instrumentation involved potentially adds a layer of complexity for respondents.

It is also extremely valuable to submit electronic instruments to *functional testing;* to evaluate whether format, order, skip logic, automated fills, and data output all operate as expected. Often this entails entering various simulated responses into the instrument to test performance under various scenarios. For specific issues to explore and methods for testing, see Tarnai and Moore (2004); Baker, Crawford and Swinehart (2004) review some specific strategies for web questionnaires. Generally such testing is performed after cognitive testing, as the final step before actually fielding an instrument. As with usability testing, functional testing pays little attention to matters such as question interpretation, so it does not replace cognitive interviewing. However, after cognitive interviewing is completed, functional testing is a vital element of quality control.

Summary and Conclusion

Cognitive interviewing methods are still relatively new, and actual practices have evolved somewhat independently in different institutions. As a result, practitioners have not reached complete consensus on best practices, and different researchers could make different decisions about how to test a particular instrument. The issues discussed above are meant to offer a range of possibilities, while also suggesting some implementation decisions that reflect current practices and the specific characteristics of ePRO instruments. In summary, here are a few key recommendations to consider:

- Make a considerable investment in questionnaire development prior to conducting cognitive interviews.

- Develop a semi-scripted interviewing protocol based on analysis of potential problems with questions.

- Recruit participants who would be appropriate respondents of the questionnaire. Target some demographic variety, but focus primarily on covering the variety of circumstances relevant to the questionnaire.

- Administer the actual questionnaire in the manner it will be administered in the field although in early phases, there may be reason for face to face interviewing regardless of the ultimate mode.

- Ask participants to answer questions to the best of their ability. Encourage them to verbalize their thought processes, but put most emphasis on probing *after* questions or sections of the questionnaire have been answered.

- Use interviewers who are as skilled and knowledgeable as possible – preferably using a team of researchers who will also serve as analysts.

- Interviewers should be on the lookout for uncertainty, hesitation, confusion, difficulty, and errors, and should explore whenever these signs are observed, deviating from the protocol as required.

- Interviewers should encourage participants to do most of the talking, and should encourage, as much as possible, elaboration/ narration on what participants mean.

- Conduct interviews in small rounds. Ideally, interviewers conduct independent analyses of their own interviews then meet to discuss findings with other team members and discuss potential changes to the questionnaire.

- Revise and re-test, ideally until interviews seem to yield few additional insights.

However cognitive interviewing is carried out, its objective is the same: to shed light on thoughts and decision processes that are not readily visible, but that can have an important bearing on the quality of responses. When we gain insights into the problems that respondents face when answering questions, we have a reasonable chance of revising our measures and overcoming these problems. Cognitive interviewing, when thoughtfully applied, can provide these insights and make an important contribution toward developing high quality questionnaires.

References

Baker, R.P., Crawford, S. and Swinehart, J. (2004). Development and Testing of Web Questionnaires. In S. Presser, J. Rothgeb, M. Couper, J. Lessler, E. Martin, J. Martin and E. Singer (eds), *Questionnaire Development Evaluation and Testing Methods*. Hoboken, NJ: John Wiley and Sons.

Beatty, P. (2004). The Dynamics of Cognitive Interviewing. In S. Presser, J. Rothgeb, M. Couper, J. Lessler, E. Martin, J. Martin and E. Singer (eds), *Questionnaire Development Evaluation and Testing Methods*. Hoboken, NJ: John Wiley and Sons.

Beatty, P. and Schechter, S. (1994). An Examination of Mode Effects in Cognitive Laboratory Research. *Proceedings of the Section on Survey Research Methods, American Statistical Association*.

Beatty, P. and Willis, G.B. (2007). The Practice of Cognitive Interviewing. *Public Opinion Quarterly*, 71: 287–311.

Belson, W. (1981). *The Design and Understanding of Survey Questions*. Aldershot, England: Gower.

Bolton, R.N. and Bronkhurst, T.M. (1996). Questionnaire Pretesting: Computer Assisted Coding of Concurrent Protocols. In N. Schwarz, and S. Sudman, (eds), *Answering Questions: Methodology for Determining Cognitive and Communicative Processes in Survey Research*. San Francisco: Jossey-Bass.

Cantril, H. and Fried, E. (1944). The Meaning of Questions. In H. Cantril, *Gauging Public Opinion*. Princeton, NJ: Princeton University Press.

Converse, J.M. and Presser, S. (1986). *Survey Questions: Handcrafting the Standardized Survey Questionnaire*. Newbury Park, CA: Sage.

DeMaio, T.J. (ed.) (1983). Approaches to Developing Questionnaires. *Statistical Policy Working Paper 10*. Washington, DC: Statistical Policy Office, U.S. Office of Management and Budget.

Dillman, D.A. (2007). *Mail and Internet Surveys: The Tailored Design Method, Second Edition*. Hoboken, NJ: John Wiley and Sons.

Dillman, D.A. and Redline, C.D. (2004). Testing Paper Self-Administered Questionnaires: Cognitive Interview and Field Test Comparisons. In S. Presser, J. Rothgeb, M. Couper, J. Lessler, E. Martin, J. Martin and E. Singer (eds), *Questionnaire Development Evaluation and Testing Methods*. Hoboken, NJ: John Wiley and Sons.

Ericsson, K.A. (1998). Protocol Analysis. In W. Bechtel and G. Graham, *A Companion to Cognitive Science*. Malden, MA: Blackwell Publishing.

Euroqol Group (1990). Euroqol – A New Facility for the Measurement of Health-Related Quality of Life. *Health Policy*, 16: 199–208.

Food and Drug Administration. Guidance for Industry: Patient-Reported Outcome Measures: Use in Medical Product Development to Support Labeling Claims (Final), December 2009. Available at: http://www.fda. gov/downloads/Drugs/GuidanceComplianceRegulatoryInformation/ Guidances/UCM193282.pdf [Accessed December 8, 2009].

Fienberg, S.E. and Tanur, J.M. (1996). Surveying and Interdisciplinary CASM. In L. Salter and A. Hearn, (eds), *Outside the Lines: Issues in Interdisciplinary Research*. Montreal: McGill-Queen's University Press.

Fowler, F.J. (1995). *Improving Survey Questions*. Thousand Oaks, CA: Sage.

Gerber, E.R. and Wellens, T.R. (1997). Perspectives on Pretesting: 'Cognition' in the Cognitive Interview? *Bulletin de Methodologie Sociologique*, 11: 18–39.

Groves, R.M., Fultz, N.H. and Martin, E. (1992). Direct Questioning About Comprehension in a Survey Setting. In J. Tanur (ed.), *Questions About Questions: Inquiries into the Cognitive Bases of Surveys*. New York: Russell Sage Foundation.

Hak, T., Van der Veer, K., Jansen, H. (2004). The three-step test-interview (Tsti): An Observational Instrument for Pretesting Self-Completion Questionnaires. ERIM Report Series Reference No. ERS-2004-029-ORG. Available at SSRN: http://ssrn.com/abstract=636782

Hansen, S.E. and Couper, M.P. (2004). Usability Testing to Evaluate Computer-Assisted Instruments. In S. Presser, J. Rothgeb, M. Couper, J. Lessler, E. Martin, J. Martin and E. Singer (eds), *Questionnaire Development Evaluation and Testing Methods*. Hoboken, NJ: John Wiley and Sons.

Jabine, T.B., Straf, M.L. and Tanur, J.M. et al. (eds) (1984). *Cognitive Aspects of Survey Methodology: Building a Bridge Between Disciplines*. Washington, DC: National Academy Press.

Jobe, J. and Mingay, D. (1991). Cognition and Survey Measurement: History and Overview. *Applied Cognitive Psychology*, 5: 175–192.

Lessler, J.T., Tourangeau, R. and Salter, W. (1989) Questionnaire Design in the Cognitive Research Laboratory. *Vital and Health Statistics*, 6(1). Hyattsville, MD: National Center for Health Statistics.

Miles, M.B. and Huberman, A.M. (1994). *Qualitative Data Analysis*. Thousand Oaks, CA: Sage.

Morgan, D.L. (1997). Focus Groups as Qualitative Research. *Qualitative Research Method Series*, 16. Thousand Oaks, CA: Sage.

O'Muircheartaigh, C. (1999). CASM: Successes, Failures, and Potential. In Sirken, M., Herrmann, D., Schechter, S., Schwarz, N., Tanur, J. and Tourangeau, R., (eds) (1999). *Cognition and Survey Research*. New York: Wiley.

Oksenberg, L., Cannell, C.F. and Kalton, G. (1991). New Strategies for Pretesting Survey Questions. *Journal of Official Statistics*, 7: 349–365.

Payne, S.L. (1951). *The Art of Asking Questions*. Princeton, NJ: Princeton University Press.

Presser, S, Couper, M.P. and Lessler, J.T. et al. (2004). Methods for Testing and Evaluating Survey Questions. *Public Opinion Quarterly*, 68: 109–130.

Ramachandran, S., Taber, T. and Craig, B.M. et al. (2005). Equivalence of Paper and Touch Screen Versions of the EQ-5D Visual Analogue Scale. Poster presented at the 12th Annual Conference of the International Society for Quality of Life Research held in San Francisco, CA, October 19–22, 2005.

Schechter, S., Beatty, P. and Willis, G.B. (1998). Asking Survey Respondents About Health Status: Judgment and Response Issues. In N. Schwarz, D. Park, B. Knauper, and S. Sudman, (eds), *Cognition, Aging, and Self-Reports*. Philadelphia, PA: Psychology Press.

Schechter, S., Blair, J. and Vande Hey, J. (1996). Conducting Cognitive Interviews to Test Self-Administered and Telephone Surveys: Which Methods Should We Use? *Proceedings of the Section on Survey Research Methods*, 10–17. Alexandria, VA: American Statistical Association.

Schuman, H. and Kalton, G. (1985). Survey Methods. In G. Lindzey and E. Aronson (eds) (1985). *The Handbook of Social Psychology*, Volume 1, 3rd edition. New York: Random House.

Schwarz, N. (1999). Self-Reports: How the Questions Shape the Answers. *American Psychologist*, 52 (2): 93–105.

Sirken, M. and Schechter, S. (1999). Interdisciplinary survey methods research. In M. Sirken, D. Herrmann, S. Schechter, N. Schwarz, J. Tanur, and R. Tourangeau (eds), *Cognition and Survey Research*, pp. 1–10. New York: Wiley.

Sudman, S. and Bradburn, N. (1982). *Asking Questions: A Practical Guide to Questionnaire Design*. San Francisco, CA: Jossey-Bass.

Sudman, S. Bradburn, N. and Schwarz, N. (1996). *Thinking About Answers: The Application of Cognitive Processes to Survey Methodology*. San Francisco, CA: Jossey-Bass.

Tarnai, J. and Moore, D.L. (2004). Methods for Testing and Evaluating Computer-Assisted Questionnaires. In S. Presser, J. Rothgeb, M. Couper, J. Lessler, E. Martin, J. Martin, and E. Singer (eds) *Questionnaire Development Evaluation and Testing Methods*. Hoboken, NJ: John Wiley and Sons.

Tiplady, B., Jamieson, A.H. and Crompton, G.K. (2000). Use of Pen-Based Electronic Diaries in an International Clinical Trial of Asthma. *Drug Information Journal*, 34: 129–136.

Tourangeau, R. (1984). Cognitive Sciences and Survey Methods. In T. Jabine, M. Straf, J. Tanur and R. Tourangeau, (eds) *Cognitive Aspects of Survey Methodology: Building a Bridge Between Disciplines*. Washington, DC: National Academy Press.

Tucker, C. (1997). Methodological Issues Surrounding the Application of Cognitive Psychology in Survey Research. *Bulletin de Methodologie Sociologique*, 11: 67–92.

Willis, G. (1994). Cognitive Interviewing and Questionnaire Design: A Training Manual. *Cognitive Methods Staff Working Paper Series*, No. 7. Hyattsville, MD: National Center for Health Statistics.

Willis, G. (2005). *Cognitive Interviewing: A Tool for Improving Questionnaire Design*. Thousand Oaks, CA: Sage.

3

Data Quality and Power in Clinical Trials: A Comparison of ePRO and Paper in a Randomized Trial

Allen L. Ganser, Stephen A. Raymond and Jay D. Pearson

Introduction

EPRO PIONEERS AND PROVING EPRO

A principal objective of the early developers of ePRO technology in the 1990s had been to overcome the many limitations inherent in paper methods. (Nived et al., 1994; Drummond et al., 1995; Raymond and Jamison, 1995; Shiffman et al., 1996; Stone et al., 1997; Raymond and Ross, 2000). Such limitations were known to result in untimely, unreadable, missing, illogical or otherwise faulty data. As engineers, given the capabilities of technologies such as telephones and handheld computers at the time, the ePRO pioneers were confident that they could accomplish their objective and would thus enable an improved quality of data provided directly by subjects of clinical investigations.

Inherent in their thinking was the assumption that improved data quality would naturally and automatically result in 'better science.' This assumption was so broadly shared by technology providers, by most sponsors of clinical trials, and by many scientists engaged in clinical studies that the idea of treating it as a hypothesis to be tested was not seen as necessary. Instead, most of the early investigative work on ePRO technologies had been focused on demonstrating that the 'data' were better (see, for example, Hyland et al., 1993; Tiplady et al., 1995). The scientific benefit of such better data seemed simply to be obvious. But in the early 2000s, the adoption of ePRO was still spotty, and for some who were then considering using the technology to demonstrate the efficacy or safety of medical products, the presumed linkage between better quality of PRO data and 'better science' became a question to be evaluated. The insomnia trial to be analyzed in this chapter (herein termed the Comparison Study) was the first controlled, randomized trial undertaken explicitly to test these expectations by comparing and quantifying the differences in data quality between electronic and paper methods and testing the assumption that if the data were better, that would lead to better science.

Organization of Chapter

We begin the chapter with an introduction to the Comparison Study, describing the background, methodology and the patient samples at different stages of the study. Secondly, we discuss the reasons why improvements in data quality and integrity with ePRO would be expected. Thirdly, we present evidence that ePRO did improve data quality, based on the differences between paper and ePRO data quality in the Comparison Study, which, when taken together with the experience in hundreds of other clinical trials, show that the ePRO pioneers clearly succeeded in delivering a technology that yields *better data* and a greater quantity of *evaluable data*. Fourthly, we examine the assumption that this better data does actually lead to better science, in particular increased statistical power. The concluding topic is a discussion of variation, variability, and signal and noise based on the analysis of the primary efficacy variable for the Comparison Study.

Background and Methodology of the Comparison Study

Studies of insomnia frequently use patient-reported outcomes, employ diary and questionnaire instruments, and have large numbers of data points. Furthermore, the PRO measures in such studies are important and often support the claims for efficacy in market authorizations. Insomnia is thus a good area in which to compare PRO methods. Our trial was designed primarily to make evident the relative capabilities of paper and electronic technologies to *yield credible conclusions*, not to yield new knowledge about medications used to treat insomnia.

The trial was a multicenter, parallel group, unblinded, and 'usual-care' design. Patients[1] who met the DSM-IV diagnosis for chronic primary insomnia and were already being treated effectively by FDA-approved prescription hypnotics (Flurazepam, Temazepam, Zaleplon, and Zolpidem) for at least 3 months as prescribed by each subject's physician, were randomized into one of two groups (arms) that used either paper forms or portable handheld electronic devices (LogPad, PHT Corporation, Charlestown, Massachusetts) for data capture. Based on previous work measuring the increase in Total Sleep Time (TST) as the primary efficacy variable, we expected that of 90 patients enrolled (half to each group), approximately 75 would complete the study and that the trial would be powered at 95 per cent to detect a 45–60 min change in mean TST with treatment. Written consent was obtained from all patients. The study was carried out between May and December, 2002, at four sites in the United States.

At the Screening Visit (Visit 1), 44 patients were allocated to paper and 46 to ePRO arms according to a computer-generated, structured, randomization schedule which balanced age and education level between each arm. All enrolled patients were included in the *data quality analysis*. Subjects were instructed to discontinue their insomnia medication for at least 7 days of washout (WO) and then resume their medication for at least 28 days of treatment. Visit 2 marked the end of WO, and was called the 'Baseline Visit'. Subjects were allowed to continue beyond Visit 2 if their diary reports during WO showed that they had:

1. a median total sleep time of ≤ 6 hours for those days;

2. a median score of fair to poor for sleep quality (poor being the worst on a four point Likert item); and

3. completed at least 4 morning diary entries for these items.

Those who continued (33 paper, 37 ePRO) resumed their usual course of medication in the evening of the day of the Baseline Visit (Day 0). At weekly clinic visits, site personnel supported subjects and encouraged compliance with diary completion and medication schedules. During the trial, nine more subjects either withdrew or were excluded for not meeting eligibility criteria. Inspection of the cleaned and locked data set led to the exclusion of an additional

---

1   Complete recruitment and eligibility criteria are available upon request from the first author (ALG).

three subjects based on protocol requirements and two because of insufficient data for the periods analyzed. Thus the final group used for the quantitative analysis of the *primary endpoint* consisted of 25 subjects in the paper arm and 31 subjects in the ePRO arm, or 62 per cent of those originally enrolled.

Although the subjects completed a full battery of insomnia assessments, for this chapter we only analyze data from one PRO instrument, the Morning Questionnaire (MQ). Subjects were requested to complete this within 1 hour after getting out of bed each morning. The MQ asked subjects to report the amount of time slept the preceding night (total sleep time or TST). This item was used to calculate the primary outcome measure. Relevant sections of the MQ in its paper and electronic forms are shown in Figure 3.1.

The primary hypotheses of the Comparison Study were that, in comparison to paper methods, ePRO would:

1.   yield data of superior quality;

2.   be superior to paper in revealing efficacy of treatment as measured by average increase in TST.

EXPECTED IMPROVEMENTS IN DATA QUALITY WITH EPRO

The data quality problems found with the paper method and the bases for expecting ePRO to address them are described in this section.

Data quality, integrity, and trustworthiness

Data quality refers to those aspects of data as they are initially captured by the subject. This includes accuracy, precision, completeness (were all questions answered? were reports lost?), consistency (logical, not out of range), attribution (did anyone but the patient write in the diary?), legibility (decipherable, unambiguous), contemporaneousness (did the patient complete three week's worth of entries just before seeing the doctor?), originality (i.e., not duplicated), sensitivity, validity, and suitability to purpose (CDISC 2008). For PRO data, quality also includes psychometric validity, compliance to the activities specified in the protocol, and logical consistency among responses.

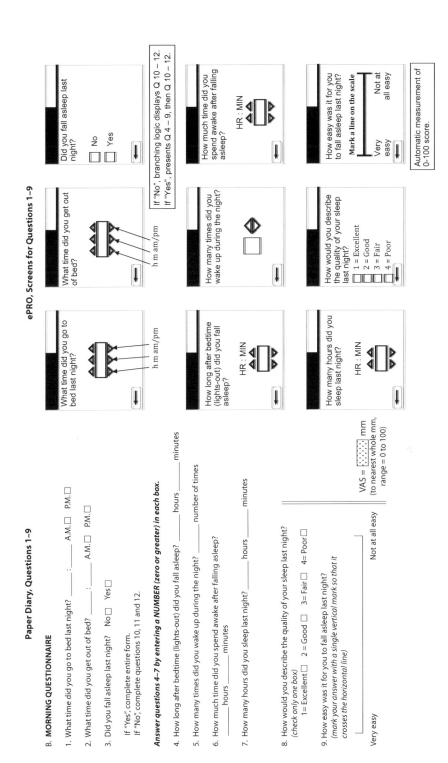

Figure 3.1 Comparison of representative images of the Morning Questionnaire for paper and ePRO

It is relevant to distinguish between data quality and data integrity, which are the two dimensions of data that determine the level of trust that policy makers can place in trial results submitted for market approval (FDA 1997; CDISC 2008). *Data integrity* refers to the preservation of the records from inception to archive. Even high quality data are not trustworthy unless they could not have been corrupted, lost, or undetectably altered. Contributing to data integrity are the systems and processes for data capture, correction, maintenance, transmission, and retention (CDISC 2008). Any findings based on data of high quality and integrity are trustworthy so long as the analyses leading to the findings are also appropriate and free of bias.

Human factors such as forgetfulness, limited thinking and processing abilities, digit preference, lack of concern and attention, and even zealousness (extra writing in the margins) contribute to the data quality problems of paper records. Paper records are replete with missing, unreadable, illogical, erroneous, extra, and retrospective values. It is a continuing expectation that all this interferes with the detection of real differences, that accuracy is less, that noise is greater, and that it is therefore harder to obtain conclusive results with paper methods.

Implementation of ePRO capabilities in the comparison study

Functionalities can be designed into ePRO technology and software that eliminate many of the familiar categories of poor data quality in clinical investigations capturing self-reports from subjects. In Table 3.1 we identify and explain the key functional capabilities relevant to the Comparison Study.

Table 3.1 ePRO solutions to data quality problems with paper methods

Aspect of Data Quality	Problem with Paper Methods	ePRO Implementation to Address the Problem
	Field(s) expected to be completed are empty in an otherwise complete report.	Completion checks disallow submission of reports with missing data fields.
	Accidentally missed fields cannot be distinguished from intentionally skipped fields ('ambiguity' of empty fields).	Accidentally missed fields are prevented while 'skip options' can mark fields that subjects skip intentionally if, for example, they consider the item too embarrassing or if none of the response options fit the situation.
Complete	Missing fields are completed after-the-fact, when study coordinators review paper records with subjects, or when site monitors attempt to correct missing fields retrospectively when neither site staff nor subject can remember the situation.	Missing fields are prevented in ePRO reports that are available for completion only during scheduled time windows. Interim access to results supports timely resolution of data errors.
	Entire report is not completed and missing because of forgetfulness or refusal.	Alarms/messages remind subjects to complete reports on schedule. Site personnel, have timely access to completion compliance metrics and can thus encourage delinquent subjects to comply.
	Finished reports are missing completely or partially because of loss by subject or investigator (for example, paper diary pages left on bus or misplaced).	A logging device can be lost or become inoperable, but only finished reports not yet transmitted will be missing; those already at a central server are not lost. Records stored centrally are backed up to protect against loss or destruction. Lost devices are replaced as easily as a set of blank paper forms.
Contemporaneous (Timely)	Data entry is performed, but not when scheduled. Subjects can misrepresent retrospective or prospective completion as if done when scheduled (Stone, Shiffman et al. 2002).	Time constraint on the availability of questions is used to make it impossible for ePRO subjects to complete scheduled diaries retrospectively or prospectively.
	No validation of time or date of entries.	All data entries are automatically time-stamped using a method validated to be accurate.

Table 3.1　*Continued*

Aspect of Data Quality	Problem with Paper Methods	ePRO Implementation to Address the Problem
	Transcription errors are made when manually transferring or scanning source data to either paper or eCRFs.	ePRO eSource data is automatically migrated to a central store and ultimately to the sponsor database by methods validated to be accurate and reliable.
	Intensity and impact of symptoms are not precisely rated because of recall difficulties. When subjects are asked to assess their current symptoms, paper methods confound data that is current with prospective (guessing) or retrospective (from memory) data.	When ePRO assessments are intended to reflect the current state of the subject, they are captured in real time or close enough for memory to be sharp. Recall bias is minimized. For example, sleep latency is required the next morning when subjects can recall the preceding night. ePRO prevents assessments made days later.
Accurate	Key behaviors required by the protocol, such as the schedule of taking study medication, are assisted only by static written instructions.	ePRO systems can request behaviors automatically at the appropriate time. Devices can also display recently logged events so that subjects can, for example, avoid taking an extra pill or reporting taking a particular pill twice.
	Subjects do not accurately interpret contingent instructions.	With a response of 'No' to 'Did you sleep last night?', ePRO skips the questions related to that nights sleep and presents subsequent items. ePRO systems can also automatically prompt subjects for contingent behaviors (for example, 'You have escalated doses 4 days in a row, please call your study nurse.').
	Annotations can show the proper formula to calculate a value to enter, but cannot assist in actually making the calculation and errors can occur in these derived fields (for example, BMI, median of total sleep time over a period of days).	Derived fields can be calculated automatically by validated methods.

Table 3.1 *Continued*

Aspect of Data Quality	Problem with Paper Methods	ePRO Implementation to Address the Problem
	Response data are factually incompatible (for example, subjects responds that 'No' they didn't sleep but also report a number of hours slept).	Software applications detect logical inconsistencies at the time of data entry and allow for corrections. The sequence of questions automatically branches depending on previous responses, so that illogical items are not presented.
Logical	Subjects fail to follow instructions on how to answer a question, such as checking both responses to an either/or question or marking more than one option of a multiple choice item where a single option is required and some options may be logically inconsistent.	ePRO system allows only one response to either/or questions and to multiple choice or rating questions that require only one answer from a list of options. For example, 'Did you sleep last night? No ☐ Yes ☐;' 'How would you describe the quality of your sleep last night? (check only one box.) 1 = Excellent ☐ 2 = Good ☐ 3 = Fair ☐ 4 = Poor ☐'
	Out of range values are entered (for example, total sleep time is greater than time in bed).	'Soft' range checks can alert responder to values likely to be out of range. 'Hard' range checks disallow values deemed impossibly out of range.
	Past, present or future dates can be entered, regardless of instructions.	Selection of dates or times that are known to be inappropriate is prevented at the moment of data entry by programmed date checks.
	Subjects may forget that they have already done a report and re-do it.	If only one report is scheduled, ePRO devices allow only one report to be completed for a particular scheduled report time.
Conforming (to protocol)	When a subject receives a set of paper forms that replaces a lost set that had been partially completed, the subject may begin with the wrong report.	ePRO replacement devices automatically guide subjects to complete the next available appropriate report.
	Paper methods cannot control, prevent, or manage illegible responses.	All fields with structured response options or free text that is typed are legible. Legibility of handwritten text data matches that of paper.
Legible	Paper records cannot be read until document has been brought to the investigator or shipped to the data entry clerk.	Completed reports are transmitted to a server that makes them readable over the Web or other network.

Table 3.1 *Continued*

Aspect of Data Quality	Problem with Paper Methods	ePRO Implementation to Address the Problem
Original	Study data are first recorded to a record that cannot be demonstrated to be original such as scraps of paper for writing measurement values or notes where dates, times and other contextual information are often not recorded.	ePRO capture devices used by subjects and observers are the first mode of capture for study data. By regulation, the temporal context and authorship must be part of each record.
	Resolution of a data mismatch between a manually compared paper CRF with paper sources may not be traceable.	ePRO records are eSource documents. The eCRF fields in ePRO systems are automatically populated from eSource data, and each field in the clinical database is therefore traceable to the original eSource.
Attributable	Data pertaining to a subject becomes associated with another subject. Source data may not include necessary identifiers and may be sorted incorrectly.	Devices with unique codes (analogous to credit cards) are assigned for the sole use of a subject. PIN or other access codes, given only to the identified user, are required for data capture. Phone numbers or IP addresses used during capture or transmission are logged. Handwritten or digital signatures are linked to eSource records. Current interim data is available for site staff to review so that data content not matching a subject's status can reveal erroneous attribution.
	Actions on data (capture, edits, approvals, etc.) may not be linked correctly to the person performing the action (for example, improperly signed or dated source documents, CRF's, edits to data).	ePRO system identifies users and links all actions on data to an identified and authorized person via a computer generated audit trail. The action cannot be completed without attribution.

Table 3.1   *Concluded*

Aspect of Data Quality	Problem with Paper Methods	ePRO Implementation to Address the Problem
	Ambiguous date formats (for example, 05/07/09 entered for July 5, 2009 could be interpreted as May 7, 2009).	Date fields are entered from a calendar, date 'spinner,' or other control that reveals month and day unambiguously and presents them in the order that is locally appropriate.
	Blank day or month numbers appear in date records where fully specified dates are required; am or pm are missing from time entries.	Devices require capture of complete dates for some fields, but could truncate full dates to hide the day and month and/or allow capture of partial dates for others. Date and time conventions are set at field, form, or study levels.
Unambiguous	For time entries, inadvertent use of am or pm, or confusion about whether midnight is 12:00 am or 12:00 pm.	Intelligent ePRO software can request assurance of am or pm entries or correction of inappropriate use of am or pm time indications.
	Differing database standards across studies hamper combining data for analysis (for example, a Yes or No response may be transcribed with 0 vs 1, 1 vs 0, or 1 vs 2 codings).	Multiple coding conventions can be supported in each study. CDISC or other standards can be enforced for original source data so that data from similar studies can be pooled for meta-analysis.
	Response mark is made between two check boxes.	Selection of response options are displayed in real time so that the subject resolves any ambiguity at the time of capture.

Bias

These types of quality problems can have very different impacts on the study outcome. Small amounts of missing data may have negligible or zero impact *provided they occur at random*. The concern is that this may not be the case. For example patients may be more likely to miss a diary entry if they are feeling well and their conditions are less salient than when they are experiencing symptoms. Or the reverse bias may occur, and they may miss entries when they are feeling poorly because they haven't the energy to do it. These two scenarios obviously introduce opposite biases and it is impossible to know a priori which is likely to occur. Occurrence may well differ from study to study. Even if there is no bias, data that are inaccurate, misremembered or invented will add a source of noise to the data that diminishes precision. Enough missing or inconsistent responses may make the data impossible to evaluate, and therefore of no value.

EVIDENCE FOR IMPROVED DATA QUALITY

Quantifying data quality: Approach and method

We relied upon the protocol and the instructions on the MQ form itself to establish expectations for data capture. The MQ is a fairly typical questionnaire, so presenting a detailed data quality analysis should provide insight into general differences in data quality (DQ) between paper and ePRO methods. The following procedure was then developed and applied to the cleaned and locked data for all subjects enrolled in the study (44 paper; 46 ePRO) to identify, count, and analyze all the ways in which any data either fulfilled or failed to fulfill these expectations.

1. Arrange all data for each subject sequentially according to the time and date of completion.

2. Review the tabulated data against the protocol and instructions to distinguish all possible types of data quality (DQ) failures and successes and develop categories that describe each kind and account comprehensively for the DQ both good and bad.

3. Develop exact rules for the assignment of each DQ category to reports and fields and systematically code each report and field as belonging to one or more DQ category.

4.   Count all instances for each DQ category both good and bad.

5.   Audit interrelated category counts to check that they match the total number determined to be possible or expected.

Reports: DQ categories and differences between paper and ePRO

The first approach to DQ was at the level of reports. At this level, we considered whether the reports were done or not in accordance with the protocol, not whether they were internally complete or consistent. DQ at the level of the individual fields or items within the report will be considered below. Distinct categories of DQ were identified to cover all the observed instances and given descriptive names, e.g., the report DQ aspect of *complete* was found to be comprised of *Reports Expected and DONE, Expected and Known NOT to be Done, Expected and MISSING*, and *NOT Expected* (but done).

The number of *Reports Expected* was 1198 for paper and 1374 for ePRO arms. The number *Expected and Done* was 1181 (98.4 per cent) for paper and 1284 (93.4 per cent) for ePRO. These percentages correspond to report completion compliance, a key performance metric. It is important to note that the Comparison Study incorporated an unusually high level of supervision of subjects using paper diaries. Subjects met with site personnel weekly and reviewed all diaries done that week. Since the paper method could not prevent retrospective or prospective completion of reports (Table 3.1.), the very high compliance of the paper arm was likely achieved in part by completions that were outside the scheduled times (Berg et al. 1998; Stone et al. 2002; Green et al. 2006). In this study, the LogPad prevented unscheduled completion by making a MQ available early in the morning of each day (5:30 am) and then withdrawing availability after 11:59 pm of that day. Higher reported compliance for paper than ePRO has also been reported in a number of previous studies, some of which have been able to show indications of better DQ for ePRO (Tiplady et al. 1995; Stone et al. 2002).

For paper subjects, there were only 16 reports categorized as *MISSING*. This category means that for such reports it was unknown whether they had been unavailable for completion; available but done and lost; or available for completion yet never done. For ePRO subjects, there were no *MISSING* reports. Although the paper MQ had a field for marking that a report was 'not done,' there was only one instance where that field was checked. Thus this report was categorized as *Expected and Known NOT to be Done*. In contrast, the ePRO arm had 90 *Expected Reports* that were *Known NOT to be Done.* These reports were known (through validation testing and ongoing monitoring of LogPad operation) to have been available but not completed.

There were a few instances where multiple MQ's were recorded as having been completed by a given subject on the same date. These were classified as *Non-Compliant with Protocol* since only 1 MQ was expected per day. All 18 reports of this category (referring to 9 days) occurred in the paper arm.

Fields: Pertinent DQ categories and salient differences between paper and ePRO

Some reports, while 'done' in the sense of containing one or more entries, are either not complete, not dated, contain irreconcilable entries, or are 'excessively complete' (e.g., containing multiple answers where one is expected). These are DQ problems that pertain to the individual *fields* that make up a *Report Expected and Done.*

When comparing ePRO and paper it is important to bear in mind that the items and fields in the two modes were the same. There were of course differences in layout and in minor details of wording, for example referring to tapping the touch screen vs. checking a box (see Figure 3.1). The structure of the data collected, however was identical for ePRO and paper.

We assigned one or more DQ categories to each field in each report. For example, when the item stem (i.e. 'question') reads: 'Did you fall asleep last night?', then the expected entry is for only one response option, either 'Yes' or 'No,' to be 'filled' or selected. With paper, both or neither option could be filled, creating a number of explicit DQ difficulties. If both 'Yes' and 'No' were to be checked, then that response would be simultaneously categorized as 'ambiguous,' non-compliant (with instructions) and logically inconsistent (both answers could not logically apply), as well as a 'filled' cell (simply responded to). All fields in all reports would thus have at least one DQ category ascribed to them, either filled or not when expected to be filled, or empty or not when expected to be empty. Some fields would have multiple categories depending on general instructions and the logical context of the particular field, as in the preceding example. Note that we use the term 'cell' to denote each particular instance where a field could have been completed or not.

Several paper reports in the Comparison Study were marked with margin notes and text explanations that were not among the structured response options. For this chapter we did not track or tally such instances of marginalia or notes.

Fields with entries that should have been blank

Blank or null entries are expected in cases where the branching logic of the questionnaire bypasses questions that are deemed not to be relevant as a result of a response to a specific question. There are two places in the MQ where this occurs.

Q. 3 asks 'Did you fall asleep last night?', with a Yes/No response. If the answer is No, the form instructs the subject to skip Q. 4–9, which ask about quality of sleep, and to continue with Q. 10–12. Thus if the answer to Q. 3 was No, any Q. 4–9 field with an actual entry was categorized as an entry completed that should have been blank. Likewise, Q. 10 asks 'Did anything unusual happen to disturb your sleep?', and requires a Yes/No response. If Yes, a description should be entered in Q. 10b; if No, Q. 10b should be blank. In both cases, if the progenitor cell (Q. 3 or Q. 10a) is blank, the expectations for the dependent cells are unknown and categorized either as Filled with Expectation Unknown or Empty with Expectation Unknown, accordingly.

The results for these two question groups are shown in Table 3.2, and are dramatically different for the two modes. Over half of the entries that should have been blank for Q.4–9 were filled in on paper. None were filled for ePRO. All entries for both questions which should have been blank for ePRO were in fact blank, indicating the correct operation of the diary software. It is interesting that the errors following the two similar questions on paper (entering fields that should be skipped) occurred almost 100 times more often following a 'No' for Q. 3 than for 'No' to Q. 10a.

What might account for the high percentage of replies describing sleep (50.7 per cent of the time) by paper subjects who had previously responded 'No' they didn't fall asleep that night? In preparing this chapter we interviewed several insomniacs informally to ask them how they might answer questions concerning such experiences as 'awakening' during a night when they also said they hadn't slept. Their explanations revealed an intriguing possible difference in the mind-set of chronic insomniacs from the mindset of those who had developed the morning questionnaire and whom we assume to have been normal sleepers. For people with chronic insomnia, a night of no sleep might also be a night of 'awakenings'; it might even be a night of many 'awakenings' that prevented 'any sleep.' It is a bit more mind boggling to see how insomniacs might feel they had not slept ('No' to Q.3) and then enter a non-zero value for total time slept (Q. 7), but it appeared from our interviews that this inconsistency was not as apparent to insomniacs as it seems to us.

Table 3.2   Counts for dependent filled cells

Category of Data Quality	Paper			ePRO		
Filled Cell Expected To Be Empty	# Cells Possible To Be Filled	# Cells Filled	Error %	# Cells Possible To Be Filled	# Cells Filled	Error %
Entries for Q. 4–9, Describe sleep, when Q. 3, Did you sleep?, is 'No'	426	216	50.7	386	0	0.0
Entries for Q. 10b, Describe unusual event, when Q. 10a, Did anything unusual happen? is 'No'	1039	6	0.58	1113	0	0.0
Filled Cell with Expectation Unknown	83	63	75.9	0	0	na

Entries NOT completed

Not all fields should be entered. The table below shows exact counts comparing cases where subjects left fields empty appropriately and inappropriately in the reports that were done.

Table 3.3   Counts for empty cells

Category of Data Quality	Paper			ePRO		
	# Cells Possible to Be Empty	# Empty	Error %	# Cells Possible to Be Empty	# Empty	Error %
Empty Cell Expected To Be Empty	1465	1243	15.2	1959	1959	0.0
Empty Cell Expected To Be Full	15095	256	1.7	17301	0	0.0
Empty Cell With Expectation Unknown	83	20	24.1	0	0	na

Cells expected to be full: In this trial, subjects did an unusually good job of completing the items in the reports they did. Only 1.7 per cent of fields that were expected to be filled were left blank by the paper subjects. For the primary efficacy value, total sleep time, there was only one paper report in the whole study where it was missing. All fields expected to be filled in any report done using ePRO were, in fact, completed, which is a reflection of the proper operation of the software application that would not allow a required item to be bypassed or left empty.

Failures to comply with instructions

As well as being logical inconsistencies, answers to questions that should have been skipped also represent a failure to follow instructions. Failure to follow instructions on a form is a familiar problem with paper methods and can lead to the lack of success of a trial. Questions 3–9 contain the most significant section of the Morning Questionnaire. These query total sleep time, which was a primary efficacy measure, as well as the secondary endpoints, sleep latency, ease of falling asleep, sleep quality, and wakefulness. In the Comparison Study the data for these key fields cannot be interpreted unless a subject had followed a particular instruction. The study team was well aware of the problem before the study began, and the training given to site investigators emphasized teaching subjects about the completion instructions for the Morning Questionnaire and also the importance of detecting any lapses during the weekly review. CRA's were also trained to attend to the issue in data cleaning. So the residual problems seen in this study may represent a lower boundary, a minimum number of possible mistakes when paper methods are used and all best practices for data cleaning are followed.

Table 3.4   Medication compliance

Category of Data Quality	Paper			ePRO		
	# Possible	# Empty	%	# Possible	# Empty	%
Non-compliance with Medication Schedule	1184	69	5.8	1284	49	3.8
Compliance with Medication Schedule Unknown	1184	17	1.4	1284	0	0.0

The counts of failure to comply with the medication schedule were drawn from reports that were done, not inferred from missing reports. Counts include instances where subjects took study medication when they should not have done so during the washout period, or where they did not take it when they should have during the treatment period. For the Comparison Study the ePRO implementation did not include an audible alarm in the evening to remind subjects specifically to take their medication before going to bed. An audible alarm did occur each morning at 11 am, and the MQ contained the item where subjects entered the information about taking the study medication the night before.

While the overall reported compliance with the medication plan was quite high in both arms, non-compliance was slightly lower in the ePRO group (3.8 vs 5.8 per cent). This may reflect the daily reminders (alarms) or it might be because ePRO subjects had to complete the MQ each day and therefore had a daily experience of encountering the medication question. Paper subjects, on the other hand, could complete several days' worth of morning diaries at a time, and thus would see the medication question on fewer days. There were no instances of unknown compliance to medication in the ePRO records.

These results show that some telling differences in DQ remain between paper and ePRO even when the self-reports are subjected to data cleaning.

Other logical inconsistencies

All subjects were instructed to complete the MQ within one hour after getting out of bed, and we categorize completion times prior to getting up as logical inconsistencies because it was a logical assumption in the study documentation that subjects would not complete their reports while still in bed. The incidence for paper and ePRO was similar (2.5 per cent vs 3 per cent). Although an edit check could have been developed for this issue, it was not implemented for the Comparison Study.

The ePRO subjects reported more instances (99 instances, 198 fields) of getting out of bed before going to bed than did paper subjects (7.7 per cent vs. 2.4 per cent of possible, respectively). The time entry items for both events were manual fields that required selection of 'am' or 'pm' (see Figure 3.1). The ePRO time entry item did not have automated consistency checks at time of entry to help subjects avoid mistaken selection of 'am' or 'pm.'

We did not include in this chapter the analysis of the numerous and sizable inconsistencies present for both paper and ePRO arms in the amount of time reported to have been spent in bed, time awake before falling asleep, time asleep, and time awake during interruptions of the night's sleep. Again, although possible, ePRO edit checks were not implemented in this case.

These findings emphasize that data from ePRO is not superior to paper simply by virtue of being electronic. Specific features implemented in the application design enable improvements in data quality to be obtained. Where an ePRO application allows inconsistent or illogical data to be entered, then at least some patients will do so.

Timeliness of data

We mention the accuracy of time, but this study did NOT yield data on the lateness of paper reports. The only documented improvement in timeliness of data was the built in constraint for the LogPad that prevented retrospective or prospective completion, thus insuring that each day's reports were completed on the scheduled day.

CONCLUSIONS CONCERNING DATA QUALITY DIFFERENCES

ePRO data were quantitatively superior to paper in the following areas:

1. Fewer fields that were expected to be completed were not completed.

2. No fields that were expected NOT to be completed were completed.

3. The incidence of logical inconsistencies in the collected data was less and was zero where automated methods were used that had been designed to prevent such inconsistencies.

4. The certainty of the time of completion was greater.

5. There were no duplicate reports.

In all categories, and for all but one item, the clinical data captured and entered on paper records were found to have higher counts and higher incidence of data quality problems than were the data captured and transmitted from ePRO electronic source records. This difference occurred even though the paper diary data were scrubbed for data quality problems. The ePRO data quality was higher, and thus a key condition needed to qualify the Comparison Study for testing of the presumption that the higher quality ePRO data would result in 'better science' was fulfilled.

Evidence for Better Science

Does the improved data quality and timeliness of entry help? Obviously increasing the percentage of evaluable data is a benefit in its own right, but what consequences does the improved quality of ePRO data have for the overall power of clinical investigations? We use *scientific power* to refer to the capability for a particular trial design (measurement methods, endpoints, number and selection of subjects, appropriate controls, baseline and treatment periods, etc.) to produce a valid, credible and statistically significant conclusion concerning the scientific question under study. The term is intended here to describe not only the relative ability to reveal a fact, but also the capacity to deepen understanding by making evident the relation of a fact to its cause or mechanism.

APPROACH

This analysis of the Comparison Study focused on the quantitative change in patient-reported total sleep time (TST) occurring between baseline and treatment. For each individual subject, we calculated the mean of the daily TST's during the wash out (WO) week and during the fourth week of treatment. The difference between these weekly means yielded a single value for the change in TST for a patient. Individual patients thus served as their own controls. The mean, median, and measures of variability of these individual changes between WO and treatment were then calculated for each arm. We then analyzed the variability from the perspective of its influence on statistical power as a way of quantifying the relative power of paper and ePRO methodologies.

The analysis included TST values as reported in Q. 7 of the MQ. Inconsistent entries were handled as follows: If Q. 7 was blank when item Q. 3 'Did you sleep last night?' was 'No,' TST was considered to be zero hours because the instructions on the paper form were to skip Q. 7 (along with several other questions). When Q. 7 had a zero entered and Q. 3 was 'No,' TST was again taken as zero hours despite the failure to comply with the instructions. If Q. 7 was blank when Q. 3 was 'Yes', a TST was regarded as missing and no imputation of a value was made. When a non-zero value for TST was entered in Q. 7 when Q. 3 was 'No,' the value was excluded from this analysis due to the evident logical inconsistency. According to the data analysis plan in the protocol, where there were < 3 TST values for any treatment week, those data were disqualified from efficacy analysis. Missing values did not invalidate any of the statistical methods used.

COMPARABLE INCREASES IN TST WITH PAPER AND EPRO

As previously stated, the sample for the power analysis consisted of 25 paper and 31 ePRO subjects. Statistical analysis, power calculations, regression curve fitting, and graphical presentation of results were performed using Prism (version 5.0b for Macintosh) and StatMate (version 2.0a91 for Macintosh) software, and online QuickCalcs, all by GraphPad Software, Inc.

Use of the mean to summarize treatment effects can aid interpretation, but can also obscure features of the data that may be important. For example, treatment could lead to an immediate improvement in sleep, which then remained at that same level (a step-function), or it could lead to progressive improvement over days or weeks. Either will lead to a change in the mean score. Likewise, the discontinuation of medication for the WO period could show an immediate, full, step-wise drop in TST or a gradual decrease over days to the untreated insomnia level. The step-function is equivalent to assuming that the use of medication on a specific treatment day or lack of use on a WO day, has no influence or carry over effect on subsequent days, i.e., the daily TSTs are independent of one another. Independence would be in keeping with the short half-lives (Passarella and Duong, 2008) of the medications[2] used by the subjects. We performed several statistical analyses that indicated the general independence of each day's TST and supported using the horizontal mean line as a reasonable model of these subjects' sleep times during WO and treatment weeks. The mean value can also be over-influenced by outliers. We have therefore presented both mean and median scores for comparison.

The changes in mean TST between baseline and treatment week 4 are presented for each paper and ePRO subject in Figure 3.2. All subjects reported an increase in mean TST in response to their medications. The amount of increase varied greatly among the subjects, from as little as 3–8 minutes to as much as 385 minutes (6.4 hours). The distributions of the increases were fairly

---

2   Half-life ranges are: 0.5–1 hr for Zaleplon, used by 3 paper and 6 ePRO subjects; 1.4–4.5 hrs for Zolpidem, used by 18 paper and 21 ePRO subjects; and 4–20 hrs for Temazepam, used by 4 paper and4 ePRO subjects.

similar for each arm and had comparable central means. The spread of data points, however, appeared greater in the paper arm (Table 3.5.).

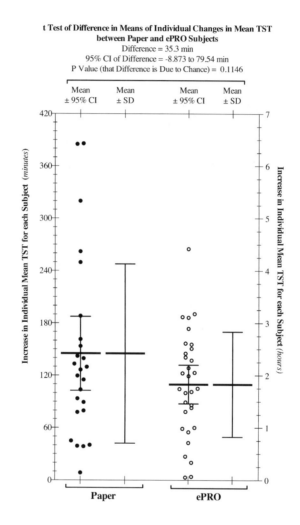

Figure 3.2   Distribution of individual changes in mean total sleep time

Note: Scatter plots of each subject's difference in mean Total Sleep Time between the washout week and week 4 of treatment; each data point indicates the change for one subject. Dark circles (left) paper; Light circles (right) ePRO. Also plotted for each arm is the overall mean increase in TST (thick center bars) along with the ± 95 per cent CI and ±SD of that mean (thin upper and lower range bars). Results of the ordinary t test (unpaired, two-tailed, P<0.05) for the equality of means are given at the top. Numerical values of these results and further statistical analysis is reported in Table 3.5.

The median increases in TST for each arm were even closer than the mean increases. The mean increases were 145 min for paper and 110 for ePRO, a difference of 35 min. The median increases were 126 min and 105 min, respectively, with a difference of 21 min (Table 3.5). We used the Mann-Whitney (or Wilcoxon) rank sum procedures to test for differences in the medians of the two arms. The test's high P value (Table 3.5) provided no evidence of a true difference making it likely that the observed difference in medians arose by chance and was not related to the method of measurement.

REDUCED VARIABILITY OF TST INCREASES IN EPRO ARM

Even though the general increase in TST associated with taking the insomnia medications, represented by means and medians, were similar when recorded by either method, the associated scatter or 'noise' around the median or mean was significantly different between paper and ePRO reporting systems. The dissimilarity in degree of variation is revealed by the sizable difference in the 95 per cent confidence interval (CI) of the means of the increases in TST between paper (84.8 min) and ePRO subjects (44.2 min) (Table 3.5.). The lower

Table 3.5   **Overall total sleep time increase and variability in paper and ePRO arms: statistical assessment and comparison**

Statistical Measure for Each Arm		Paper	ePRO
Mean of individual subject increases*	Time (*min*)	145.1	109.7
95% CI of the mean	Range (*min*)	102.6 to 187.5	87.6 to 131.8
	± Range (*min*)	± 42.4	± 22.1
	± Range as percent of mean	± 29.3%	± 20.2%
SD	Time (*min*)	102.8	60.3
	95% CI of SD (*min*)	80.3 to 143	48.2 to 80.6
CV		70.9%	55.0%
Median of individual subject increases*	Time (*min*)	126.4	105.0
	25% to 75% Interquartile range (*min*)	78.8 to 174.9	60 to 150.6
	Absolute value of the 25% to 75% interquartile range (*min*)	96.1	90.6
Number of values		25	31
Normality Test (D'Agostino and Pearson Omnibus K2)			
K2** value		6.73	0.506
P value for normality		0.0346	0.7765
Pass normality test? (alpha=0.05)		No	Yes

Table 3.5 *Concluded*

Tests for Differences between Paper and ePRO Arms		
Unpaired t Tests for Difference in *Means*	Assuming Equal Variances	Using Welch's Correction for Unequal Variances
Difference between means, paper minus ePRO (min)	35.3	35.3
95% CI of the difference (min)	-8.9 to 79.5	-11.8 to 82.5
P value (two-tailed) that difference is due to chance	0.1146	0.1372
Are the means significantly different at P < 0.05?	No	No
R^2 (fraction off total variability due to difference in means)	4.55%	6.03%
Mann-Whitney Rank Sum Test for Difference in Medians * **		
P value (two-tailed) that difference is due to chance	Gaussian Approximation	
Exact or approximate P value?	Gaussian Approximation	
Are medians significantly different? (P<0.05)	No	
F Test for Unequal Variances		
F ratio (larger variance/smaller variance)	2.908	
P value that F ratio is due to chance (two-tailed, standard Gaussian approximation)	0.0062	
Are the variances significantly different at P < 0.05?	Yes	

*Individual increases in TST were the difference between the mean of in treatment week 4 minus the mean of WO week TSTs for each subject.

**K2 combines computation of kurtosis and skewness into one value that quantifies how far the distribution deviates from Gaussian.

***This is a non-parametric test and only if the distributions of the data points in the two groups have the same shape (see Figure 3.2) can you interpret this test as comparing medians.

scatter in the ePRO arm was also shown by quantifying the variability as a standard deviation (SD) of the individual increases around their means. The SD for paper subjects was 102.8 min and 60.3 min for ePRO subjects (Table 3.5.). The difference between the SDs is apparent in the difference between the 95 per cent CIs of the two SDs (Table 3.5.) and was found to be statistically significant by the results of the F test for unequal variances, where the F ratio, the ratio of the larger to the smaller variance, was 2.9. (P value of 0.0062, Table 3.5.). The 42.5 min difference in SD between paper and ePRO arms corresponded to a 41 per cent reduction in SD and a 65.6 per cent reduction in variance in the ePRO arm. The lower variability in the ePRO arm was also revealed by the lower coefficient of variation (CV, 55.0 per cent for ePRO, 70.9 per cent for paper). Strong evidence that ePRO methodology resulted in less scatter in the measurement of the primary efficacy endpoint, the general change in TST, is very relevant to each of the primary hypotheses of the Comparison Study.

VARIATION, VARIABILITY, SIGNAL AND NOISE

But is the daily fluctuation within a subject in reported sleep times an accurate reflection of that subject's nightly sleep? Or is it contaminated by some amount of spurious noise arising from the method of measurement? Similar questions may be asked for other types of PRO and several published studies have addressed this. McKenzie et al. (2004) compared paper and ePRO data collection in overactive bladder, though using historical controls rather than a randomized design. They found a reduction in variability of scores with ePRO as compared to paper. Such a reduction translates into an increase in the statistical power of the study or a reduction in the required number of patients for a given power. This can be substantial. A reduction in SD on the scale found for the Comparison Study would allow the 95 per cent power to be reached with fewer than half the number of subjects using ePRO as would be needed for subjects using paper methods, and McKenzie et al. calculated that the sample size could be reduced by about 50 per cent. In the first publication of the results of the Comparison Study (Raymond and Pearson, 2004), it was noted that the standard deviation around the overall change in mean TST from baseline was less for ePRO than for the paper arm. Here we have re-analyzed and confirmed that finding, and have also shown evidence that the difference in SD is statistically significant. Similar findings of diminished variation around mean efficacy endpoints with ePRO have been reported in most of the published studies on this topic. Why is that?

The Comparison Study did not directly measure sleep and thus was not designed to determine if the variation from night to night in self reported TST's corresponded to objective fluctuations in time slept. In our study there is no reason to think the actual amount of time slept each day, nor its variability from day to day, nor the increase due to treatment, would be substantially different among paper and ePRO subjects. In fact the average increase in TST was the same for both methods. We suggest that the significantly greater variation reported in the Comparison Study when using paper must then include some component of misreporting, failed reporting, minimizing or exaggeration.

The principal methodological factor that most influences the difference in variances has been presumed to be that ePRO eliminates the retrospective or prospective completion of reports. A consequence is that subjects assess and report on the variable of interest (time slept) in the morning after the night in question. They would be expected to have better insight and recollection than would some subjects using paper who might be reporting retrospectively or prospectively.

Should we, however, also expect the variation in the reported assessment to be universally less for ePRO than for paper methods? Considering this question in view of the results of our study, we find first of all that most individual paper and ePRO subjects reported great variability in the amount of time slept from night to night. Based on our expectation that ePRO subjects should be able to report each day's TST more accurately, they should also convey more truthfully their sleeping behavior from night to night. The reported variation from night to night for an individual ePRO subject would thus be expected to more closely follow the true biological variation. And if this is correct, that the natural variation is large and is more accurately reported by ePRO subjects, then there is certainly the possibility that recalled or prospective assessments done by subjects using paper methods could *under-report* such variation. In this case, the method less able to accurately reveal the true experience of subjects could conceivably be the method with the lower scatter around a mean, while the more accurate method could show higher scatter. We can certainly imagine the possibility that true variation for intensity of some symptoms (osteoarthritic pain, shortness of breath with COPD, and others) will be large from day to day. In such cases we wonder whether subjects using paper to make reports in batches might report values that discount the variation (or possibly over emphasize it) and yield a consistency (or lack of it) that is a false representation of experience and feelings.

Thus while it has been demonstrated that ePRO methods can reduce variability around a treatment mean, and thus increase study power, we are skeptical about generalizing to the assumption that lower variation around a population mean will *always* result from the use of ePRO methods. Nonetheless, given that accuracy of measurement of a variable includes the accurate measurement of its variation over time, it seems persuasive that ePRO is a better scientific measuring method than paper.

For power calculations of sample size for clinical studies it will help to have preliminary results using the same method. A satisfactory solution is to use ePRO methodology in phase two of a program and then rely on the results of these studies to power phase three confirmatory research. An alternative, and possibly more efficient, approach, given access to ePRO data in real time, is to measure the standard deviation of the primary efficacy variable as the study progresses and thus determine sample size adaptively.

Such thinking has led us to a somewhat radical perspective concerning signal and noise. The accurate recording of individual symptom levels, even as they vary, is deemed noise only if the objective is to arrive at a difference in mean values for two populations. Trial design emphasizes such mean differences because they are the hallmark of effective treatments, and profoundly informative in comparison to untested claims of efficacy. From the patient perspective, however, it is also important to know what actually happens when using a therapy. More specifically, patients deserve to know what might happen to them if they use a therapy. A statement such as: 'on average, this medication has led to an increase of 2 hours and 5 minutes of total sleep time' tells them something. But reviewing the longitudinal daily records of the individual subjects in the Comparison Study provides a much richer picture of the range of personal experience of those using insomnia medications. For some patients the medications had little effect. Others had wide swings from night to night. It is also telling that the effect occurred nearly in full force on the first night of treatment. The big news for ePRO is that it documents in a trustworthy fashion what happens when individuals take a medication. The wealth of information in such experiences of individual subjects should, in our view, work its way into the documentation available to physicians who are considering and patients who have been prescribed therapies for which clinical investigations have been done.

Conclusion

Our consideration of paper and electronic methods of PRO data collection in this chapter identified many of the improvements in data quality expected by pioneers of ePRO. Such improvements were achieved in a study specifically designed to compare ePRO with paper PRO. Analysis of the data from this Comparison Study led to an approach for defining and categorizing data quality issues comprehensively so that PRO data quality could be quantified. We believe this approach and the metrics developed may be of value to researchers engaged in trial design who may rely on data quality measures as a tool for successive optimization of processes and PRO instruments.

Improvements in data quality with ePRO also were found to be associated with greater statistical power, or the possibility of sample size reduction for equivalent power, when ePRO was used to measure the primary endpoint. While the findings of the Comparison Study do not establish that such improvement in statistical power can be generalized to all trials using ePRO, this particular tangible example is important since the Comparison Study was a parallel, controlled, and randomized trial specifically intended to discover and measure any benefits of ePRO in comparison to matching paper methods. For endpoints where day-by-day variation is high, the more accurate ePRO method might yield a high variation that paper methods might obscure. Daily reports from both methods were very revealing of individual subject differences in the impact of treatment and, for reasons we have discussed, we believe the ePRO reports were the more trustworthy. To optimize scientific power and credibility of PRO data, we recommend that clinical researchers incorporate ePRO into drug development programs in Phase two trials so that confirmatory trials can be optimized for data quality and scientific power.

Acknowledgements

We are grateful for the assistance of Sandy Lewis, who helped describe the training of subjects and sites on PRO questionnaires and Dr. Bing Cai of Merck, who helped provide data sets and explanations of analyses done by Merck at the time of the original study. Thanks also to Harvey Motulsky, Ph.D., President of GraphPad Software, for much helpful advice on statistical analysis.

References

Berg, J., Dunbar-Jacob, J. and Rohay, J.M. (1998). 'Compliance with inhaled medications: the relationship between diary and electronic monitor.' *Ann Behav Med*, 20(1): 36–38.

CDISC (2008). CDISC Clinical Research Glossary, Version 7.O. Applied Clinical Trials. December, 2008: 12–52.

Drummond, H.E., Ghosh, S. and Ferguson, A. et al. (1995). Electronic quality of life questionnaires: a comparison of pen-based electronic questionnaires with conventional paper in a gastrointestinal study. *Qual Life Res*, 4(1): 21–26.

FDA (1997). 21 CFR Part 11. Electronic Records; Electronic Signatures Final Rule. 62 Federal Register 13430, March 20. Preamble, and Section 11.1.

Green, A.S., Bolger N., Shrout P., Rafaeli, E., Reis, H. (2006). Paper or plastic? Data equivalence in paper and electronic diaries. *Psychol Methods*, 11(1): 87–105.

Hyland, M.E., Kenyon, C.A. and Allen R. et al. (1993). Diary keeping in asthma: comparison of written and electronic methods. *BMJ*, 306(6876): 487–489.

McKenzie, S., Paty, J. and Grogan, D. et al. (2004). Proving the eDiary dividend. *Applied Clinical Trials*, 13(6): 54–68

Nived, O., Sturfelt, G. and Eckernas, S.A. et al. (1994). A comparison of 6 months' compliance of patients with rheumatoid arthritis treated with tenoxicam and naproxen. Use of patient computer data to assess response to treatment. *J Rheumatol*, 21(8): 1537–1541.

Passarella, S. and Duong, M.T. (2008). Diagnosis and treatment of insomnia. *Am J Health Syst Pharm*, 65(10): 927–934.

Raymond, S.A. and Pearson, J. (2004). Does better data from electronic Patient Reported Outcomes (ePRO) methodology actually improve clinical research? Results from a randomized trial comparing paper and ePRO diaries. ISOQOL 2004 Symposium Abstracts *Advancing Outcomes Research Methodology and Clinical Applications*, Boston MA. 2004: 28.

Raymond, S. and Jamison, R. (1995). Electronic Diary and Computer-Assisted Management in a Pilot Trial of Oral Opioids for Back Pain. *IBC International Forum on Remote Data Entry*. Orlando, FL.

Raymond, S. and Ross, S. (2000). Electronic Subject Diaries in Clinical Trials. *Applied Clinical Trials*, March, 2000.

Shiffman, S., Paty, J.A. and Gnys, M. et al. (1996). First lapses to smoking: within-subjects analysis of real-time reports. *J Consult Clin Psychol*, 64(2): 366–379.

Stone, A.A., Broderick, J.E. and Porter, L.S. et al. (1997). The experience of rheumatoid arthritis pain and fatigue: examining momentary reports and correlates over one week. *Arthritis Care Res*, 10(3): 185–193.

Stone, A.A., Shiffman, S. and Schwartz, J.E. et al. (2002). Patient non-compliance with paper diaries. *BMJ* 324(7347): 1193–1194.

Tiplady, B., Crompton, G.K. and Brackenridge, D. (1995). Electronic diaries for asthma. *BMJ*, 310(6992): 1469.

4

Regulation and Compliance: Scientific and Technical Regulatory Issues Associated with Electronic Capture of Patient-reported Outcome Data

Sonya Eremenco and Dennis A. Revicki

INTRODUCTION

Patient-reported outcome (PRO) measures of symptoms and health status are increasingly incorporated into clinical trials evaluating new and existing treatment interventions. These PRO endpoints often cover symptom experience, perceptions of health-related quality of life, functioning and well-being and treatment satisfaction (Coons et al. 2009; Revicki et al. 2000; Willke et al. 2004; Rothman et al. 2007; Revicki 2007). In many cases, such as pain and fatigue assessment, the patient's perception of outcome is the only available clinical trial endpoint. PRO endpoints are also used in clinical drug development programs to demonstrate the benefits of new treatments. Willke et al. (2004) found that PRO endpoints were included in 30 per cent of product labels examined between 1997 through 2002, and that for 11 per cent of products, PROs were the only endpoints reported.

Given this increased activity, in 2009 the Food and Drug Administration (FDA) released the final guidance for industry on PRO endpoints to provide insight to researchers as to the evidence requirements necessary for successful labeling and promotional claims (FDA 2009). The final FDA guidance was created to make the process of developing and reviewing PRO measures more efficient for both the FDA and clinical trial sponsors by outlining basic evidentiary standards. Nevertheless, this process continues to evolve and remains challenging given the large number of available PRO measures, the need for various language and cultural adaptations and the multiple existing and emerging methods of data collection.

Simultaneously with the increased use and significance of PROs in clinical trials has been the steady growth in electronic data capture (EDC) in clinical trials (Coons et al. 2009). Adaptation of case report forms to electronic formats in the clinical trial setting, including electronic methods of PRO data collection (ePROs), requires that sponsors provide evidence that the data collected using different platforms or methods are equivalent or account for any identified differences. Consequently, the FDA PRO guidance raised specific issues associated with ensuring the comparability of paper and electronic-based PRO measures (FDA 2009). To date most of the problems with ePRO endpoints have been associated with failure of electronic devices and with the perceived lack of adequate technical support for clinical investigators (Wiechers et al. 2002; Saponjic et al. 2003; Getz 2006).

This chapter specifically addresses the regulatory requirements for ePRO instruments from the perspective of the US FDA and European regulatory authorities (FDA 2009; EMEA 2005). The chapter is divided into two sections: the first section discusses regulatory related scientific issues associated with ePRO endpoints and the second section deals with technical requirements for ePRO measures.

Scientific Regulatory Issues for Electronic Pro Endpoints

Most PRO instruments were originally developed for paper-based administration but are increasingly adapted to ePRO formats. EDC adaptation of existing PROs may lead to reduced administrative burden, high patient compliance and acceptance, prevention of secondary data entry errors, increased understanding of when patients complete responses, easier implementation of complex skip patterns, reductions in missing data and more accurate data (Taenzer et al. 1997; Bloom 1998; Velikova et al. 1999; Stone et al. 2002; Bushnell et al. 2006; Gwaltney et al. 2008). The FDA has indicated support for the application of ePRO measures in clinical trials (Patrick et al. 2007). Nonetheless, ePRO instruments will require the same evidentiary requirements as any paper-based measure (Patrick et al. 2007; FDA 2009). In addition, evidence will be required to demonstrate the comparability of content validity and the psychometric qualities between the original paper version and the ePRO version. It is not recommended to migrate a poorly developed paper-based PRO measure with little psychometric evidence that does not adequately meet the FDA guidance criteria to an electronic format for use as primary or key secondary endpoints in clinical trials. More recently developed PRO instruments are often designed for ePRO applications or are simultaneously developed for both ePRO and paper data collection methods (Leidy et al. 2008; Thakkar et al. 2008; Kleinman et al. 2008; Cella et al. 2007). For example, the EXACT-PRO instrument developed by Leidy et al. (2008) was developed for electronic administration from the outset. Figure 4.1. depicts two items that were included in the development of this scale but not selected for the final EXACT-PRO instrument. In addition, the NIH sponsored Patient-Reported Outcome Measurement Information System (PROMIS) was designed for flexible data collection using paper or electronic, including computer adaptive testing, formats (www.nihpromis.org).

Electronic PRO Data Collection Devices/Systems

There are two main categories of ePRO data collection platforms: voice/auditory devices and screen text devices (Coons et al. 2009). Voice/auditory devices are primarily telephone based and are referred to as interactive voice response (IVR). IVR systems are automated telephone-based systems that interact with respondents using pre-recorded voice questions and responses. Advantages of IVR include that only a telephone is needed, limited respondent training is required, data can be directly stored to a central database, that IVR

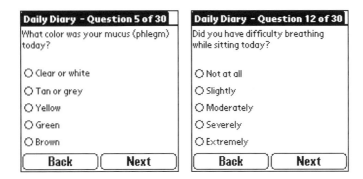

Figure 4.1   Sample items from the EXACT validation study not included in the final version

systems can also record voice responses (Coons et al. 2009), and IVR systems can be used with low literacy participants (Henriksen 1999). The system can be programmed to call the participants or to allow the study participants to call into the IVR system. The auditory presentation of IVR systems departs from the vision-oriented paper format but is analogous to telephone interview-administered data collection. Adapting a visual-oriented paper-based method to an auditory-based IVR method may introduce problems with data collection and respondent burden (Weiler et al. 2004). Studies of IVR systems demonstrate evidence supporting the reliability and feasibility of the IVR systems (Krystal et al. 2003; Mundt et al. 2002).

Screen text devices provide the respondent with a computerized version of the questionnaire items and responses in a visual text format. Screen text devices include desktop and laptop computers, which may include a touch-screen; tablet or touch-screen notebook computers; handheld/palm computers; web-based systems (Coons et al. 2009) and more recently mobile telephones. Touch-screen tablet or laptop systems are usually computers that have few practical limits on the number of questions, graphical displays (for example, visual analog scales), computational complexity, data storage, or data transfer options. Because tablet or laptop computers offer more screen space than other screen-based options, the question and response text can usually be presented in larger font and displayed on the same screen.

With hand-held computer systems/devices, data are entered via the touch sensitive screen using a special pen/stylus. Handheld computers offer the advantage of being lightweight and the most portable of the screen text devices, but the drawback can be limited screen space. This may require that the individual question text and response scales appear on different screens, and often limits font size and formats. The portability of the handheld computer gives it the advantage of being potentially more useful for real-time assessment of patient experience using daily diaries (Shiffman et al. 2001; Stone et al. 2002; Dale et al. 2007). Mobile telephones are also being used as handheld devices for PRO data collection, as the programming capabilities of these phones now include Windows Mobile as well as custom software programs that enable data to be entered and transmitted to a central database with little intervention by the subject (Schreier et al. 2008).

In addition, audiovisual computer-assisted self interviewing (A-CASI) platforms are available. This is an EDC device that combines screen text and voice/auditory functionality into one platform. Respondents are presented with a visual format of the PRO measure on a computer monitor accompanied by an audible reading of the questions and responses. These hybrid devices provide flexibility in PRO data collection which can help when assessing low literacy or visually impaired groups (Hahn et al. 2004).

Selection between the different ePRO methods for a study should consider the type of PRO measure being adapted, the target population, the complexity of data collection needs or scoring calculations, the timeframe required for patient reporting, frequency and location of assessment and requirements for visual elements such as a visual analog scale (see Chapter 5 for more discussion of selection of appropriate ePRO solutions). For the ePRO methods where the data are not stored immediately in a central database, once the data are collected they should be transferred as soon as possible via internet, intranet, or server-based system to a centralized storage and processing facility (Coons et al. 2009).

Equivalence between Electronic and Paper Methods of PRO Data Collection

Several studies have compared the equivalence of PRO data collected with electronic versus paper-based method. Recently, Gwaltney et al. (2008) completed a meta-analysis that included 46 studies designed to assess the equivalence between electronic and paper-based PROs. They found that the mean difference between the electronic and paper data collection methods were minimal (0.2 per cent of the scale range) and that 94 per cent of the observed correlations were > 0.75 (mean weighted r = 0.90). No substantive differences were seen between handheld devices (mean weighted r = 0.91) and larger screen computers (mean weighted r = 0.90). Research has demonstrated that there is little evidence that the size of the computer screen, respondent age, or amount of computer experience meaningfully influenced the equivalence of ePROs (Gwaltney et al. 2008).

In comparison to screen text devices, relatively few studies have directly compared IVR and paper-based versions of PRO measures. Agel et al. (2001), Brodey et al. (2005), Lam et al. (2009), Lundy and Coons (2008), Weiler et al. (2004) and Dunn et al. (2007) provide published examples. Studies completed to date suggest that there are strong correlations and no significant differences between IVR and paper-based methods of data collection. Perhaps the most comprehensive comparisons were performed by Lam et al. (2009) and Lundy and Coons (2008) in their studies demonstrating the equivalence of paper and IVR versions of the Short Inflammatory Bowel Disease Questionnaire (SIBDQ) and the EQ-5D questionnaire respectively. Further research is needed to generalize the findings of these studies and to assess whether and under what conditions (for example, length of assessment or item, number of options, respondent cognitive capacity) transfer from PRO paper to IVR methods yields equivalent data. For these reasons, the degree of equivalence evidence required when transferring an instrument from paper to IVR may be comparatively higher than for the conversion of a paper scale to a screen text device (see later in this chapter, and Chapter 9 in this book).

The research literature has also focused on other endpoints such as time to completion, satisfaction/ease of use, and missing data between ePROs and paper-based PROs (Coons et al. 2009). The results on time to completion are variable, and the implications of observed differences are not clear. In several studies, respondents were faster on the paper–based version than the electronic version (Bliven et al. 2001; Caro et al. 2001; Crawley et al. 2000) while in other studies participants were faster with the electronic version (Velikova et al. 1999; Bushnell et al. 2003; Ryan et al. 2002). Results have indicated that less computer experience, greater age, impaired health status, and less education were associated with greater time needed to complete the ePRO (Velikova et al. 1999; Crawley et al. 2000; Allenby et al. 2002). Some studies found that although patients took longer to complete the ePRO form, they also reported that they thought completion took less time for ePROs compared with the paper version (Kleinman et al. 2001).

Guidelines on Modification of PRO Instruments for Electronic Formats

Paper-based PRO measures sometimes need to be modified for electronic format applications. Frequently, changes to how the participant records a response choice to splitting instructions, item stems and response categories across several screens are needed when migrating paper-based questionnaires to handheld devices. Sometimes the actual item content is altered to fit on small screens, which can have implications for PRO assessment. The impact of these modifications on the measurement equivalence between paper-based and electronic PROs depends on how substantive the changes are. Recently, Coons et al. (2009) provided definitions regarding the different levels of modification and guidelines on how to handle these modifications to evaluate equivalence. The amount of modification during migration to the electronic platform/device determines the amount of evidence necessary to demonstrate that the modification did not introduce response bias and/or negatively impact the content validity or psychometric properties of the instrument.

A *minor modification* is one not expected to change the content or meaning of the question stems or response scales. Simply placing a scale from a paper-and-pencil format into a screen text format without significantly reducing font size, altering item content, recall period, or response options represents a minor modification (Coons et al. 2009). The existing research literature on adapting paper-based to electronic-based formats suggests that these common modifications will not impact the measurement equivalence between the paper and electronic based measures (Gwaltney et al. 2008). It is recommended that a cognitive interview study, also known as cognitive debriefing, be completed to ensure that participants understand the instructions, item stems, and response scales in the ePRO format. Cognitive interview studies involve small groups of subjects (n = 5-10) where each participant is interviewed after completing the ePRO instrument and queried on their level of understanding and interpretation of the instructions, items and response scales (Willis 2005; Willis et al. 2005) as well as their ability to use the ePRO technology, called usability testing. These studies also help to confirm that the content validity of the ePRO instrument is comparable to other data collection methods in use (FDA 2009). See Chapter 2 of this book for more detail on cognitive interviewing.

A *moderate level of modification* may change the meaning of the assessment items, and this change may be quite subtle. Examples of changes to items that could fall in this category include splitting a single item into multiple screens, significantly reducing font size, requiring the patient to use a scroll bar to view all item text or responses, or modifying the order of item presentation. When these types of modifications are made to a PRO, it is advisable to formally establish the equivalence of the electronic measure with the paper version. Either randomized cross-over or parallel groups designs can be used to evaluate measurement equivalence between paper-based on ePRO measures (Coons et al. 2009). Transferring a paper-based PRO to IVR also represents a moderate modification since it is not clear whether there are reasons to be concerned about the changes involved in moving from paper to IVR (for example, visual to aural presentation) and the available literature supporting the equivalence between IVR and paper-based formats is inconclusive (Coons et al. 2009). In addition to assessing measurement equivalence, cognitive interviews and usability testing should be conducted in the target population.

Substantial modifications are likely to change the content or meaning of the PRO assessment. Examples of changes that could fall into this category include removing items to decrease the amount of time it takes to complete an assessment or making significant changes to item content, such as removing references to a recall period or scale anchors, in order to fit an item on a screen (Coons et al. 2009). This level of modification really should be treated as the development of a new PRO measure, and the criteria recommended in the final FDA guidance will need to be addressed (FDA 2009; Patrick et al. 2007). Studies designed to assess the content validity and measurement properties, the reliability and validity, of the new measure are required along with cognitive interviews and usability testing in the target population.

Translation and Cultural Adaptation Issues

Language translation and cultural adaptation issues for ePROs are the same as for paper based PROs. Careful attention needs to be given to the translation of instructional and training materials associated with ePROs. Translations need to be completed using a systematic and standardized approach (Eremenco et al. 2005; Wild et al. 2005; Cull et al. 2002). A systematic and complete translation of an ePRO instrument involves:

1. Two independent forward translations, completed by two professional translators who are native speakers of the target language, with an in-depth knowledge of the source language and culture and experience with PRO translations.

2. Reconciliation of the forward translations by another native speaker or by consensus between the forward translators.

3. At least one back translation by a professional translator who is a native speaker of the source language, with an in-depth knowledge of the target country's language and culture and who has no prior knowledge of, or has never seen, the source measure. If two back translations are completed, a reconciliation of the back translations is required.

4. Assessment of conceptual equivalence between source and back translation, and resolution of issues in forward and backward translations by the project team.

5.   Harmonization of translations across languages for multi-country studies.

6.   Whenever possible, at least five cognitive debriefing interviews with patients who live in the target country.

7.   A final review and proofreading of the translation by clinical or outcomes experts in the target country.

8.   Complete a report and produce a translation certificate.

It is also essential to translate any patient training materials and instructions for the use of the ePRO solution. Ideally, whenever possible evidence supporting the psychometric characteristics of the translated PRO measures should also be completed. The evaluation of psychometric properties can be accomplished through a blinded secondary analysis of the clinical trial data if there are sufficient samples for each translation.

Regulatory agencies have expressed concerns about the quality of translations of PRO instruments, and need documentation that language translations were completed by trained professional translators using systematic methods. The FDA's main concerns relate to demonstrating that the original and translated versions of the PRO instrument are capturing the same concepts and that the data across translations can be pooled together in the clinical trial.

FDA PRO Dossier Template

A clear and concise summary of the rationale for PRO assessment, instrument development methods and the psychometric characteristics and interpretation guidelines for PRO instruments, regardless of whether they use ePRO or paper-based data collection methods, are required if a labeling claim is desired (Revicki et al. 2007). More recently, the FDA has recommended the application of a PRO dossier template to standardize evidentiary submissions on PRO endpoints for labeling or promotional claims (Patrick et al. 2007; FDA 2009). Appendix 1 outlines a working version of the PRO evidence dossier template based on further recommendations for sponsors. In any case, the same standards of evidence are required for electronic PRO and paper-based PRO instruments. The template information and documentation of evidence may also assist in submissions to the EMEA and European regulatory authorities.

Completion of the PRO dossier template is needed for all ePRO endpoints where the sponsor wants a labeling or promotional claim. Documentation is necessary on the ePRO's content validity and conceptual framework, as well as providing information as to the ePRO endpoint's place in the hierarchy of clinical trial endpoints (i.e., endpoint model). Evidence documenting the content validity of the ePRO measure, based on qualitative research in the target population is essential. Based on current experience with ePRO and paper based PRO instruments, the FDA focuses most of its review on the content of the instrument and on the content validity of the measures.

Next, all available evidence supporting the internal consistency and test-retest reliability, construct validity, and responsiveness of the ePRO instrument needs to be summarized. Ideally, the evidence supporting the psychometric characteristics of the ePRO instrument should be in place before the pivotal phase three clinical trials are started. However, sometimes all the necessary information is not available. In this situation, the PRO dossier should include information on the planned activities to secure the needed psychometric data.

Evidence on measurement equivalence between the ePRO and paper based instrument needs to be provided if moderate to substantial changes are made (see Chapter 9 for a review of equivalence testing methodology). Responsiveness is critically important for clinical trials, and anchor-based methods should be used to evaluate responsiveness and to develop guidelines for interpretation of PRO scores (Revicki et al. 2008). More recently, the FDA is focusing more on responder analyses for PRO endpoints, and clearly documented responder definitions are needed for all PRO endpoints. Information on language translation and the cultural adaptation of the ePRO instruments needs to be provided, including documentation that all language versions have content validity based on qualitative research.

Finally, information should be summarized as to the methods and timing of data collection, with some rationale for data collection procedures. It is not recommended to mix methods of PRO data collection within a clinical trial, such as using paper and electronic or using two forms of electronic such as IVR and handhelds. However, in cases where this is unavoidable, evidence needs to be provided that the different modes of administration result in equivalent measurement so that the data can be pooled for analysis and to assess any variance in treatment effect due to method or mode (FDA 2009). The clinical trial protocol and planned statistical analyses for the PRO measures need to be summarized. For the protocol data collection, information should be provided on the methods of data collection, investigator and patient training, and methods for minimizing bias. The statistical analysis plan should include methods for handling multiplicity of PRO endpoints, handling missing data, and the main treatment comparisons.

A number of appendices should be attached to the PRO template, including qualitative research study reports, all cited publications, unpublished psychometric analyses and reports and other documentation. Patient transcripts from qualitative studies are not included unless the FDA specifically requests this information.

The intent of the PRO template is to provide a clear and concise summary of the rationale for the PRO endpoint and necessary documentation on the development, content validity and measurement characteristics of the PRO measure, and on the clinical trial program and data analysis plans. This document should provide information on the PRO assessment strategy for securing a labeling or promotional claim for a new or existing product.

Regulatory-related Technology Issues

The previous section focused on the content and presentation of ePRO questionnaires using a variety of technologies, also known as the 'front-end' of the system. This section summarizes issues related to the 'back-end' of the system, the underlying database and associated systems into which ePRO data are entered. Because the collection of ePRO data inherently involves the use of computer systems to store and retrieve the data, ePRO systems are subject to a number of federal and international regulations and guidelines which discuss requirements to ensure that the data are collected, stored and accessed in a way that ensures their accuracy and integrity. This section will provide an overview of the different regulations and guidelines which pertain to ePRO computer systems; will discuss issues related to the implications of ePRO as source data and provides recommendations for the development of a validated system which meets the requirements of the various regulatory bodies.

REGULATIONS AND GUIDANCES PERTAINING TO EPRO DATA

The regulatory requirements which follow apply to data collection in the context of clinical trials for regulatory submission and approval. It is important to keep this context in mind as these requirements might not be absolutely necessary for use of ePRO computer systems that are part of studies outside of the regulatory arena. The two most relevant documents referenced in the development of ePRO computer systems are the International Conference on Harmonisation - Guideline on Good Clinical Practice (ICH 1997) and Title 21 of the Code of Federal Regulations; Electronic Records; Electronic Signatures (21 CFR Part 11; FDA 1997) . The ICH-GCP Guideline was developed to provide a unified standard for clinical trial data to be accepted by regulatory agencies in the United States, European Union (EU) and Japan (FDA 1996; ICH 1997). This guideline for good clinical practice covers the entire process of conducting a clinical trial and is broader in scope than the use of ePRO data collection methods in trials. The FDA has also issued a number of regulations regarding the principal record keeping requirements for clinical investigators and sponsors: 21 CFR 312.50, 312.58, 312.62, 312.68, 812.140, and 812.145 which are consistent with the ICH-GCP Guideline. 21 CFR Part 11 is an FDA regulation with a narrower scope, focusing on the use of electronic records and electronic signatures in the submission of data for regulatory review.

21 CFR Part 11

Often referred to as Part 11, this regulation became effective on August 20, 1997. The intent of this regulation is to enable the submission of electronic records as source data instead of paper data to the FDA as well as the use of electronic signatures in lieu of handwritten signatures, and to explain the requirements that need to be met to ensure the accuracy and integrity of the electronic records and signatures. This regulation applies to the use of computerized systems that are used to create, modify, maintain, archive, retrieve, or transmit clinical data to the agency (FDA 1997). Regardless of the platform used to collect them, ePRO data become part of the case history of the clinical trial and are therefore subject to the same requirements as any other data collected for the trial. Under this regulation, sponsors are expected to demonstrate that their computerized systems were developed according to the data standards described in the rule, that these systems were validated according to the requirements used to develop them, and that these processes are documented. In addition, Part 11 requires that the system provide a mechanism for documenting any changes made to the data such as a date and time stamped audit trail and a process for record retention and copying that allows for the data to be accessed at a later date by the FDA for source data verification purposes (FDA 1997).

In order to assist with the implementation of Part 11 requirements, the FDA issued a number of guidelines to industry including *Guidance for Industry,*

Part 11, Electronic Records; Electronic Signatures, Maintenance of Electronic Records (FDA 2002a) and compliance policy guide, *CPG 7153.17: Enforcement Policy: 21 CFR Part 11; Electronic Records; Electronic Signatures.* One of the major difficulties industry faced in light of these regulations and guidelines was the fact that legacy computer systems which were developed before Part 11 was instituted and therefore may not have been compliant with its requirements, had already been in use for a number of years. Concerns were also raised regarding the expense of becoming Part 11 compliant and the burdens on industry to implement new technology in light of the regulation. In February 2003, FDA announced in the Federal Register that the agency intended to re-examine Part 11 requirements and also withdrew the previously issued guidance and compliance policy documents. In August 2003, the Agency issued a revised *Guidance for Industry Part 11, Electronic Records; Electronic Signatures — Scope and Application* (FDA 2003) to explain how Part 11 would be enforced during this re-examination period. In this revised guidance, the Agency narrowed the scope of records to which Part 11 applies and also stated that the Agency is using 'enforcement discretion', meaning that it will not take action to enforce compliance with the validation, audit trail, record retention and record copying requirements of the regulation, although it expects that sponsors will follow these requirements (FDA 2003). For legacy systems in use before August 20, 2007, compliance with Part 11 requirements will not be enforced but the Agency expects the system to comply with predicate rule requirements and to be documented as fit for use (FDA 2003). Records subject to Part 11 compliance include those that are required under predicate rules and electronic records used in place of paper or in addition to paper for regulatory purposes.

A key point that predates Part 11 is that whether the FDA will accept data from clinical trials for decision-making purposes depends on its ability to verify the quality and integrity of the data via inspections and audits (FDA 1999). These quality standards apply regardless of the method of data collection and whether recorded electronically or on paper, and are known as the ALCOA principle of data quality and integrity, that data should be Accurate, Legible, Contemporaneous, Original, and Attributable (FDA 1999; EMEA 2007) . With regard to system validation, the revised guidance reiterates that the objective of validation is to ensure the accuracy, reliability, integrity, availability, and authenticity of required records and signatures (FDA 2003) which reinforce the ALCOA principle.

Although the FDA is not currently actively enforcing compliance with Part 11 requirements, it is recommended to sponsors that any new computer systems for clinical trial use be developed according to the requirements of the regulation to ensure they are Part 11 compliant. For further information on validation processes and requirements, sponsors can refer to the guidance document titled *General Principles of Software Validation* (FDA 2002) and industry guidance *GAMP 4 Guide* (ISPE/GAMP Forum, 2001).

ISSUES RELATED TO EPRO AS ESOURCE DATA

One aspect of ePRO data that is more complicated than the same situation with paper is the question of what is the source data, where does it reside and who is responsible for it ? With paper data collection, the paper documents are the source data which the investigator retains for future verification and audit purposes even when the data are then entered into a database for subsequent analysis. However, in most cases, data collected from the patient electronically is transmitted directly into a database system without requiring the investigator's intervention. While much more streamlined and efficient, the unintended result of ePRO data collection is that the investigator no longer has direct control over the patient data. However, the investigator is still held legally responsible for its accuracy and integrity (ICH, 1997; Directive 2001/20/EC5; Directive 2005/28/EC6; CPMP/ICH/135/95). According to the ICH-GCP guideline, the investigator is responsible for ensuring the accuracy, completeness, legibility, and timeliness of the data reported to the sponsor in CRFs and all required reports (ICH 1997, GCP Section 4.9.1). On the other hand, the sponsor's responsibilities include validating the system; maintaining SOPs for the use of the system; maintaining an audit trail of data changes ensuring that there is no deletion of entered data; maintaining a security system to protect against unauthorized access; maintaining a list of the individuals authorized to make data changes; maintaining adequate backup of the data and safeguarding the blinding of the study (ICH 1997, GCP Section 5.5.3). Other important aspects of the system are keeping the original data separate from any transformed data so that comparisons between them can be made and to ensure that an unambiguous subject identification code allows identification of all the data reported for each subject (ICH 1997).

Recommendations for addressing the issues inherent in eSource data have been developed by a number of organizations to enable industry to continue to use electronic data capture methods for all data while still being compliant with GCP guidelines and other regulations. Electronic source documents include electronic case report forms (eCRFs), electronic patient diaries and other instruments such as those used to capture biomarker measures (for example blood glucose, peak expiratory flow readings, etc). It is important for the investigator to maintain control and access to the data to protect it against unauthorized changes, by having either the original electronic data or a certified copy (EMEA 2007; CDISC 2006). If the source data are stored on a central server, then the method of investigator retaining control needs to be demonstrated (EMEA 2007; CDISC 2006) in order to comply with this requirement. Another important requirement is that the sponsor should not have exclusive control of a source document, in order to prevent inappropriate modification of the source data by unauthorized individuals (EMEA 2007; CDISC 2006). In the case of ePRO studies, the roles are further complicated by the presence of service providers such as contract research organizations (CROs) who are directly involved in the execution of the clinical trial itself and technology providers who are responsible for development and implementation of the ePRO electronic systems and data storage and transfer. While these types of organizations play an important role in the use of ePRO instruments in clinical trials, neither bears the same legal responsibilities for the conduct of the trial as the sponsor and investigator. The general recommendation is that the study protocol or separate document clearly specify how the electronic PRO source data will be maintained and protected by the investigator and how the sponsor, CRO and technology provider will be involved while retaining separate roles and responsibilities for the data according to GCP requirements (EMEA 2007).

Summary of Technology Issues: Developing a Validated System for Data Collection

The following are key points to keep in mind for developing a validated computer system that is GCP and Part 11 compliant (FDA 1999; FDA 1997; EMEA Annex 11, FDA 2009).

1. Follow the ALCOA principles.

2. Develop according to the life cycle of a computer system; planning, specification, programming, testing, commissioning, documentation, operation, monitoring, modifying and decommissioning.

3. Include processes for quality assurance and validating the system.

4. Restrict who is authorized to enter data into the system and modify the data.

5.   Have an audit trail to track such changes especially after data leave the ePRO data collection device.

6.   Have backup and disaster recovery plans.

7.   Maintain investigator accountability for the source data, working with technology providers to safeguard the data and prevent direct access by the sponsor.

8.   Prevent loss of adverse event data and ensure timely transmission to the clinical investigator when safety information is transmitted directly to sponsors, clinical research organizations, and/or other third parties.

9.   Ensure an FDA investigator is able to inspect, verify, and copy the data at the clinical site during an inspection.

Conclusion

This chapter presents the current thinking of various regulatory bodies with regard to the scientific and technological issues around using data collected with ePRO instruments in clinical trials. While regulations and laws are subject to change, the principles presented here are based on appropriate scientific and good practice guidelines for ensuring the most accurate and reliable data possible and are less likely to change in the future. Whenever PRO data are collected using electronic technologies, it is important to document any changes and adaptations to the PRO measures necessary for implementation on the ePRO device. Depending on the nature and extent of these modifications, sponsors may need to provide evidence that the electronic version captures the same information as a paper version. If significant changes are made to the PRO instrument, then psychometric evidence (i.e., reliability, validity, responsiveness) may also need to be generated. However, increasingly new PRO instruments are developed for electronic methods of data collection and psychometric evaluations are completed on either only the electronic version or on both electronic and paper versions of the questionnaires. For ePROs, the key is documenting usability, feasibility and measurement properties including content validity of the electronically administered instrument. Finally, reliable systems need to be in place to maintain the integrity of the electronic data and quality control procedures are necessary for maintaining data storage and quality. Patient-reported outcomes are important for understanding the comprehensive effects of new and existing treatment interventions. Electronic modes of PRO data collection allow for the flexible and reliable collection of this information, allowing the patient's perspective on the outcomes of treatment to be assessed.

References

Agel, J., Greist, J.H. and Rockwood, T. et al. (2001). Comparison of interactive voice response and written self-administered patient surveys for clinical research. *Orthopedics*, 24: 1155–57.

Allenby, A., Matthews, J. and Beresford, J. et al. (2002). The application of computer touch-screen technology in screening for psychosocial distress in an ambulatory oncology setting. *Eur J Cancer Care*, 11: 245–53.

Bliven, B.D., Kaufman, S.E. and Spertus, J.A. (2001). Electronic collection of health-related quality of life data: validity, time benefits, and patient preference. *Qual Life Res*, 10: 15–21.

Bloom, D.E. (1998). Technology, experimentation, and the quality of survey data. *Science*, 280: 847–8.

Brodey, B.B., Rosen, C.S. and Brodey, I.S. et al. (1995). Reliability and acceptability of automated telephone surveys among Spanish- and English-speaking mental health services recipients. *Mental Health Services Research*, 7: 181–184.

Bushnell, D.M., Martin, M.L. and Parasuraman, B. (2003). Electronic versus paper questionnaires: a further comparison in persons with asthma. *J Asthma*, 40: 751–62.

Bushnell, D.M. and Reilly M.C., et al. (2006). Validation of electronic data capture of the Irritable Bowel Syndrome—quality of life measure, the work productivity and activity impairment questionnaire for Irritable Bowel Syndrome and the EuroQol. *Value Health*, 9: 98–105.

Caro Sr, J.J., Caro, I. and Caro, J. et al. (2001). Does electronic implementation of questionnaires used in asthma alter responses compared to paper implementation? *Qual Life Res*, 10: 683–91.

Cella, D., Yount, S. and Rothrock, N. et al. (2007). The patient-reported outcomes measurement information system (PROMIS): progress of an NIH roadmap cooperative group through its first two years. *Med Care*, 45(1): S3–S11.

Clinical Data Interchange Standards Consortium (CDISC). CDISC e-source standard requirements. Version 1.0, 20 November 2006.

Coons, S.J., Gwaltney, C.J. and Hays, R.D. et al. (2009). On behalf of the ISPOR ePRO Task Force. Recommendations on evidence needed to support measurement equivalence between electronic and paper-based Patient-Reported Outcome (PRO) measures: ISPOR ePRO good research practices task force report. *Value Health*, 12(4): 419–429.

Crawley, J.A., Kleinman L. and Dominitz J. (2000). User preferences for computer administration of quality of life instruments. *Drug Information Journal*, 34: 137–44.

Cull, A., Sprangers, M. and Bjordal, K. et al. (2002). *EORTC Quality of Life Group Translation Procedure.* 2nd edn Brussels, Belgium: EORTC Quality of Life Group.

Dale, O. and Hagen, K.B. (2007). Despite technical problems personal digital assistants outperform pen and paper when collecting patient diary data. *J Clin Epidemiol*, 60: 8–17.

Dunn, J.A., Arakawa, R. and Greist, J.H. et al. (2007). Assessing the onset of antidepressant-induced sexual dysfunction using interactive voice response technology. *J Clin Psychiatry*, 68: 525–32.

EMEA. (2005). *Reflection Paper on the Regulatory Guidance for the use of Health-related Quality of Life (HRQL) Measures in the Evaluation of Medicinal Products.* London, UK: EMEA.

EMEA. GCP Inspectors Working Group. Reflection Paper on Expectations for Electronic Source Documents Used in Clinical Trials, 2007. Available at http://www.emea.europa.eu/Inspections/docs/50562007en.pdf [Accessed July 11, 2008].

EMEA. Note for Guidance on Good Clinical Practice (CPMP/ICH/135/95) Volume 3C Efficacy, Rules Governing Medicinal Products in the European Union.

Eremenco, S.L., Cella, D. and Arnold, B.J. (2005). A comprehensive method for the translation and cross cultural validation of health status questionnaires. *Eval Health Professions*, 28(2): 212–232.

European Commission. Directive 2001/20/EC of the European Parliament and of the Council of 4 April 2001 on the approximation of the laws, regulations and administrative provisions of the Member States relating to the implementation of good clinical practice in the conduct of clinical trials on medicinal products for human use (*Official Journal L 121, 1/5/2001:34–44*).

European Commission. Directive 2005/28/EC of 8 April 2005 laying down principles and detailed guidelines for good clinical practice as regards investigational medicinal products for human use, as well as the requirements for authorisation of the manufacturing or importation of such products (*Official Journal L 91, 9/4/2005: 13–19*).

European Commission. Eudralex Volume 4 Medicinal Products for Human and Veterinary Use: Good Manufacturing Practice – Chapter 4 Documentation and Annex 11 Computerised Systems. Available at http://ec.europa.eu/enterprise/pharmaceuticals/eudralex/vol-4/pdfs-en/anx11en.pdf [Accessed October 30, 2008].

Food and Drug Administration. 21 CFR Part 11, Electronic Records; Electronic Signatures; Final Rule. *Federal Register,* 62(54): 13429, March 20, 1997.

Food and Drug Administration. General Principles of Software Validation; Final Guidance for Industry and FDA Staff, 2002. Available at http://www.fda.gov/cdrh/comp/guidance/938.html [Accessed October 30, 2008].

Food and Drug Administration. Guidance for Industry, Computerized Systems Used in Clinical Trials, 1999. Available at: http://www.fda.gov/ora/compliance_ref/bimo/ffinalcct.htm [Accessed October 30, 2008].

Food and Drug Administration. Guidance for Industry, E6 Good Clinical Practice: Consolidated Guidance, 1996. Available at http://www.fda.gov/cder/guidance/959fnl.pdf [Accessed October 30, 2008].

Food and Drug Administration. Guidance for Industry, Part 11, Electronic Records; Electronic Signatures, Maintenance of Electronic Records, 2002a. Available at http://www.21cfrpart11.com/files/fda_docs/draft_guidance_for_ind_july2002.pdf [Accessed July 11, 2008].

Food and Drug Administration. Guidance for Industry, Part 11, Electronic Records; Electronic Signatures — Scope and Application, 2003. Available at (http://www.fda.gov/Cder/guidance/5667fnl.htm [Accessed July 11, 2008].

Food and Drug Administration. Guidance for Industry: Patient-Reported Outcome Measures: Use in Medical Product Development to Support Labeling Claims (Final), December 2009. Available at: http://www.fda.gov/downloads/Drugs/GuidanceComplianceRegulatoryInformation/Guidances/UCM193282.pdf [Accessed December 8, 2009].

Getz, K.A. (2006). The imperative to support site adoption of EDC. *Applied Clinical Trials*, 15(1): 38–40.

Gwaltney, C.J., Shields, A.L. and Shiffman, S. (2008). Equivalence of electronic and paper-and-pencil administration of patient-reported outcome measures: A meta-analytic review. *Value Health*, 11: 322–33.

Hahn, E.A., Cella, D. and Dobrez, D. et al. (2004). The talking touch screen: a new approach to outcomes assessment in low literacy. *Psycho-oncology*, 13: 86–95.

Henriksen, B. (1999). Three dimensions of vocabulary development. *Studies in Second Language Acquisition*, 21: 303–17.

International Conference on Harmonisation. Good Clinical Practice: Consolidated Guideline. Federal Register Vol 62, No. 90, 25711, May 9, 1997.

ISPE/GAMP Forum. The Good Automated Manufacturing Practice (GAMP) Guide for Validation of Automated Systems, GAMP 4, 2001. Available at http://www.ispe.org/gamp/ [Accessed October 30, 2008].

Kleinman, L., Benjamin, K. and Viswanathan, H. et al. (2008). The Anemia Impact Measure (AIM): Development of an instrument to evaluate symptoms and symptom impacts of chemotherapy-induced anemia (CIA). Presented at the American Society of Hematology Annual Meeting, San Francisco, California, December 2008.

Kleinman, L., Leidy, N.K. and Crawley, J. et al. (2001). A comparative trial of paper-and-pencil versus computer administration of the Quality of Life in Reflux and Dyspepsia (QOLRAD) questionnaire. *Med Care*, 39: 181–9.

Krystal, A.D., Walsh, J.K. and Laska, E. et al. (2003). Sustained efficacy of eszopiclone over 6 months of nightly treatment: results of a randomized, double-blind, placebo-controlled study in adults with chronic insomnia. *Sleep*, 26: 793–9.

Lam, M.Y., Lee, H. and Bright, R. et al. (2009). Validation of interactive voice response system administration of the Short Inflammatory Bowel Disease Questionnaire. *Inflamm Bowel Dis*, 15: 599–607.

Leidy, N.K., Powers, J.H. and Howard, K.A. et al. (2008). For the EXACT-PRO Study Group. The EXACT-PRO Initiative: Development of a standardized outcome measure for evaluating exacerbations of chronic obstructive pulmonary disease. Poster presented at the American Thoracic Society International Conference, Toronto Canada, May 2008.

Lundy, J.J. and Coons, S.J. (2008). Testing the measurement equivalence of paper and Interactive Voice Response (IVR) versions of the EQ-5D. Poster presented at The International Society for Pharmacoeconomics and Outcomes Research (ISPOR) 11th Annual European Congress, Athens, Greece, November 2008.

Mundt, J.C., Marks, I.M. and Shear, M.K. et al. (2002). The work and social adjustment scale: a simple measure of impairment in functioning. *Br J Psychiatry*, 180: 461–4.

Patrick, D.L., Burke, L.B. and Powers, J.H. et al. (2007). Patient-reported outcomes to support medical product labeling claims: FDA perspective. *Value Health*, 10(2): S125–S137.

Revicki, D.A. (2007). FDA draft guidance and health-outcomes research. *Lancet*, 369(9561): 540–542.

Revicki, D.A., Gnanasakthy, A. and Weinfurt, K. (2007). Documenting the rationale and psychometric characteristics of patient reported outcomes for labeling and promotional claims: the PRO Evidence Dossier. *Qual Life Res*, 16(4): 717–723.

Revicki, D.A., Hays, R. and Cella, D. et al. (2008). Recommended methods for determining responsiveness and minimally important differences for patient-reported outcomes. *J Clin Epidemiol*, 61(2): 102–109.

Revicki, D.A., Osoba, D. and Fairclough, D. et al. (2000). Recommendations on health-related quality of life research to support labeling and promotional claims in the United States. *Qual Life Res*, 9: 887–900.

Rothman, M.L., Beltran, P. and Cappelleri, J.C. et al. (2007). Patient-reported outcomes: conceptual issues. *Value Health*, 10(2): S66–S75.

Ryan, J.M., Corry, J.R. and Attewell, R. et al. (2002). A comparison of an electronic version of the SF-36 General Health Questionnaire to the standard paper version. *Qual Life Res*, 11: 19–26.

Saponjic, R.M., Freedman, S. and Sadighian, A. (2003).What monitors think of EDC: results of a survey of U.S. monitors. *Applied Clinical Trials*, 12(5): 50–2.

Schreier, G., Modre-Osprian, R. and Kastner, P. (2008). ePRO makes strides with the mobile phone. *Applied Clinical Trials*, 14–17.

Shiffman, S., Hufford, M.R. and Paty, J. (2001). Subject experience diaries in clinical research, Part 1: The patient experience movement. *Applied Clinical Trials*, 10(2): 46–56.

Stone, A.A., Shiffman, S. and Schwartz, J.E. et al. (2002). Patient noncompliance with paper diaries. *BMJ*, 324: 1193–4.

Taenzer, P.A., Speca, M. and Atkinson, M.J. et al. (1997). Computerized quality-of-life screening in an oncology clinic. *Cancer Practice*, 5: 168–75.

Thakkar, R., Revicki, D.A. and Davidson, M.H. et al. (2008). Psychometric qualities of the Flushing Assessment Tool (FAST). Australian Atherosclerosis Society Annual Scientific Meeting 2008, Sydney, Australia, October 2008.

Velikova, G., Wright, E.P. and Smith, A.B. et al. (1999). Automated collection of quality-of-life data: a comparison of paper and computer touch-screen questionnaires. *J Clin Oncol*, 17: 998–1007.

Weiler, K., Christ, A.M. and Woodworth, G.G. et al. (2004). Quality of patient-reported outcome data captured using paper and interactive voice response diaries in an allergic rhinitis study: is electronic data capture really better? *Ann Allergy Asthma Immunol*, 92: 335–339.

Wiechers, O.A. (2002). The move to EDC. *Applied Clinical Trials*, 11(11): 38–40.

Wild, D., Grove, A. and Martin, M. et al. (2005). Principles of good practice for the translation and cultural adaptation process for patient-reported outcomes (PRO) measures: report of the ISPOR Task Force for Translation and Cultural Adaptation. *Value Health*, 8(2): 94–104.

Willis, G. (2005). *Cognitive interviewing: A Tool for Improving Questionnaire Design*. Thousand Oaks (CA): Sage Publications, Inc.

Willis, G.B., Reeve, B.B. and Barofsky, I. (2005). Invited Paper C: The use of cognitive interviewing techniques in quality of life and patient-reported outcomes assessment. In: Lipscomb J, Gotay CC, and Snyder C. *Outcomes Assessment in Cancer*. Cambridge: Cambridge University Press.

Willke, R.J., Burke, L.B. and Erickson, P. (2004). Measuring treatment impact: a review of patient-reported outcomes and other efficacy endpoints in approved product labels. *Control Clin Trials*, 25: 535–52.

Appendix 1: FDA PRO Submission Template

1. **Instrument(s): (review cannot begin without a copy of the proposed instrument)**

    1.1. Exact version of the instrument proposed/used in clinical trial (protocol) under review and all instructions for use. Include screen shots or interviewer scripts, if relevant.

    1.2. Prior versions, if relevant.

    1.3. Instructions for use: An instrument user manual can be provided as Appendix A and referenced here.

        1.3.1. Administration timing, method (for example, paper or pencil, electronic), and mode (for example, self-, clinician- or interviewer-administered).

        1.3.2. The scoring algorithm.

        1.3.3. Training method and materials used for questionnaire administration.

            1.3.3.1. Patient training – summarize here and include a copy of all materials in Appendix A1.

            1.3.3.2. Investigator training – summarize here and include a copy of all materials in Appendix A2.

            1.3.3.3. Other training – summarize here and include a copy of all materials in Appendix A3.

2. **Targeted Claims or Target Product Profile (TPP)**

Include language describing all specific targeted labeling claims related to all clinical trial endpoint measures, both PRO and non-PRO, and specific to:

- disease/condition with stage, severity, or category, if relevant.
- intended population (for example, age group, gender, other demographics).

- data analysis plan.

3.　Endpoint Model

3.1.　Relationship (known and hypothesized) among all clinical trial endpoints, both PRO and non-PRO. These may include physiologic/ lab/physical, caregiver, or clinician-reported measures in addition to PROs.

3.2.　Hierarchy of all PRO and non-PRO endpoints intended to support claims corresponding with the planned data analyses.

4.　Conceptual Framework of the PRO Instrument(s)

4.1.　Diagram of hypothesized (proposed) or final PRO instrument conceptual framework showing relationship of items to domains and domains to total score. Ensure that the conceptual framework of the PRO instrument corresponds to the clinical trial endpoints described in the clinical trial protocol and proposed as labeling claim(s).

5.　Content Validity Documentation: *Evidence that instrument captures all of the most clinically important concepts and items, and that items are complete, relevant (appropriate), and understandable to the patient. This evidence applies to both existing and newly created instruments and is specific to the planned clinical trial population and indication. Documentation includes:*

5.1.　Literature review and documentation of expert input.

5.2.　Qualitative study protocols and interview guides and summary of results for:

5.2.1.　Focus group testing (include transcripts in Appendix C1).

5.2.2.　Open-ended patient interviews (include transcripts in Appendix C2).

5.2.3.　Cognitive interviews (include transcripts in Appendix C3).

5.3.　Origin and derivation of items with chronology of events for item generation, modification and finalization.

Item tracking matrix for versions tested with patients showing items retained and items deleted providing evidence of saturation. Summarize here and include complete materials under Appendix B.

5.4. Qualitative study summary that supports content validity for:

> 5.4.1. item content;
> 5.4.2. response options;
> 5.4.3. recall period;
> 5.4.4. scoring.

5.5. Summary of qualitative studies demonstrating how item pool was generated, reduced, and finalized. Specify type of study (i.e., focus group, patient interview, or cognitive interview) and characteristics of study population. Include full transcripts and datasets in Appendix C. Transcripts, if requested by FDA.

6. **Assessment of Other Measurement Properties**: *Assuming content validity is established in the intended population and application, evidence that the instrument is reliable, valid and able to detect change. Same version of instrument to be used in the clinical trial must be used to assess measurement properties.*

6.1. Protocols for instrument testing.
6.2. Summary of testing results for each domain or summary score proposed as support for claims:

> 6.2.1. Reliability (Internal; Test-retest);
> 6.2.2. Construct validity (Convergent, Discriminant, Known-Groups);
> 6.2.3. Ability to detect change.

7. **Interpretation of Scores**

7.1. Summary of the logic and methods used to interpret the clinical meaningfulness of clinical trial results.
7.2. Responder definition (i.e., definition of meaningful within-person change specific to the clinical trial population).

8. **Language Translation and Cultural Adaptation**

8.1. Process used to translate and culturally adapt the instrument for populations that will use them in the trial.
8.2. Description of patient testing, language- or culture-specific concerns, and rationale for decisions made to create new versions.

8.3.   Copies of translated or adapted versions.

8.4.   Evidence that content validity and other measurement properties are comparable between the original and translated instrument(s).

9.   Data Collection Method

9.1.   Process used to develop data collection methods (for example, electronic, paper, etc.) intended for use in the clinical trial. If electronic data collection is used to assess PRO endpoints, procedures for maintenance, transmission and storage of electronic source documents must comply with requirements.

9.2.   Evidence that content validity and other measurement properties are comparable between all methods of data collection.

9.3.   User manual for each additional method of data collection.

10.   Modifications: *any change in the original instrument for example, wording of items, response options, recall period, use in a new population or indication, etc.*

10.1. Rationale for and process used to modify the instrument.

10.2. Copy of original and new instruments.

10.3. Evidence that content validity and other measurement properties are comparable between the original and modified instrument(s) (including use in a new indication or population).

11.   PRO-Specific Plans Related to Clinical Trial Design and Data Analysis

11.1. Clinical study protocol. Ensure in the protocol that:

- Each PRO endpoint is stated as a specific clinical trial objective and multiplicity concerns are addressed.
- The clinical trial will be adequately blinded.
- Procedures for training are well-described:

  - patients;
  - study interviewers;
  - clinical investigators.

- Plans for instrument administration are consistent with instrument's user manual.

- Plans for PRO instrument scoring are consistent with those used during instrument development.
- Procedures include assessment of PRO endpoint prior to or shortly after a patient withdraws from the clinical trial.
- Frequency and timing of PRO assessments are appropriate given patient population, clinical trial design and objectives, and demonstrated PRO instrument measurement properties.
- Clinical trial duration is adequate to support PRO objectives.
- Plans are included for handling missing data.
- Plans are included for a cumulative distribution function comparison among treatment groups
- Data collection, data storage, and data handling/transmission procedures, including ePROs, are specified.

11.2 Statistical analysis plan (SAP). Ensure the SAP includes:

- Plans for multiplicity adjustment.
- Plans for handling missing data at both the instrument and patient level.
- Description of how between-group differences will be portrayed (for example, cumulative distribution function).

12. **References**: List and attach all relevant published and unpublished documents

13. **Appendix A**: User Manual

    A1: Patient training;
    A2: Investigator training;
    A3: Other training.

14. **Appendix B**: Item Tracking Matrix
15. **Appendix C**: Transcripts

    C1: Focus groups;
    C2: Open-ended patient interviews;
    C3: Cognitive interviews.

5

Selection of a Suitable ePRO Solution: Benefit, Cost and Risk

Mikael Palmblad

> *'Cheshire Puss,' began Alice, rather timidly, 'Would you tell me, please, which way I ought to go from here?'*
>
> *'That depends a good deal on where you want to get to,' said the Cat.*
>
> *'I don't much care where--' said Alice.*
>
> *'Then it doesn't matter which way you go,' said the Cat.*
>
> *'--so long as I get somewhere,' Alice added as an explanation.*
>
> *'Oh, you're sure to do that,' said the Cat, 'if you only walk long enough.'*
>
> *Lewis Carroll,* Alice's Adventures in Wonderland

Introduction

This book explores all the aspects of electronic capture of Patient Reported Outcomes. After reading it, you should have a good understanding of what ePRO is, and how it is used. The next step is to use it yourself.

There are many ePRO solutions on the market and more opportunities arise as technology and the global technological infrastructure develops. Which one should you use?

Unfortunately, there is no easy answer to this question. Fortunately, many have made choices in the past, both good and bad. Therefore, we can present some of the experiences from these and suggestions for how to make a decision.

Basically, the selection process should consider three main aspects of using ePRO: benefits, cost and risk. First you look at why you wish to use ePRO, then you find out what it will cost and lastly you evaluate the risks in using it. Combining these three types of information will give you a solid foundation for the decision.

Benefits

Which way you want to go depends on where you want to get. Equally, selecting a suitable ePRO solution depends on why you wish to use it. Quite often you will find that you are more interested in one or a few of the benefits of ePRO and then you can focus your selection on those.

Why do you want to use an ePRO solution?

Will the selected solution give you that?

So, what are the potential benefits of using ePRO? As shown in Figure 5.1. below, there are three main benefits: reduce cost in the clinical trial, shorten the time to results and improve the science. Depending on what you are researching and where you are in the clinical research process you may wish to focus on one or more of these benefits.

As an example of improving the science, consider PRO data collection from patients in an everyday life setting, for example symptom diaries collected on a daily basis. In this situation, the key benefits will probably relate to patient compliance – both *improving* compliance compared to paper, for example using feedback and reminders, and, equally important, *documenting* compliance using the time-stamping that electronic solutions provide. Without such documentation it could be difficult to demonstrate to a reviewer that entries were made according to the study design.

Good compliance can lead to another important benefit; timely records are generally more accurate than late ones particularly in a condition that fluctuates in severity and fluctuating disease severity is often one of the reasons for using a daily diary rather than recall at a clinic visit. This can lead to substantial improvements in the precision of the study result, or to reductions in sample size if the PRO data are primary outcome measures. These issues are discussed more fully in Chapters 1, 3 and 6 of this book.

In this situation, the other benefits of ePRO are still valid and may be important, but these two issues will likely be critical.

If, on the other hand, your study involves collecting PRO data in a supervised environment, for example when a patient visits the clinic, documenting compliance is less important, as the clinic staff will give the patient the questionnaire and record the patient details and the date and time. In this situation, paper PRO data collection can give good quality data. The issues here are likely to relate to the clinical study process.

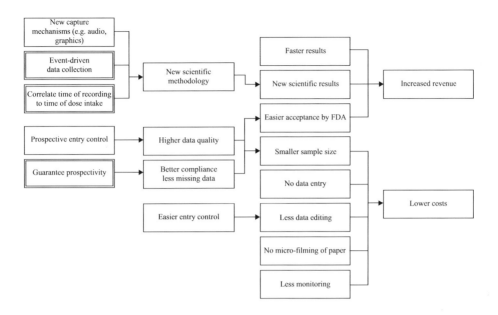

Figure 5.1   Potential benefits of using ePRO

Obtaining good quality paper questionnaire data, even in a supervised environment, takes a good deal of work. Left to themselves, some patients will leave questions blank, write a description of their problem rather than ticking a box, or mark between boxes. Fallowfield and colleagues have identified such problems as the main quality problem in quality of life data (Fallowfield, 1996; Bernhard et al., 1998). Clinic staff can check questionnaires and ask patients to correct or complete such entries, but this is time-consuming both for the staff and for the patient, who must remain available until checks have been completed.

Electronic systems can manage these procedures quickly and accurately, making the monitoring work much easier. There are no data to check or query except for ensuring that the data are recorded to the correct patient number. Data entry is not needed at all. The whole paper management issue with printing, distribution, collection and archiving disappears. It is not certain that these cost reduction elements in themselves outweigh the cost of the ePRO solution, and this will vary from context to context, but they will contribute significantly to the cost/benefit picture.

Using ePRO correctly can, if the setting is right, significantly reduce the time to delivery of results. Having data immediately available shortens the time to database lock in a traditional study, but combining ePRO with an adaptive study design may shorten the timelines much more.

In addition to these more prosaic benefits, an electronic questionnaire can be 'loaded' with much more knowledge than a paper questionnaire. This knowledge is also executable, i.e. the electronic system can apply the knowledge based on the situation and the interaction with the patient. This means that it is possible to create completely new measurement regimen compared with paper.

Here are some examples:

1.   questions asked or not depending on previous answers or time of day;

2.   randomised selection of questions from a larger question base;

3.   randomised selection of measurement times over 24 hours;

4.   randomised order of questions;

5.   'auction' type questions;

6.   questions based on audio and/or graphics for patients who due to age, training, culture or disease cannot use standard questionnaires.

These examples mean that it is possible to measure more aspects of the patients' burden of illness. The first example, conditional navigation, makes it possible to query individual situations in more detail without jeopardizing the whole data set. On paper this requires navigation choices by the patient such as – 'If "Yes" continue with the next question, otherwise go to question 37'. Except in the simplest cases these designs invariably confuse many patients and lead to bad data. With electronic systems the navigation process is invisible to the patient, who simply sees a series of questions and often need not even be aware that choices are being made (see e.g. Norman and Pleskac, 2002).

The second example, Computer Adaptive Testing, has not been greatly used in clinical research, but has an extensive literature in areas such as educational and vocational testing (Wainer, 1990).

The third example comes within the scope of ecological momentary assessment (EMA), and is discussed by Alan Shields and colleagues in Chapter 1 of this book. Early work in this area successfully used paper collection with various forms of timers and alarms, but again electronic devices allow a great expansion of the method and increased trust in the results. By distributing the questions and collection times in a controlled way across patients and over the patient's day it is possible to acquire a more complete picture of their situation without unnecessarily burdening each of them with a multitude of questions.

The fourth example, randomized question order, can reduce, or at least be used to investigate, bias due to the effect of one question on another (see e.g. Couper et al., 2001).

Different types of questions can allow investigations into new aspects of the drug. In the fifth example, auction type questions have been used to evaluate how much a patient is prepared to pay for a new treatment (van Steenberghe et al., 2004). The process begins with a specific cash value and the patient is asked if she/he would be willing to pay this. The amount is then increased or decreased depending on the responses. Clearly the initial bid could affect the outcome, and to avoid bias the initial bid should be randomized. This can be done with paper, but is cumbersome. Electronic methods allow the starting bid to be automatically selected randomly, and then to be increased or decreased as the result of the patient's willingness or not to pay the specified amount.

The last example, using different modes of question presentation, shows how new patient groups can be investigated using ePRO. For example, solutions have been developed for patients who are illiterate, or visually disabled, as well as for children (see e.g. Hahn et al., 2004; Butz et al., 2005).

All these benefits can lead to a stronger case for the drug when submitting for regulatory approval or for price negotiations or, in some cases, differentiation against competitors.

In some settings, following a patient's symptoms daily could increase the safety of the patient in the trial. The investigator will have access to the data and can look at trends to see if the patient's condition is worsening. If so, the patient could be called to an extra visit or the treatment regimen can be changed over the phone. This approach has so far been mainly used in a telemedicine setting (see e.g. Wainwright and Wootton 2003), but is potentially valuable in clinical trials also.

Selection of the best solution may involve quantification of the benefits. This is useful if there are several solutions that only partially meet the requirements. By quantifying the benefits it is easy to rank the solutions by value.

To quantify the benefits start by creating two future scenarios. One describes what happens if ePRO is not used and the other if ePRO is used. The difference between these scenarios is what drives the benefits. If the revenue benefits are interesting, describe what happens to the sales curve. If the treatment effects are better documented you could expect a faster ramp-up and a higher peak sales. If you achieve faster results and, therefore, a shorter time to market, the start of sales will be earlier. Calculate the expected net present value of the product in the two scenarios. The difference between the two is the benefit of the faster results, the better science and the easier acceptance by the authorities.

If the cost reduction benefits are interesting, describe how the sample size will differ and how the work will be done with and without the ePRO solution. The reduced sample size will reduce patient fees and possibly reduce the number of investigational sites. The rest of the benefits will drive a reduction in work load. In some cases this will be on behalf of the investigator or a CRO, in which case the external costs will be reduced. In other cases it will be the internal work load that will decrease.

Select the desired benefits in the benefit graph.

List these on one axis of a table and the proposed solutions on the other axis.

As you review the solutions, write a comment in each intersection.

If no solution is adequate in all aspects, you should quantify the value of the benefits in order to decide which solution gives the most value.

The solutions that best fulfil the benefit criteria go on to the next step.

Cost

This brings us to the cost of implementing the ePRO solution. Are the benefits you aspire to worth the cost?

Depending on the supplier and the type of technology you will have different types of acquisition costs. A commercial supplier may charge a licence fee per user, per patient or per data point. Other cost models are also available. This means that the design of the clinical trial will affect the cost evaluation of the solution.

How much does the solution cost in all?

Are the benefits worth this much?

A trial with many patients but few data points per patient may benefit from a cost model per data point, while a trial with few patients and many data points will be suitable for a per patient fee.

In addition to the acquisition cost you will need different services, including but not limited to trial setup and validation, logistics, first and second line support and training. It is important to decide whether you will supply the services yourself or purchase them from the ePRO system supplier or another vendor. Either way, they will incur a cost. When deciding this, consider whether you are already providing that service for other parts of the study. For example, if you are using device-based ePRO, and you have set up logistics for delivering study medication it might be possible to use the same service to deliver ePRO devices. If you are using an IVR service for patient randomization, it may be cost-effective to use the same system for ePRO. Some of these costs may differ significantly between solutions. Support and training costs are strongly affected by the usability of the solution. User Interface issues are discussed by Brian Tiplady in Chapter 8 of this book.

You may also need to modify your internal processes to be able to deliver the benefits of ePRO. Manuel Morales has proposed the equation:

$$OP + NT = VEOP$$

This is to be read as Old Process plus New Technology equals Very Expensive Old Process, and indicates that if a process is faulty, then throwing new tools at it will cost money and not bring the hoped-for improvements. On the other hand if the process is sound, and it is the existing tools that are faulty, then replacing them with better tools will bring benefits. It is necessary to understand the processes and tools to know which is which! A practical example of the implementation and analyses of process and tool changes in clinical research is given by Brandt et al. (2004, 2006).

In practice, tools and processes often interact, and new tools may allow some parts of an old process to be discarded. An example already mentioned is that when patient data is collected electronically, the data entry and most of the data checking associated with paper diaries is no longer necessary. Bear in mind though, that new tasks may be required, for example software testing. When process changes are being considered there should be an analysis of system needs. On occasion this may suggest changes that benefit the old process. Thus software developers are extremely familiar with the idea of testing applications before they are released. There is a much greater emphasis than there used to be on the need for usability testing of paper questionnaires and it may be that the skills and attitudes of computer and web developers have contributed to this change.

The last part of the cost equation is tied to systems integration. Depending on which of the benefits you are interested in, you may need to invest in integrating the selected system with your internal computer systems: monitoring, data management etc. If you are interested in lead-time benefits from your ePRO investment, you may lose them if you have a complicated, manual data transfer process between the ePRO solution and your central database. Even the work load savings may diminish if users need to log into several systems and possibly even copy data manually from one to another. Manual data transfer also extends the risk of error. This will raise the cost in terms of increased manual control and/or more error resolution.

The CDISC initiative provides a set of standards that is increasingly being used in this type of integration. The use of CDISC to facilitate the interchange of laboratory data is described by Bassion (2002), and such methods are being increasingly used for other types of clinical data, including ePRO.

There are also costs related to the management of your partners; the solution vendor and any service collaborators you have. You must invest time and money in keeping the relationship with them alive and well. In some cases you may also need to monitor their performance and financial status to avoid unpleasant surprises.

List all the cost items. Estimate the value of each item for each of the proposed solutions. Vary the assumptions (e.g. the number of patients) to see how the different cost models react to changes.

Items include:

- licence fees (per trial, per user, per patient, per data point);
- setup and validation (don't forget internal costs for validation);
- logistics;
- support and training (these can differ, depending on the usability of the solution);
- process changes;
- systems integration (or costs for manual transfer, including quality control and error resolution);
- vendor and partner management.

Risk

Now you know what you want and have an idea of   *What will go wrong with*
what it will cost. That's fine, but there is still much   *this ePRO solution?*
left to do before you have delivered the benefits. To
actually get there you need to acquire the solution, have it delivered, implement it including changes to other applications, make the necessary process changes in your and other organisations and follow up the execution of those processes. To put it bluntly, there will be many things that can go wrong along the way.

Therefore, the final question we will ask is: *What will go wrong with this ePRO solution?*

In order to answer this question we will look at a number of dimensions that illuminate the process of acquiring and implementing an ePRO tool. For each dimension we will see what can go wrong and how you might go about validating the suitability of the solution you are looking at. The dimensions that we will consider are:

- the supplier;

- the system;

- the science;

- the data flow;

- the usability.

It is both advisable and practical to set up a risk register for each of the proposed solutions. The risk register should record every damaging event that could happen, with an evaluation of the consequences of the damage and the probability of it happening. A table comparing the risks of all the solutions is a good way of seeing the whole picture. Even if the picture is complicated, it is still useful and possible to quantify the risks. The damage can be quantified in terms of increased cost or lengthened time lines and the probability is estimated as a percentage: if you used this solution in ten trials, in how many would you expect the event to occur? Multiplying the damage with the probability gives the expected cost of that risk. Just remember to update the evaluation of the damage or the probability as you put risk reduction measures in place. There is an extensive literature on risk management that has recently been reviewed from a drug development perspective by Saari (2004).

THE SUPPLIER

A supplier of ePRO solutions can be a commercial vendor, either a general vendor or one specialised in software for clinical research. It could also be a department internal to your own business or an outsourcing/offshoring partner.

The first thing you need to do is to identify the supplier clearly and list what you expect from that supplier.

- delivery of technology?

- computer operations?

- logistics?

- support?

- data management?

- etc

Depending on what services you require, the supplier evaluation may be more or less demanding. For example, if you are only buying the technology and will deploy and support it yourself, it will not be critical for a specific clinical trial if the supplier goes out of business. On the other hand, if you depend on the supplier for computer operations, you will want to evaluate and monitor its financial state to ensure that nothing adverse happens. In any event, there should be an analysis of the impact of supplier failure and of measures in place to minimize it, such as having application source code and documentation in escrow.

Basically, the supplier evaluation is a standard supplier audit, covering their business operations and regulatory compliance (e.g. Li et al., 2007). It is important to focus on the expectations you have on the supplier you listed. Can you trust them to fulfil these expectations throughout the duration of the trial? One aspect often missed in evaluations is the supplier's own approach to risk management. Do they have active risk management, proactively identifying, evaluating and managing risks? Remember, any risk that affects their business will affect yours.

THE SYSTEM

There is always a risk, some would say a certainty, that the system will break down during the trial. To manage this, you need to evaluate the system itself and the procedures that the supplier uses in systems development and management. This evaluation will give you an idea of the risk level and also about what support to expect if something adverse happens.

Many problems that show up during systems use are not due to errors in implementation but rather to incorrect specifications. Many quality systems assume implicitly that the specifications are correct and only check that the specification has been correctly implemented. You should carefully evaluate the specifications to ensure the system is expected to do what you require.

THE SCIENCE

An ePRO solution is not just a data entry or communications tool. It is a scientific instrument. Therefore it must be evaluated from a scientific point of view. Will the instrument record what you expect?

Will the capture method introduce bias? Questionnaires are subject to psychological processes in the patient. The design of the questionnaire and how it is administered can affect the answers. If you are using device-based ePRO, the device itself could introduce anxiety in the patient. If anxiety is part of what is being assessed by the questionnaire, then this might skew the results (see e.g. Tseng et al., 1997).

Often the study protocol requires that patients answer questions morning and evening. Why morning and evening? Are the results different if a patient answers all questions once daily, half of them after 12 hours? In some cases they will not be, in others they will.

If you have paper-based data to compare with, is the electronic data different? There has been a substantial amount of work done in recent years, reviewed by Gwaltney et al. (2008). They show that, in general, the results were very similar between the two modes, indicating that migration from paper to electronic does not in itself change the results. But this does not mean that your specific instrument has not been affected by the change from paper to electronic. There are a number of ways such differences could arise.

A questionnaire administered on paper often has many questions on one page. It is also possible to turn the pages to see all the other questions. Each question is therefore set in the context of all other questions. Device-based questionnaires, particularly on small devices, are often designed so that only one question is visible at a time. IVR systems also present one question at a time. Furthermore, it is possible to stop patients from going back and changing the answer to a previous question. Even if they can do so, they may be less likely to navigate back to a previous question on an electronic system than to turn a paper page. This means that the context of the question is reduced to itself and any previous questions. This may be a good thing, reducing the 'halo' effect, or the tendency for respondents to answer grouped questions more similarly than questions presented separately, or it may be tend to increase question order effects (see e.g. Couper et al., 2001). In your specific PRO application, might this factor affect the results?

You will need to address the issue of 'equivalence of measure', i.e. how data captured on paper compares to data captured through your selected ePRO solution. This is similar to the testing required after translating a questionnaire into a new language and culture. In some cases there will be previous studies that show equivalence. In others, you will need to run a study of your own.

There are two main approaches to comparing electronic and paper questionnaires. The first, cognitive interviewing, is described in detail by Paul Beatty in Chapter 2 of this book and uses interviews with patients who have completed paper and electronic versions of scales to explore possible differences in the ways patients understand the questions and response options and the way they use the scales. The second is similar to evaluating test-retest reliability of a scale, comparing scores obtained by patients who have completed both forms, usually within a short time of each other in randomized order. A review of such studies has already been referred to (Gwaltney et al., 2008) and the methodology is discussed in more detail by Damian McEntegart in Chapter 9 of this book.

Equivalence studies are sometimes combined with efficacy studies to avoid the cost and possible delay of carrying out a separate study before the efficacy studies get under way. What is the risk that such a study will show non-equivalence? How would you handle that and what would it cost?

If the ePRO solution gives any feedback to the patient, you need to understand if this introduces any behavioural changes. If so, there is a risk that the behavioural changes will add to the placebo effect thereby diluting the study results.

THE DATA FLOW

The whole data flow, from the moment the patient answers the question to the study database and, indeed, the investigators' and sponsors' archive as required by GCP, must be validated. This is an area where technology is moving much faster than guidelines so it is important to understand the basics.

The most fundamental requirement on data is called 'ALCOA'. This is an acronym for Attributable, Legible, Contemporaneous, Original, Accurate. If you can conserve these attributes in the data, and document that you have conserved them, then you have a validated data flow.

Attributable means that any mechanism you use to verify that an approved user has entered the data also passes on this information to posterity. If you require the user to log on to the system you can use the log on data (who, when). If you use the fact that the patient has a device in his/her possession as evidence of authenticity (e.g. when using a mobile phone or PDA) then you need to document the ID of the device, and the date and time of its issue to the patient, and match these to the data entered. It is also a good idea to ensure that the same device is returned by the patient at the end of the study.

Legible seems to be less of a problem using ePRO than with paper, but you may code the answers, e.g. 1 for yes, 0 for no, during capture. In this case, legible means that the code is available when the data are to be analysed. To preserve the contemporaneous aspect of the data you must ensure that the time stamp is preserved. It is also important to verify that the device, whether it be a PDA or a server, was set at the correct time.

Originality is preserved if you show that no unaudited changes can be made throughout the data flow. On the device and server sides this is achieved through a computer generated audit trail. During transit this may be handled by encryption and/or digital signatures. Accuracy in PRO data can be verified as with other data, through statistical checks that verify the distribution.

Test the data flow from start to finish before you begin the trial. Use both realistic and extreme volumes. Do not forget there may be bottlenecks when many individuals try to transmit data simultaneously.

While analysing the data flow, set up and manage a risk register. If you find anything that resembles a weak point, add that to the risk register and investigate how you can eliminate, mitigate or observe the risk depending on its potential impact. One way of eliminating the risk is to choose another solution.

Make a special note of manual steps. These may always induce mistrust. Therefore, if you cannot automate them, ensure you have a system of checks and balances to be able to verify that the manual work has been consistent and does not adversely affect ALCOA.

THE USABILITY

The last, but by no means least important, part is about how the solution will work in real life, with real people. If the solution is not designed for these people, things will go wrong. These things will definitely cost you, but at worst they may jeopardize the study results.

When you evaluate usability, it is important to remember that this is a vertical application. Different rules apply to the usability design compared with an application designed for broad use such as a word processor. Test the solution in real-world situations. How will a patient live his or her life with the diary? Where will the patient make the entries? If you are asking for entries at different, perhaps random, times of day, when the patient may not be at home or have access to a phone, then a small portable device is probably needed. If entries can be made at home or at work, then IVR or a larger device may be appropriate.

The illness itself may also be a factor. If you are studying Parkinson's disease, will the patient's tremor make it difficult to use the ePRO system? If using diaries for patients with migraine, would an alarm be bothersome to someone having an attack?

If using a clinic-based system, how will if fit in with work practices? Will it impose changes in the way investigators and nurses manage the patients? How much training is needed? The cost of the study will increase if a solution requires a lot of training of patients or staff. Also, a solution that requires a lot of initial training will most often need re-training if the solution isn't used often. This is especially important to consider for investigative staff. In some studies the frequency of patient visits may be so low that they will have ample time to forget how to manage the ePRO solution in between. Staff turnover at the clinic will also increase the training requirement, as new staff will need to be initiated into system use.

If using devices, then you need to think about power – or, rather, lack of it. Mobile phones need charging at least once a week and modern PDAs more often. How will this work for the patient or in the clinic? What happens when the batteries run out? Some devices store information in non-volatile memory, while others will lose both application and data if the battery goes flat. This is less of a problem than it used to be, but you need to know!

If the batteries run out, even if the data are secure, there may be other problems. Will the device need re-setting, and can patients manage this, themselves? What happens to the clock? We started by saying that one of the major benefits of ePRO was the ability to know exactly when the patient answered the questions. If a device is without power for a half a day, will the clock still show the correct time? Will it be set back half a day or will it default to a start date (e.g. Jan 1, 1900)? Can the patient set the clock and how do you audit that?

The last issue to watch out for, especially when using devices such as electronic diaries, is how data are protected at the source. This is an ALCOA issue, but can also have effects on the usability. It is possible to require a password or PIN code for everything a patient does. It is also possible to accept that possession of the device is sufficient guarantee for authenticity. This depends on the design of the study. If the study calls for entries once daily, the device will often be left at the bedside table for most of the time. In this case a password is not too cumbersome and may be considered necessary. If the study requires entries as the patient experiences events, say pain, the patient should keep the device with him/her and in that case possession may be enough.

Remember that if you use passwords or PIN codes it will be necessary to have good password management, including an easy way to reset the password after verifying that it is the right person requesting the password reset.

Analyse the risks by describing the harmful event and evaluating the damage should it occur and the probability of it happening. Examples of events include:

Supplier risks: The supplier goes out of business, loses key competence, reneges on the contract, is struck by misfortune (fire, burglary, terrorism, etc).

System risks: The system does not fit reality, fails in specific circumstances (high user load, high data load, etc), depends on specific hardware or software that goes out of production during the trial or is hard to update.

Science risks: Bias, non-equivalence to prior data, psychological context, introduction of behavioural changes.

Data risks: Failure to conserve ALCOA. Lack of validated electronic archiving.

Usability risks: Patients, or investigational staff, do not want to use the solution. Patients or investigational sites decline to take part in the study due to the ePRO solution. Usability problems (e.g. power, clock, or handling issues) affect the data quality.

Decisions in Practice

As an example of the kind of practical evaluation that   *How do benefits, cost*
is often made in study planning, consider a decision   *and risk compare?*
as to whether to use a handheld or a telephone-based
solution for patient diary data in a clinical trial. Telephone systems, based on a
spoken script to which the patient responds by pressing buttons on the phone
keypad, are often referred to as interactive voice response (IVR) systems. The
ubiquity of the telephone can make these systems an attractive choice both
because patients are familiar with phones, and because they can use their own
phones in the study, which may reduce costs. But a number of factors have to
be taken into account that illustrate many of the points made above.

The cost models for the two systems are quite different. An IVR solution
generally has a lower start-up cost per patient because there is no need to
supply hardware, but the volume costs for data management are higher. So IVR
would be more cost-effective in a study collecting relatively small amounts of
data per patient, while a handheld would be more suitable where data volumes
were large.

Questions of usability are also important. IVR systems can be easy for the
patient to use, but do not readily offer features such as alarms or reminders.
So if it is important to obtain data at well-defined times, a handheld would
have advantages. For a diary, where the patient records data at the end of the
day and the exact time is not important, either method would be suitable.
Both methods provide time-stamping of data, so compliance can be reliably
documented whichever option is chosen (Stone et al., 2002).

IVR uses a spoken script, while handhelds use visual presentation. If an
instrument has been migrated from another modality this may be a relevant
consideration. For some paper instruments the visual aspect may be essential (as
with body diagrams) or valuable (e.g. where different questions have different
response options). There are also a lot of measures that are designed to be
presented verbally, typically by a clinician. There is, for example a substantial
literature on the use of IVR to administer psychiatric rating scales (Moore et al.,
2006), as discussed by Byrom and colleagues in Chapter 7. In these cases, the
choice of electronic modality needs to take the original method of presentation
of the instrument into account.

Practically, preparing for the decision means collecting all the information about benefits, cost and risk in one place and structuring it so that a comparison is possible. For qualitative data, tables are useful. When comparing two alternatives it is often possible to say that one item in a column is equal to another item in the other column. These can then be struck out from the comparison. If two on one side are equal to one on the other all three can be struck out (Franklin, 1772).

In more complex cases or when a more systematic analysis is needed, quantification of benefits, cost and risks can support the analysis. Modern quantification methods, e.g. Monte Carlo simulation using calibrated estimates (Hubbard, 2007), can model uncertainty in a systematic way.

Obviously there are no 'one size fits all' solutions to be had when choosing an ePRO solution. But provided we are clear about where we want to go, we will be able to get there.

Summary

Selecting a suitable ePRO solution depends on why you wish to use it. In different research situations different features of the ePRO system will be important, for example documenting protocol compliance, improving data completeness and quality, shortening the time to data lock or even enabling previously impractical measures in the study. Cost may be a primary factor, in that ePRO is being used to reduce overall cost. In other situations the cost will be weighed against the other benefits being obtained. Risks will be very different in different settings, for example in unsupervised situations versus use in a hospital clinic, or in the likelihood and consequences of a vendor going out of business. These factors cannot be assessed once and for all, but must be assessed for the specific goals and circumstances of the project and the environment in which it is run. However the framework for assessing benefits, cost and risk is well-established. Its use will allow informed decisions about ePRO system selection and ensure that study goals are met in a cost-effective fashion.

References

Bassion, S. (2002) Standardizing laboratory data interchange in clinical trials, *Journal of the Association for Laboratory Automation*, 7: 62–64.

Bernhard, J., Cella, D.F. and Coates, A.S. et al. (1998) Missing quality of life data in cancer clinical trials: serious problems and challenges, *Statistics in Medicine*, 17: 517–532.

Brandt, C. A., Argraves, S. and Money, R. et al. (2006) Informatics tools to improve clinical research study implementation, *Contemporary Clinical Trials*, 27: 112–122.

Brandt, C.A., Gadagkar, R. and Rodriguez, C. et al. (2004) Managing complex change in clinical study metadata, *Journal of the American Medical Informatics Association*, 11: 380–391.

Butz, A.M., Donithan, M. and Bollinger, M.E. et al. (2005) Monitoring nebulizer use in children: comparison of electronic and asthma diary data, *Ann Allergy Asthma Immunol*, 94: 360–365.

Couper, M.P., Traugott, M.W. and Lamias, M.J. (2001) Web survey design and administration, *Public Opinion Quarterly*, 65: 230–254.

Fallowfield, L. (1996) Quality of quality-of-life data, *The Lancet*, 348: 421–422.

Franklin, B. (1772) A letter to Joseph Priestley, Sept. 19, 1772, http://www.franklinpapers.org/franklin/

Gwaltney, C.J., Shields, A.L. and Shiffman, S. (2008) Equivalence of electronic and paper-and-pencil administration of patient-reported outcome measures: a meta-analytic review, *Value in Health*, 11: 322–333.

Hahn, E.A., Cella, D. and Dobrez, D. et al. (2004) The talking touch screen: a new approach to outcomes assessment in low literacy, *Psychooncology*, 13: 86–95.

Hubbard, D.W. (2007) *How to Measure Anything*, John Wiley & Sons, Inc., Hoboken NJ.

Li, H., Hawlk, S. and Hanna, K. et al. (2007) Developing and implementing a comprehensive clinical qa audit program, *Quality Assurance Journal*, 11: 128–137.

Moore, H.K., Mundt, J.C. and Modell, J.G. et al. (2006) An examination of 26,168 Hamilton Depression Rating Scale scores administered via interactive voice response across 17 randomized clinical trials, *Journal of Clinical Psychopharmacology*, 26: 321–324.

Norman, K.L. and Pleskac, T. (2002), 'Conditional branching in computerized self-administered questionnaires: an empirical study', Proceedings of the human factors and ergonomics society, 46th annual meeting, Baltimore, pp. 1241–1245.

Saari, H.-L. 2004, Risk management in drug development projects, Helsinki University of Technology Laboratory of Industrial Management, Helsinki, Report No: 2004/1.

Stone, A.A., Shiffman, S. and Schwartz, J.E. et al. (2002) Patient non-compliance with paper diaries, *British Medical Journal*, 324: 1193–1194.

Tseng, H.-M., Macleod, H.A. and Wright, P. (1997) Computer anxiety and measurement of mood change, *Computers in Human Behavior*, 13: 305–316.

van Steenberghe, D., Bercy, P., De Boever, J., Adriaens, P., Geers, L., Hendrickx, E., Adriaenssen, C., Rompen, E., Malmenas, M. and Ramsberg, J. (2004) Patient evaluation of a novel non-injectable anesthetic gel: a multicenter crossover study comparing the gel to infiltration anesthesia during scaling and root planeing, *J Periodontol*, 75: 1471–1478.

Wainer, H. (1990) *Computer Adaptive Testing: A Primer*. Lawrence Erlbaum, Hilldale, NJ.

Wainwright, C. and Wootton, R. (2003) A review of telemedicine and asthma. *Disease Management & Health Outcomes*, 11: 557–563.

6

Patient Compliance in an ePRO Environment: Methods for Consistent Compliance Management, Measurement and Reporting

Alan L. Shields, Saul Shiffman and Arthur Stone

Introduction

Migration to 'ecologically valid' or real world based models of clinical data collection holds the promise of overcoming biases and inaccuracies associated with data gathered retrospectively. Translating that *promise* into *reality*, however, carries its own challenges. Diary methods of data collection can, for example, place burdens on patients that may interfere with their ability to comply with measurement instructions, such as complete a pain inventory before going to sleep or a voiding diary following each micturition. It has long been observed that patients are noncompliant with measurement instructions and complete the diary cards either before or after the time specified by the protocol. This not only violates the protocol, but is a major impediment to validity. In this way, the rationale for using diary methods is subverted, as the retrospectively completed records fall prey to the very inaccuracies and biases that motivated the use of diaries in the first place. Considerable evidence confirms that while patients *report* compliance with paper diary assessment procedures, the objectively validated and *actual* rates of their compliance are typically much lower (for example, Stone et al., 2002). In fact, a review of studies comparing patient reported compliance with objectively monitored compliance found that nearly 40 per cent of paper diary entries were indeed falsified (Hufford, 2007). Fortunately, when objective compliance monitoring is built into a diary protocol, typically through electronically instrumented devices, patient compliance can be both thoroughly monitored and, with the addition of certain procedures, enhanced (for example, Broderick et al., 2004).

These methods are carried out in an unsupervised everyday environment, for example at home or work, and therefore rely upon patients' compliance with the measurement instructions and data collection protocol. This chapter is divided into three sections that address patient compliance in an eDiary environment. In the first, we briefly describe the development of diary and eDiary methods and discuss why they place such a high premium on patient compliance. The second outlines factors that may contribute to non-compliance as well as approaches toward achieving high compliance. The third describes published accounts of investigators' methods for monitoring patient compliance, as well as recommendations for consistent compliance measurement and reporting.

Collection of PRO Data via Diary Methods

HISTORICAL DEVELOPMENT: A BRIEF REVIEW

Patient Reported Outcome (PRO) data are common and important in clinical research (Wilke et al., 2004). For many research questions, patient self-report is the key source of data. For example, research subjects are frequently asked to report on the occurrence of objective events, such as an episode of urinary incontinence or an asthma attack. In these instances, participants are acting as a proxy for the researcher, recording the occurrence and details of events that could, in principle, be observed by others. A more realistic representation of these events can be obtained, however, if patients self-monitor and record these events as they occur during the normal course of daily activities in the patients' typical environment. Patients are also frequently asked to report on their subjective state. In these instances the patient is the sole source of data. Common examples of subjective self-report include pain, fatigue, and mood states. Lastly, patients are also asked to make global evaluations about their well-being and health-related quality of life (HRQoL).

Though the use of PRO data in clinical research has always been standard practice, the Food and Drug Agency (FDA) has only recently released final guidance on PRO assessments and on the development and use of methods used to collect PRO data (FDA, 2009). This document, 'Patient Reported Outcome (PRO) Measures: Use in Medical Product Development to Support Labeling Claims,' commonly referred to as the *PRO Guidance*, lays out the type and quality of information that clinical researchers will need to provide to justify the use of a particular PRO instrument in a trial and promises to make for more efficient and effective use of these tools.

The importance of PRO data to clinical research is clear. As such, researchers must strive to overcome a number of methodological challenges to collect this data in a reliable and valid way. Historically, researchers collected PRO data retrospectively and in summary during clinic visits. While potentially useful, we now know that PRO data gathered in this way can be limited in important ways. For example, empirical research on autobiographical memory has documented a wide range of inaccuracies and biases that can affect recall data. This issue was briefly summarized in Chapter 1 and we reiterate that the inaccurate recall of past experiences is not simply a result of the fading of memory over time. Instead, recall relies heavily on the use of heuristic strategies or mental shortcuts to *reconstruct* the past (Bradburn, Rips and Shevell, 1987). This reconstructive process is imperfect and subject to a range of biases resulting from the layers of processing necessary to answer the typical research inquiry. Each step of the recall process has the potential to introduce significant inaccuracy and bias into recall data.

A key objective of diary methods is to collect data closer to real time, and thus to minimize recall bias. The importance of this objective is illustrated by the fact that diaries have been used for well over half a century to collect PRO data from hundreds of thousands of patients in clinical research (Verbrugge, 1980).

The most common type of diary used in clinical research is a paper diary. This methodology requires patients to record their experiences on diary cards, typically for a single day, and return them to a research site. The use of paper diaries promised several advantages relative to data gathered retrospectively at the research visits. Most importantly, the patient's experience and behavior could be assessed in near real time, avoiding or significantly reducing the problems associated with recall. Additionally, the multiple assessments inherent in most diary designs had the potential to provide more reliable and statistically powerful data by virtue of their repeated measures over different time periods. These assessments would also be sensitive to transient medication effects or other phenomena that may exert their influence over time and are of significant interest to clinical researchers. The net effect of collecting real-time data repeatedly from patients in their natural environment could be a more rich, ecologically valid, statistically powerful and reliable assessment of the phenomenon of interest.

THE IMPORTANCE OF PATIENT COMPLIANCE IN DIARY RESEARCH

Paper diaries have not lived up to their promise. Specifically they have yielded poor compliance, which undermines the core objective of diary methods. In this context, patient compliance refers to the extent to which the research participant follows the guidelines of the research protocol. Compliance to the diary protocol is absolutely critical from both a scientific and commercial perspective as patient non-compliance may diminish the validity of PRO data and, in short, render data inaccurate or impossible to interpret. In other words, as will be discussed below, patient non-compliance can yield results different from results obtained from a compliant patient group or preclude our ability to draw *any* trustworthy substantive conclusions from a given study (for example, Broderick et al., 2004).

When using paper, researchers rely on the patient to faithfully comply with the diary protocol by completing the diary cards as instructed (for example, at the end of the day or after the target event, such as a hot flash, and to honestly and accurately report when the diaries were completed. Compliance rates with paper diary studies have been reported as quite high (Norman et al., 1982; Sherliker and Steptoe, 2000). But it is important to recognize that these estimates of compliance are simply based on the patients' reports, usually as indicated by how they complete their diary cards. Because there has been no practical way of authenticating patient reported compliance rates, they have been called unconfirmed compliance rates.

More recently, Stone et al. (2002) used an instrumented paper diary to assess more objectively patient compliance with paper diaries. This covertly-instrumented paper diary system was equipped with photosensors that recorded the opening of the diary booklet – a prerequisite to completing diary cards – so that the researchers could estimate actual rates of compliance. Thus, they were able to compare *patient reported compliance*, the time and date that patients reported completing their diary cards and *actual compliance,* the electronic records of the paper diary having been opened or closed. In this study, a group of pain patients ($n = 80$) were asked to complete three fixed-time assessments at 10 am., 4 pm. and 8 pm. of their pain each day for three weeks. Patients in the trial returned 90 per cent of their paper diary cards with entries implying that they had been completed in a timely way, per-protocol. However, evaluation of the objective data from the instruments indicated that only a small portion,20 per cent, could actually have been completed within 90 minutes of the assessment window. In other words, the vast majority of the dates and times were falsified. Moreover, on 32 per cent of days, the paper diary was not opened at all. Yet on those days, patients had a *reported compliance* of 96 per cent. Over all, while *patient reported compliance* was 90 per cent consistent with patient-based reports in many other paper diary studies, *actual compliance* with the paper diary was estimated at 11 per cent. Data indicated that patients both back-filled paper diary entries, completing multiple diary cards for several previous days at one time, and forward-filled them, completing multiple diary cards for several days in the *future*, which obviously rendered the data invalid. Broderick et al (2004) subsequently showed that adding an audible reminder to complete the paper diary boosted actual compliance only modestly. As we discuss below, however, an electronic diary with compliance-enhancing features yielded actual, verified, compliance of 94 per cent.

The compliance findings reported above have stirred debate among diary researchers who contend that either paper diary compliance is reasonable and/or that poor protocol compliance may not have a significant impact on diary data (Green et al., 2006; Tennen et al., 2006). Nevertheless, the results, along with other literature documenting falsified paper diary entries (Hufford, 2007), suggest that diary compliance cannot simply be assumed – even when patients are well-instructed, monitored periodically, and provided with real-time prompts to complete the diary.

Without being able to document and verify timely compliance with diary completion, the validity of diary data is suspect. Paper diaries are so vulnerable to back- and forward-filling that the burden of proof must fall on the sponsor and investigator to objectively document the timeliness of diary entries. Indeed, the FDA's PRO Guidance explicitly states that:

> *If a patient diary or some other form of unsupervised data entry is used, we [the FDA] plan to review the clinical trial protocol to determine what steps are taken to ensure that patients make entries according to the clinical trial design and not, for example, just before a clinic visit when their reports will be collected.*

> (FDA, 2009, p. 14)

Therefore, from a scientific and regulatory standpoint, compliance monitoring and verification are essential elements of diary protocols.

Despite challenges, confidence in diary data can be achieved when compliance verification methodology is employed. This can be accomplished via electronic data gathering systems. Electronic or eDiaries are capable of providing a detailed account of patient compliance, as they can time and date stamp all data entries, log missed assessment opportunities and track the timeliness of patient responses, which are all important aspects of monitoring compliance. This is discussed later in greater detail. An example of such tracking is in the 40 patients in Stone et al. (2002) who recorded their pain in an ePRO diary. It prompted for assessments at the times required by the protocol and did not allow entries outside the designated time windows. These patients *actually* completed 94 per cent of their assigned assessments on time, as evidenced by the electronically time and date stamped records of each eDiary entry, an 83 per cent improvement in overall compliance relative to the paper diary system.

Achieving Patient Compliance

High rates of actual subject compliance have been consistently reported in clinical research using eDiary technology (Hufford and Shields, 2002). Nevertheless, strong compliance is not an invariable result of using these methods and simply relying on 'e' technology to make research subjects comply with assessment is no guarantee of success. Instead, compliance is dependent upon the thoughtful application of the technology in the context of a good understanding of other factors that contribute to both compliance and non-compliance (Hufford, 2007; Hufford and Shiffman, 2003). Therefore, we now consider some of the reasons and underlying processes that may lead to non-compliance. Next, we outline strategies that clinical researchers can employ to enhance patient compliance.

REASONS FOR PATIENT NON-COMPLIANCE

We stress that non-compliance is not caused by 'bad' people or 'bad' study participants, or by errors or omissions on the part of the researchers. The vast majority of research subjects have a genuine interest in helping researchers and fully participating in the protocol. One source of non-compliance is participants' everyday schedules, which can interfere with the patient's intrinsic desire to be 'compliant.' This is simply a reality of conducting research in the context of everyday life. Paradoxically, a patient's desire to participate in clinical research and be a 'good study participant' may actually motivate him or her to 'make up' missed diary entries by recording them retrospectively. The patient is unlikely to realize that the recalled responses are contaminated by recall bias and, instead, considers the retrospective reporting to be the most responsible action.

A second reason for non-compliance is simple forgetfulness. Patients may be asked to make entries for various events, at various time intervals and at various times of day. These protocols require patients to remember when to make diary entries and, especially for protocols that require multiple entries per day, the demand on working memory can be overwhelming. Given the limitations of human memory and the complexities of daily living, it is not surprising that many subjects simply forget to make diary entries. This is especially true without cues for assessment, such as 'beeps' that prompt patients to complete a record.

The eDiary burden may increase as the severity or frequency of the symptoms monitored increase. When diary entries are supposed to be cued by events, in other words monitoring is event-driven, such as by an exacerbation of symptoms, the patient's diary burden can become too great. In other words, an increasing rate or intensity of the symptoms may actually discourage patients from completing their assessments, especially if they are being asked to record each occurrence. Such increased subject burden has the potential to introduce bias into the data as subjects may systematically stop entering symptoms because of reporting fatigue.

Somewhat surprisingly, the number of daily assessments appears to be unrelated to subject compliance, even after controlling for the length of the monitoring protocol. Empirical support for this is found in a study by Kamarck et al. (1998) where there was 99 per cent compliance with a protocol requiring 12 or more assessments each day. In this study, however, patients only participated for a few days. Stone et al. (2003), however, did demonstrate that the number of daily assessments was unrelated to patient compliance to the assessment procedures and that this was true over a 14 day protocol. In this study, 68 chronic pain patients were randomized to receive 3, 6, or 12 assessment prompts per day for two weeks and compliance with assessment was at or above 94 per cent for each of these groups. Additionally, no statistically significant differences were observed among groups for observed behavior indicative of patient frustration with an increased sampling density. Patients in the more heavily sampled group did not suspend, delay, or otherwise opt out of assessments at rates any higher than the less heavily sampled groups. Nevertheless, the circumstances under which patient burden begins to interfere with patient compliance are unclear.

COMPLIANCE ENHANCEMENT

As noted, one advantage of eDiaries over paper is that their systems can easily accommodate automated compliance monitoring and these methods can time and date stamp data entries. Even within an eDiary protocol, however, there are a variety of additional techniques that clinical investigators can use to further enhance compliance.

BUILD COMPLIANCE INTO THE PROTOCOL

Compliance considerations must be part of design, execution, and write up of a research program using diary methods (Stone and Shiffman, 2002). Compliance enhancement features of any diary system must be considered from the perspective of the patient. Considering and anticipating the needs, limitations, and strengths of research participants prior to data collection can foster effective 'partnering' with them in the larger research endeavor. This partnering with patients, a task easily overlooked in a busy research environment, serves many important functions. Chief among them is that it can enhance the patients' intrinsic desire to be responsible participants, as defined by the investigator.

PROMOTE PATIENT ACCOUNTABILITY

Patients who feel a sense of accountability for the data will be more compliant with the protocol (Rabin et al., 1996; Urquhart, 1994). Creating a sense of accountability can be initiated during patient training and should be carried through the duration of the protocol. Empirical evidence confirms that patients' compliance can be related to whether they are aware that the researcher is tracking their compliance over the course of the study. For example, Broderick et al. (2004) sampled female fibromyalgia patients and randomized them to 'Aware' or 'Unaware' conditions. The Aware group was trained to understand that their compliance with the measurement strategy was being monitored while the Unaware group was ignorant of the objective compliance verification procedures. In this way, the Unaware subject protocol more closely mirrored a typical research protocol in which compliance is based on unconfirmed patient reports, the 'honor system'. For this study, an eDEM™ electronic monitor cap (Aardex Ltd., Switzerland) would record each time the cap was opened and closed to provide information about adherence to the sampling protocol – self-administration of an oral cotton swab. Objective compliance for the Unaware condition was 71 per cent while their self-reported compliance was 93 per cent. In contrast, aware participants' objective compliance was 90 per cent which was consistent with self-reported compliance of 93 per cent. In other words, subjects who were aware of the compliance monitoring procedures were significantly more compliant with measurement relative to the group which was unaware of them. Moreover, these researchers showed that reliance on the non-compliant data yielded results different from results obtained from the more compliant patient group which, in turn, could alter the substantive conclusions drawn from the study.

The results presented by Broderick et al. (2002) are consistent with other reports and reviews on patient non-compliance with diary assessment procedures (Hufford, 2007). Patients *report* being far more compliant with research procedures than objective assessment of their *actual* compliance would suggest. But when objective compliance monitoring is built into the protocol and patients are made aware of these procedures, they are able to comply with the protocol in ways that yield more valid data. Put another way, patients will tend to be more compliant when they know their compliance is being monitored and how it is being monitored.

Include user-friendly interface and 'livability' functions

eDiaries, like any other PRO instrument, should be easy to use. As suggested in Tiplady (2007), the eDiary should be developed with the patient's point of view in mind. An important compliance-enhancing feature is a user interface that is intuitive to the particular patient sample being tested. Livability functions reflect components of the assessment protocol that allow patients to seamlessly integrate the eDiary into their daily lives (for example, Shiffman, 2000). For example, in protocols that prompt patients for assessment, it is helpful to allow patients to briefly postpone an assessment (for example, while they are taking a nap). Of course, the researcher should be aware that postponing assessments for too long may invalidate the protocol requirements. For that reason, we encourage researchers to thoughtfully consider both the reasons for and consequences of any livability functions added to an eDiary protocol.

'Drive' the protocol

Programmed reminders when the diary needs to be completed can improve compliance (Hufford and Shields, 2002), but do not guarantee it (for example, Broderick et al., 2003). For example, real-time compliance reminders can be built into some PRO methods of data collection, such as eDiaries, to prompt subjects to complete entries. But these prompts do not force subject compliance. In addition to prompting or pre-programmed assessment reminders, clinical researchers should thoughtfully consider the sampling strategy that may be most appropriate or the 'best fit' for the target of assessment. For example, if the researcher suspects and/or anticipates non-compliance due to reporting fatigue, the researcher may need to reduce the burden to maximize compliance. ePRO methods make data available to researchers for review in near real time and this allows the staff of a clinical trial site to identify patients with compliance or training issues and offer prompt help and support.

Guide subjects through assessments

Study patients may make mistakes and become frustrated if there are difficult decisions about whether to complete or skip certain items based on their responses to other items. Frustration will be reduced and compliance will be enhanced if the PRO data collection method clearly specifies complex branching found within many assessment strategies. Electronic diary systems can be programmed to respond to a patient's response pattern and administer the correct items in the correct logical sequence, with no additional effort from the patient.

Train the patients

Patients should be trained in the use of the diary. Adequate training procedures are associated with high rates of patient compliance in the field (Hufford and Shields, 2002). This is sensible, as compliance can only be observed if patients understand what is being asked of them. As suggested already, any eDiary or other ePRO data collection method should be simple and intuitive and require little training regarding the system's basic functions. However, orienting the patient to the protocol, the assessment, and the diary, helps promote compliance. A practice period in which patients get experience with the diary prior to data collection can improve compliance.

Training can also specifically emphasize compliance, including making patients aware of the objective compliance monitoring features of the protocol (for example, Broderick et al., 2004). Lastly, compliance training should not be viewed as a one-time offering. By providing patients with frequent, real time compliance reminders and feedback on their actual ongoing compliance performance, eDiaries can encourage the type of device interactions that are characteristic of effective computer interfaces (Raskin, 2000).

MONITORING PATIENT COMPLIANCE

Diary protocols seek data generated in the real world and near real time to an event (for example, a symptom exacerbation) or time (for example, at the end of each study day) of interest. Therefore, the primary diary compliance question is, *did the patients complete the assessment at the time we asked them to do so?* In order to answer this question, the researcher must know when responses are supposed to be completed by research subjects and when they are actually completed. In a paper diary system, the research typically knows only when responses are supposed to be completed and when patients say they completed the responses which are usually hand written on a record form; actual compliance cannot be monitored. Moreover, as has been shown, patient-reported compliance rates are often much higher than actual compliance rates and are, therefore, suspect. Electronic diaries, on the other hand, are capable of characterizing actual compliance, as all responses can be time and date stamped and skipped assessments can be logged. Without such procedures, researchers cannot know the true degree of compliance.

Stone and Shiffman (2002) have suggested and defined two specific types of compliance data that should be reported in any eDiary report. Specifically, *compliance rates* are the proportion of scheduled assessment opportunities that were completed. For example, a 95 per cent compliance rate would be reported for a patient who completed 20 of 21 scheduled, nightly reports, assuming that the date stamps indicate the patient completed an assessment on each of the study nights. Second, *compliance verification data* provide an estimate of the timeliness of the report. For example, the electronic time stamps can verify that the 20 completed reports were all recorded within the 2-hour time window, say between 7:00 and 9:00pm, permitted by the protocol. In order to make interpretation of the literature more systematic, we encourage the use of these definitions as benchmarks for eDiary protocol compliance. Stone and Shiffman (2002) offer other guidance for complete and consistent reporting of diary data.

Clinical investigators are also encouraged to explore other means of monitoring compliance. For example, Smith and Safer (1993) reviewed sleep/ wake cycles and how often entries were made into the eDiaries throughout the course of a day. If the number of entries, say 2–3, matched the behavior of interest (for example., number of meals consumed in a day), then patient compliance was inferred. Further, Rosenfalck and Bendston (1993) evaluated compliance by whether a study patient made a 'minimum' number of electronic entries over the course of the protocol.

Monitoring and documentation of compliance is most directly accomplished when the protocol specifies the number and timing of entries, which will typically be the case when entries are tied to time (for example, once daily at bedtime, or hourly). When the protocol focuses on monitoring clinical events (for example, asthma attacks, headaches), however, compliance is difficult to verify independently because there is usually no independent record of those events against which diary entries can be compared. In some cases, biochemical markers may be used to document the occurrence of certain events as acute myocardial infarction (c.f., Adams and Miracle, 1998) or drug use (Shiffman and Paty, 2006), but many events targeted by diary assessments leave no such traces. In these instances, patient entries can be compared against expectations (for example, people usually eat at least twice daily) or against patient-specific norms (for example, the patient's own report of typical headache frequency), but these comparisons are fraught with error. Objective assessment of compliance with event entries is limited.

In summary, the most common and successful way to ensure and document timely PRO compliance with time-based entries is by using eDiaries or other ePRO methods that can tag each record with time of entry, and thus allow for detailed analysis of compliance as described. eDiary studies that do document compliance rates report them to be around 90 per cent (Hufford and Shields 2002). Nevertheless, good compliance with eDiaries is not universal, as some studies report much lower compliance levels (for example, Jamison et al., 2001; Totterdell and Folkard, 1993). Therefore, we remind our readers that use of 'e' technology does not, by itself, result in strong patient compliance rates. It is the thoughtful application of electronic methods in combination with the compliance enhancing techniques discussed in Section 2 that have allowed eDiary systems to achieve high compliance.

Conclusion

Past reports of eDiary and ePRO methods suggest patients can successfully self-monitor with electronic devices anywhere from a day to a year or more (Hufford and Shields, 2002). Furthermore, even in protocols where patients can temporarily disengage electronic monitoring capabilities (for example, suspending prompting), patients make only sparing use of that facility, suspending monitoring only 10 per cent of the time or less (Porter et al., 2000; Schwartz et al. 1999; Stone et al., 1998). Even when given a choice to self-monitor or not, patients tend to want to make themselves available for assessment. Nevertheless, whether they actually complete assessments in a timely fashion is a more difficult question to answer and non-compliance with real world data collection methods, especially those using paper systems, have been well documented (for example, Stone et al., 2002). The results of these studies are clear: patient-reported compliance rates are often dramatically lower than the objectively monitored or actual compliance (Hufford, 2007). Fortunately, eDiary systems can easily integrate automated compliance monitoring systems that time and date stamp data entries. Because of this, researchers can reliably track patient compliance with assessment and, importantly, use this data to document compliance in ways that are consistent with scientific principles (Stone and Shiffman, 2002) and regulatory guidelines (FDA, 2009).

The mere use of 'e' technology is, though, no guarantee that high compliance will be achieved. We believe that an electronically instrumented diary system is a necessary, yet insufficient, condition for achieving satisfactory patient compliance. However, when applied in the context of other compliance enhancing components of a protocol, the eDiary system can have a positive and synergistic influence on patient compliance. Indeed, clinical researchers employing eDiary systems across a wide variety of therapeutic areas and patient populations have documented excellent assessment compliance rates that are generally 90 per cent or better (Hufford and Shields, 2002). This lends confidence to the validity of the data thus collected.

References

Adams, J.E. III and Miracle, V.A. (1998). Cardiac biomarkers: past, present, and future. *American Journal of Critical Care*, 7: 418–23.

Bradburn, N., Rips, L. and Shevell, S. (1987). Answering autobiographical questions: the impact of memory and inference on surveys. *Science*, 236: 157–61.

Broderick, J.E., Arnold, D. and Kudielka, B.M. et al. (2004). Salivary cortisol sampling compliance: comparison of patients and healthy volunteers. *Psych oneuroendocrinology*, 29: 636–650.

Broderick, J.E., Schwartz, J.E. and Shiffman, S. et al. (2003). Signaling does not adequately improve diary compliance. *Annals of Behavioral Medicine*, 26: 193–48.

Food and Drug Administration. Guidance for Industry: Patient-Reported Outcome Measures: Use in Medical Product Development to Support Labeling Claims (Final), December 2009. Available at: http://www.fda.gov/downloads/Drugs/GuidanceComplianceRegulatoryInformation/Guidances/UCM193282.pdf [Accessed December 8, 2009].

Green, A.S., Rafaeli, E. and Bolger, N. et al. (2006). Paper or plastic? Data equivalence in paper and electronic diaries. *Psychological Methods*, 11: 87–105.

Hufford M.R. (2007). Special methodological challenges and opportunities in Ecological Momentary Assessment. In A.A. Stone, S. Shiffman, A.A. Atienza and L. Nebeling (eds) *Science of Real-Time Data Capture: Self-Reports in Health Research*, pp. 54–75. New York: Oxford University Press.

Hufford, M.R. and Shields, A.L. (2002). Electronic diaries: an examination of applications and what works in the field. *Applied Clinical Trials*, 11: 46–56.

Hufford, M.R. and Shiffman, S. (2003). Patient-reported outcomes: assessment methods. *Disease Management and Health Outcomes*, 11: 77–86.

Jamison, R.N., Raymond, S.A. and Levine, J.G. et al. (2001). Electronic diaries for monitoring chronic pain: 1-year validation study. *Pain*, 91: 277–285.

Kamarck, T.W., Shiffman, S. and Smithline, L. et al. (1998). Effects of task strain, social conflict, and emotional activation on ambulatory cardiovascular activity: Daily life consequences of recurring stress in a multiethnic adult sample. *Health Psychology*, 17: 17–29.

Norman, G.R., McFarlane, A.H. and Streiner, D.L. (1982). Health diaries: strategies for compliance and relation to other measures. *Medical Care*, 20: 623–629.

Porter, L.S., Marco, C.A. and Schwartz, J.E. et al. (2000). Gender differences in coping: A comparison of trait and momentary assessments. *Journal of Social and Clinical Psychology*, 19: 480–498.

Rabin, J.M., McNett, J. and Badlani, G.H. (1996). 'Compu-voiding II': The computerized voiding diary. *Journal of Medical Systems*, 20: 19–34.

Raskin, J. (2000). The *Humane Interface: New Directions For Designing Interactive Systems.reading*, MA: Addison Wesley Longman, Inc.

Rosenfalck, A.M. and Bendston, I. (1993). The Diva® system, a computerized diary, used in young type 1 diabetic patients. *Diabete & Metabolisme*, 19: 25–29.

Schwarz, J.E., Neale, J. and Marco, C. et al. (1999). Does trait coping exist? A momentary assessment approach to the evaluation of traits. *Journal of Personality and Social Psychology*, 77: 360–369.

Sherliker, L. and Steptoe, A. (2000). Coping with new treatments for cancer: a feasibility study of daily diary measures. *Patient Education and Counseling*, 40: 11–19.

Shiffman, S. (2000). Real-time self-report of momentary states in the natural environment: computerized ecological momentary assessment. In A.A. Stone, J.S. Turkkan, C.A. Bachrach, J.E. Jobe, H.S. Kurtzman and V.S. Cain (eds), *The Science of Self-report: Implications for Research and Practice*, pp. 277–296. Mahwah, NJ: Lawrence Erlbaum Associates, Publishers.

Shiffman, S. and Paty, J. (2006) Smoking patterns and dependence: contrasting chippers and heavy smokers. *Journal of Abnormal Psychology*, 115: 509–523.

Smith, W.B. and Safer, M.A. (1993). Effects of present pain level on recall of chronic pain and medication use. *Pain*, 85: 355–361.

Stone, A.A., Broderick, J.E. and Schwartz, J.E. et al. (2003). Intensive momentary reporting of pain with an electronic diary: Reactivity, compliance, and patient satisfaction. *Pain*, 104: 343–351.

Stone, A.A., Schwartz, J.E. and Neale, J.M. et al. (1998). A comparison of coping assessed by ecological momentary assessment and retrospective recall. *Journal of Personality and Social Psychology*, 74: 1670–1680.

Stone A.A., and Shiffman S. (2002). Capturing momentary, self-report data: a proposal for reporting guidelines. *Annals of Behavioral Medicine*, 24: 236–43.

Stone, A.A., Shiffman S. and Schwartz, J.E. et al. (2002). Patient non-compliance with paper diaries. *British Medical Journal*, 324: 1193–94.

Tennen, H., Affleck, G. and Coyne, J.C. et al. (2006). Paper and plastic in daily diary research: comment on Green, Rafaeli, Bolger, Shrout, and Reis. *Psychological Methods*, 11: 112–18.

Tiplady, B. (2007). ePROs: Practical issues in pen and touchscreen systems. *Applied Clinical Trials*, March 2nd.

Totterdell, P. and Folkard, S. (1992). In situ repeated measures of affect and cognitive performance facilitated by use of a hand-held computer. *Behavior Research Methods, Instruments and Computers*, 24: 545–553.

Urquhart, J. (1994). Role of subject compliance in clinical pharmacokinetics: a review of recent research. *Clinical Pharmacokinetics*, 27: 202–215.

Verbrugge, L.M. (1980). Health diaries. *Medical Care*, 18: 73–95.

Wilke, R.J., Burke, L.B. and Erickson, P. (2004). Measuring treatment impact: a review of patient reported outcomes and other efficacy endpoints in approved product labels. *Controlled Clinical Trials*, 25: 535–552.

7

Computerised Clinical Assessments: Derived Complex Clinical Endpoints from Patient Self-report Data

Bill Byrom, Keith Wenzel and James Pierce

Introduction

As we have read in previous chapters, electronic solutions present important advantages compared to paper and pencil in the collection of PRO data including less administrative burden, high subject acceptance and more accurate and complete data. They can eliminate conflicting or ambiguous data and, importantly, measure and monitor the required diary reporting schedule so that those performing clinical trials can provide a measure of the contemporaneousness of their PRO data. However, in addition to enhancing the quality and integrity of data collected, technology solutions have additional features that enable us to record far more than we ever could using pencil and paper. The digital pen, for example, does not simply provide the end result of a patient recording but also information on how the end result was achieved in terms of the pen strokes, pressure and the speed of the writing or drawing process. These measures can be of value in certain situations, for example, cognitive function tests requiring measures of speed and accuracy such as maze tests where subjects must plot a course through a circuit or maze with the optimal speed without touching an obstacle or meeting a dead end (Tiplady et al., 2004). Continuing this example, cognitive function testing usually involves measurement of response times in addition to accuracy. Most modern ePRO solutions have sufficient precision to measure response time, such as the delay in pressing a button after receiving a stimulus, in order to be able to demonstrate clinically relevant treatment-related changes. In addition to the digital pen, cognitive testing has been successfully administered using mobile phone (Tiplady et al., 2009), Interactive Voice Response (Byrom (2006), Girdler et al. (2002)) and PDA (Tiplady (1994); Cameron et al. (2001); Lamond et al. (2005)), all of which facilitate home testing and suggest that cognitive tests can be applied cost-effectively on a much larger scale than conventional clinic-based PC testing in specialist studies.

ePRO solutions have the unique ability to make novel measurements and also to assimilate complex data. In this chapter, we review the development and validation of computerised clinical assessments for use in clinical trials. In particular we focus on use of computerised methods to make subjective assessments normally confined to an expert rater or an investigator. Many of the instruments we discuss in this chapter are not, therefore, simply patient diaries or questionnaires converted from a paper version to computerised delivery, but are validated computerised clinical assessments replacing rating normally conducted by a clinician with a computer-delivered interview and associated scoring algorithm.

Much of the key work performed to date in this area relates to the assessments made in the Central Nervous System (CNS) area, and in particular the measurement of severity and diagnosis of depression and anxiety. This chapter reviews key validation studies demonstrating the equivalence of computerised assessments to clinician-made subjective assessments, with particular focus on the Hamilton Depression and Anxiety rating interviews. We also review the results of studies using these techniques, illustrating their particular utility in limiting the potential for inclusion bias in CNS clinical trials and providing particularly sensitive measures of change. We also comment on the regulatory acceptance of this methodology and the current direction of future research in this area. The observations and conclusions made by looking at these specific examples have application to other therapy areas where disease severity and improvement are conventionally assessed by an expert rater.

Parts of this chapter contain material previously published in the review article by Byrom and Mundt (2005), and the interested reader is directed to that article in Current Opinion in Drug Discovery and Development for additional information.

The Case for Computerised CNS Clinical Assessments

It is widely known that failure rates in CNS trials are somewhat higher than what is observed in other therapeutic areas and this is likely due to the reliance on subjective or observer rated assessments. In contrast to trials with objective physiologic measures, many endpoints in CNS are observer rated and involve subjective interpretation of a subject's health status. Some evidence has suggested the quality of and/or lack of standardised methods for these ratings is associated with the overall precision of the clinical trial. An analysis of new drug applications approved by the FDA between 1985 and 1997, performed by Khan and colleagues (2002a), reports that less than half of adequate-dose new antidepressant treatment arms showed statistically significant separation from placebo, with over 30 per cent showing no significant difference. Their similar review of new anxiolytic drug approvals reported that only 48 per cent of adequate dose new drug treatment arms were shown to be statistically superior to placebo (Khan et al., 2002b). These results are in addition to development programs that may have been unnecessarily halted due to poor results prior to regulatory submission. Large placebo response rates in depression and anxiety studies are suspected to be another key reason for failing to detect significant separation of active treatment arms from placebo (Byrom and Mundt, 2005). It is becoming increasingly clear that methods that eliminate observer rated error can ultimately improve signal detection in CNS trials.

Subjective investigator ratings generally form the basis of primary efficacy measurement in clinical drug trials in depression, anxiety, schizophrenia and many other CNS disorders. These ratings are made following semi-structured interviews with the patient, after which clinicians rate the severity of symptoms exhibited on an ordinal scale against a number of individual scale items. Item scores, subscale totals and total scores form the basis of clinical measurements. Standard instruments for depression include the Hamilton Depression Rating Scale (HAM-D) (Hamilton, 1960) and the Montgomery-Åsberg Depression Rating Scale (MADRS) (Montgomery and Åsberg, 1979); and for anxiety the Hamilton Anxiety Rating scale (HAM-A) (Hamilton, 1959). Numerous additional scales for these and other CNS disorders exist, some of which are listed later in Table 7.2. In clinical trials, these instruments are valuable both in assessing the baseline disease severity to determine study eligibility and in measuring treatment-related changes to the severity of symptoms.

The subjective nature of investigator ratings may be one of the factors influencing the proportion of studies that are unable to demonstrate significant treatment effects over placebo for a number of reasons including:

- inflated variance of the study endpoint due to subjective differences between investigators (inter-rater variability);

- time constraints preventing the investigator from delivering rating interviews effectively;

- pressure to recruit on time leading to subjective bias in baseline assessments (see later section).

There is significant published work that illustrates how computerised interviewing as an alternative or adjunct to investigator ratings is able to limit or overcome these potential issues by standardizing methods for collecting data from patients without subjective interpretation from an observer. Variability in ratings or inter-rater differences cannot be ignored. The absence of inter-rater agreement essentially decreases both the precision in determining a dose-response relationship and chances of accurately detecting a difference between active drug and placebo when one actually exists. To illustrate this point, Muller and Szegedi (2002) reported results suggesting that poor reliability of rating scales is correlated with reduced statistical power and increased type II error – concluding that a treatment had no effect when in reality it was superior to its comparator. Computerised interviews, in contrast, provide a standardized assessment and eliminate the potential issue of between-rater differences. In clinical trials using investigator ratings as primary endpoints, the issue of inter-rater reliability is well known to the regulators. Regulatory guidance (EMEA, 2002) requires study sponsors to measure and control the effects of inter-rater variability by conducting pre-study training to standardize ratings. However, it has been reported that such training can in fact have minimal effect on providing standardised and consistent ratings across study sites. Demitrack et al. (1997) studied the variance between expert raters during a training event reviewing recorded interviews for Hamilton Depression Scale Rating. They found the difference between minimum and maximum total scores of 86 raters obtained across four recorded Hamilton interviews varied from 14 to 21 points. This size of difference represents a huge variance relative to the range of scores likely in a depressed population – where most patients would be scored between 10 and 35.

Time constraints experienced by busy investigators may also play a role in how effective investigator ratings can be. The recommendation for a HAM-D rating interview is to spend 25–30 minutes with the patient. Add to this the time required for other assessments and it is not surprising that this may not be practical for some raters. One investigation revealed, for example, that 35 per cent of interviews in one study were conducted in under 10 minutes (Feiger et al., 2003). These limitations can be addressed by validated computer interviews which deliver completely standardised assessments on each application, and can be delivered without the requirement for the investigator to be present throughout.

Finally, the evidence surrounding the merits of the computerised interview in eliminating inflation of baseline scores to meet inclusion criteria is dramatic. We discuss this in more detail later in this chapter. First we consider the validation work evidencing that computerised interviews and scoring algorithms can provide equivalent measures to subjective investigator ratings.

Practical Steps to Developing Computerised Clinical Assessments

When developing ePRO instruments that can be used as a replacement for clinician interview-based ratings, a computerised clinical assessment must be both clinically appropriate and easy to use by the patient. Key elements for any such system include: emulating the questioning and follow up probes of an expert rater; applying appropriate rules to assign item scores; and pausing, repeating and/or elaborating on the information being elicited from the study subject or patient.

The development of a new computerised clinical assessment can be broken down into four discreet components which sometimes can be completed one at a time, but are more often inter-related and iterative. For purposes of discussion, these are described as independent steps and include:

1.   interview design considerations;

2.   scoring algorithm design and testing;

3.   pilot testing;

4.   formal validation testing.

INTERVIEW DESIGN CONSIDERATIONS

When designing a computerised interview, the objective is to develop a questioning strategy that is able to obtain sufficient information adequately to elicit the desired symptoms or severity data such that an item can be appropriately rated or, in some cases, scored. Care should be taken to create a set of questions that elicits responses without burdening the patient with excessive questioning or by requiring answers to inappropriate or redundant questions. This can be achieved by branching logic, whereby the next question delivered is dependent on the patient's previous responses.

For example, item 12 of the 17-item HAM-D instrument assesses gastrointestinal somatic symptoms and specifically appetite. A rating of zero reflects no loss of appetite, whereas ratings of 1 or 2 represent 'loss of appetite but eating without encouragement', and 'difficulty eating without urging' respectively. Structured interview guides for the HAM-D, see Williams (1989) for example, propose initial questioning around this item should ascertain whether patients are experiencing a change in their normal appetite. An initial question, for example, may be: 'Have you been eating more or less than usual over the past week?' The response to that question will determine whether the computerised interview should ask additional questions to determine the severity of the item to aid the scoring. If, for example, the patient indicates a lessening of normal appetite then additional questions might assess whether others have needed to urge the patient to eat and how often over the week the patient has eaten less or skipped meals. From these responses the rating of 1 or 2 will be determined.

Where duplicate information is required to validate a previous response, it is sometimes appropriate to phrase the question slightly differently and/or to provide context in the instructions so that the patient understands that he/she may encounter seemingly duplicate questions.

Much as with a human-to-human interview, the computerised clinical assessment should be designed to provide the context for the respondent as well as to accommodate the possible needs to pause the interview, to repeat the question and/or to provide context-specific help. Ease of use by the respondent is critical. The computerised clinical assessment should begin with instructions for the patient explaining what information is needed, the time period to be used for responses (e.g. during the last seven days) and what to do if the question needs repeating or additional information is needed. The assessment must be designed to accommodate the need for the interview to be interrupted while appropriately balancing the fact that a patient's health status may change during a paused assessment. The designer will need to evaluate the potential for a change in the health status and factor that into whether the assessment can be continued from the point of interruption or whether the assessment must be restarted from the beginning.

A computerised clinical assessment should include the ability to repeat questions and, ideally, to provide context-specific help. For example, when assessing respiratory symptoms, context-specific help might provide examples of different forms of breathing difficulty. Such an assessment should also orient respondents as to the expected length of the interview and inform them of their progress, e.g. 'You are half way through today's assessment.' For computerised clinical assessments that collect longitudinal data, such as weekly, one of the closing salutation statements should include a reminder of the date/day of the next scheduled assessment.

With respect to question responses, Likert type scales must have appropriate, understandable anchor points for each unique response option. Visual Analogue and Verbal Numeric Scales, such as 0–10 pain ratings, must have detailed instructions so the respondent is oriented with respect to the two extremes and understands how to indicate the appropriate response across the continuum.

Because of the requirement to mimic an expert assessment, these questionnaires cannot be constructed without the involvement of expert raters. Developers must understand the mind set and logic applied by expert raters in their delivery of patient interviews and appropriately emulate this via the computerised approach.

SCORING ALGORITHM DESIGN AND TESTING

Investigator-assessed instruments normally expect the investigator to rate the patient against a number of items using an ordinal scale, for example 0 to 3. Item scores are important in their own right, but normally scale or sub-scale totals are also computed and have meanings pertinent to the disease or condition assessed. Instrument definitions of severity categories for each item are the starting point for developing an algorithm to automate the rating alongside a computerised interview.

Again, the interpretation and know-how of expert raters is a vital component and developers require their insights and internal logic to derive the automated scoring algorithm. Once in place, algorithms and interviews can be pilot tested to give an early indication of their acceptability and any areas that require revision in the algorithm logic. A number of iterations may be required to arrive at a final algorithm as described below. A formal validation study is probably required to confirm the reliability and validity of the scoring algorithm(s) through comparisons of not only the total and subscales scores, but also the items scores for the clinician and computerised clinical assessments.

USER TESTING

While there are neither agreed industry standards nor any specific regulatory guidance with respect to the types and extent of user testing required, there are generally agreed categories of user testing. They are:

1. Functionality testing;

2. Usability testing;

3. Pilot testing;

4. Cognitive debriefing.

Functionality testing

Once the computerised clinical assessment is programmed, testing needs to be conducted to ensure that all of the major components of the original computer assessment design are administered accurately. The assessment must appropriately welcome and orient the respondent, it must accurately administer each item through the question and associated response options and then it must branch appropriately to the succeeding question(s). Behind the scenes, the computerised assessment must: date and time stamp the assessment; store each response and increment/weight appropriate subscale and total scores; store any changes to previous responses as well as time latencies between the end of a question and the entry of the response. Functionality testing is also known as system validation; the goal is to test and document that the computerised clinical assessment is performing as originally conceptualised.

Usability testing

With the move from human administration to a computerised clinical assessment, it is important to ensure that the users understand how to use the computerised assessment appropriately. For example, usability testing would document how easily a user interfaces with the computer-based method and identify enhancements to improve ease of use prior to launch of the system. There are five components that should be assessed in usability testing of a computerised instrument:

- *Learnability*. How easy is it for users to complete the instrument on their first encounter?

- *Efficiency*. How much time does it take to complete the computerised assessment?

- *Memorability*. How easy is it for respondents to complete a computerised instrument after a period of time not using the system?

- *Errors*. How many errors are made completing the computerised instrument? How severe are these errors and can they be overcome?

- *Satisfaction*. How pleasant is it for subjects to complete the computerised assessment?

Coons et al. (2009) describe methods for user testing as it relates to computerised versions of commonly used health related questionnaires. Briefly, they reported user testing allows one to determine a respondents' ability to navigate/use the electronic platform and questionnaire, as well as comprehend, retain, and accurately follow instructions. The overall goal of this evaluation is to demonstrate that respondents can complete the computerised assessment as originally intended. As an example, usability testing should include the extent to which patients can easily use the response scales as directed (e.g. touching the screen to select a response) and can move from one screen to the next. Just as the level of evidence to support data equivalence of a computerised version of a questionnaire should reflect the amount of change in the text and content from the paper to the electronic versions, the amount of usability testing required should also reflect the amount of change in difficulty or cognitive processes from the standard mode of administration.

As a final note, it is important to distinguish between usability testing and user acceptance testing (UAT). UAT is designed to determine compliance with required system specifications or user requirement documents. Accordingly, UAT has no relationship to ease of use, but rather that the system or software validation process has been performed. UAT will not be discussed in this chapter.

Pilot testing

Pilot testing is normally carried out on a very small number of patients in which both a clinician interview and rating is performed in addition to the computerised approach. The objective is to get an early indication of areas that require revision. Ideally, clinical interviews and ratings should be performed by expert raters not involved in the algorithm development, although this is not essential in early pilot testing. The results of early tests will identify areas where the algorithm and computer interview require development. Once the developers are comfortable with the overall performance of the computerised assessment, it should be subjected to formal validation activities. There are no clear lines of demarcation with respect to where Usability Testing ends and Pilot Testing starts; both types could be combined.

Cognitive debriefing

Cognitive debriefing is described in detail by Paul Beatty in Chapter 2. In essence, it is valuable in assessing that the understanding of questions is consistent with their intended meaning and can be conducted in a small sample of the target population. In validating computerised assessment versions of clinical ratings, cognitive debriefing can give an early indication of areas that may require revision prior to final formal validation.

FORMAL VALIDATION

We describe some of the validation work performed on computerised clinical assessments in the following section of this chapter. However, the general steps in validating a computerised assessment against an investigator subjective assessment are in common with the steps in validation described in Chapter 9 of this book. In general, a small cross-over study in a modest sample of patients (perhaps 40 to 60) should be performed. Patients should represent the cross-section of severities for which the assessment is intended in practice. Each patient should be assessed by clinician and computer in a random order. Patients, or a sub-sample, should also be re-tested within an appropriate time interval to assess test-retest reliability. The ideal time interval should be long enough that the responses to individual questions are not immediately recalled, but short enough to ensure the condition has not changed significantly between test applications. The objectives of the study will be to:

- demonstrate equivalence of item and total scores;

- demonstrate equivalent internal consistency and construct validity of the instrument;

- demonstrate appropriate test-retest reliability;

- assess acceptability of the approach for use by the target population.

It should be noted that in many validation exercises, we aim to show equivalence against an original or accepted approach. Where this is not achieved, it is not always a failing in the new approach and may illustrate a limitation in the original version.

There is evidence, for example, that in comparison to face-to-face interviews, patients may exhibit increased honesty when responding to sensitive, emotional or embarrassing questions using computer assessments. Millard and Carver (1999), for example, found that patients were less reserved in reporting emotional concerns and mood to a computer compared to a human interviewer in their study comparing the equivalence of SF-12 quality of life data collected via a live telephone interview and using an automated interview delivered via a telephone-based Interactive Voice Response (IVR) system. Kobak et al. (1997a) reported that IVR administration had greater sensitivity in detecting alcohol problems, and Turner et al. (1998) reported higher prevalence of sexual behaviours and drug abuse amongst adolescents when audio-assisted computer interviewing was used. With this in mind it is important not to lose sight of the fact that altering the mode of administration may actually improve the ability of an instrument to measure according to its intended purpose. Researchers should always refer to the conceptual framework about which the instrument was initially developed when evaluating the significance of differences between versions.

The Validity of Computerised Assessments Compared to Clinician Ratings

Much work has been done in translating the semi structured interviews and item scoring performed by trained clinicians when assessing patients using the HAM-D, MADRS and HAM-A instruments into fully-structured computerised interviews with non-linear scoring algorithms to produce equivalent measures. Unlike questionnaire delivery where an ePRO solution will run through a defined sequence of questions in turn, these interviews are highly branched enabling the computerised approach to drill into specific areas dependent upon answers to earlier questions. This fine detail enables the underlying scoring algorithm to fine-tune the scores determined for each measurement item. Considerable data has been collected over more than ten years to support the clinical utility of this approach.

A particularly significant example is the summary of computerised HAM-D validation evidence published by Kobak et al. (2000) . They report a summary of 10 studies performed between 1990 and 1999 comparing their computer interview version of the HAM-D to investigator rating. Early versions of this instrument were delivered using a PC with later studies employing a telephone version using an Interactive Voice Response (IVR) system, which automated the interview. This simple interface was attractive as it provides particular convenience enabling assessment from home as well as clinic, but there is no reason why these complex assessments could not be performed using a PDA in the clinical trial setting. Because currently there are few examples of delivering complex CNS clinical assessments in place of the clinician using any other electronic solution, much of the review that follows refers exclusively to instruments delivered via IVR technology.

In their article, Kobak et al. (2000) reported a high correlation between clinician and computer HAM-D scores (n=1791, r = 0.81, p<0.001). Considering all 17 scale items (Table 7.1), internal consistency measures of scale reliability (Cronbach, 1951) supported the use of the computer-administered HAM-D. Cronbach's alpha, for example, ranged from 0.60 to 0.91 across the 10 studies for the computerised HAM-D, compared to a range of -0.41 to 0.91 for clinician ratings, with Cronbach's alpha for computer rating exceeding that for clinician rating in 8 of the 10 studies. The researchers also found that the test-retest reliability for scores obtained by computer interview were in the same range as those measured for the clinician assessments. It is important to remember that the patient self-assessment version is not simply a rating against 17 items, but that each item score is calculated from the response to a number of questions. Overall, this represents a high number of questions during each computer interview, and because of the response-specific branching, questions may be different on subsequent administrations. For that reason, it is likely that the computerised assessment approach is less prone to memory artificially inflating correlations between assessments repeated over a short time period, compared to clinician memory of individual item ratings.

Other studies have also examined and demonstrated good equivalence between electronic and clinician rated scores for the Hamilton Anxiety Rating Scale (Kobak et al., 1993; Kobak et al., 1998), Montgomery Åsberg Depression Rating Scale (MADRS) (Mundt et al., 2006), Yale-Brown Obsessive Compulsive Disorder Scale (Y-BOCS) (Kobak et al., 1997b) and the Leibowitz Social Anxiety Scale (LSAS) (Kobak et al., 2002). These latter two instruments, however, are essentially clinician-checklists which makes the equivalence between clinician and self-report less surprising. Assessments that have been adapted and used via IVR relevant to CNS studies are listed in Table 7.2.

Table 7.1   Items comprising the Hamilton depression rating scale (HAM-D)

1	Depressed mood	10	Psychic anxiety
2	Guilt	11	Somatic anxiety
3	Suicide	12	Appetite
4	Initial insomnia	13	Somatic symptoms, general
5	Middle insomnia	14	Genital symptoms
6	Terminal insomnia	15	Hypochondriasis
7	Work and interests	16	Weight loss
8	Psychomotor retardation	17	Insight
9	Psychomotor agitation		

Table 7.2   Assessments that have IVR adaptations relevant to CNS clinical trials

Brief Social Phobia Scale (BSPS)

Changes in Sexual Functioning Questionnaire (CSFQ)

Cognitive Function Test battery (Cognitive Drug Research Ltd/ClinPhone)

Daily Telephone Assessment (DTA) – for depression

Davidson Trauma Scale (DTS)

Hamilton Anxiety Rating Scale (HAM-A)

Hamilton Depression rating Scale (HAM-D)

Liebowitz Social Anxiety Scale (LSAS)

Memory Enhanced Retrospective Evaluation of Treatment (MERET)

Mental Heath Screener (MHS)

Montgomery-Åsberg Depression Rating Scale (MADRS)

Quality of Life Enjoyment and Satisfaction Questionnaire (Q-LES-Q)

SF-12, SF-20 and SF-36 quality of life scales

Symptoms of Dementia Screener (SDS)

Work and Social Adjustment scale (WSAS)

Yale-Brown Obsessive Compulsive Disorder Scale (Y-BOCS)

Source: Table reproduced, with permission from The Thomson Corporation and Bill Byrom and James C Mundt: The value of computer-administered self-report data in central nervous system clinical trials. *Current Opinion in Drug Discovery and Development* (2005) 8(3): 365–373. Copyright 2005, The Thomson Corporation.

Validated computer assessments may offer many advantages to researchers. In particular, the use of a standardised interview delivered via computer eliminates inter-rater variability observed in multicenter clinical trials. As discussed later in this chapter, it can also eliminate the sources of rater bias, importantly the inflation of scores at baseline when assessment instruments are also used to define study eligibility. The ability to perform clinical assessments from home rather than at clinic when using remote electronic solutions such as IVR or PDA provides many benefits to study designs. It enables efficacy data to be collected more frequently to investigate, for example, speed of onset and to collect data in study phases where regular clinic assessments are not convenient, such as during long term safety extensions. Clearly these instruments are not intended to replace the regular requirements for a clinician-patient meeting. Computer-administered ratings can, however, reduce the time required for lengthy rating interviews, permitting more time for clinicians to focus on the care and treatment of the patient.

USABILITY

A final aspect of instrument validity that has been reported measures the usability of computerised assessments in clinical trials. In a study of social anxiety disorder patients using IVR versions of the HAM-D and LSAS (Katzelnick et al., 2001), 90 per cent of 874 patients rated computer assessment as 'very easy' or 'easy' (Greist et al., 2002). Similar results have been reported in another, smaller, study of 74 patients using the IVR HAM-D assessment (Ewing et al., 1998), see Figure 7.1. In this study, 76 per cent of patients agreed that the questions were clearly stated and understandable, 93 per cent agreed that the assessment was easy to complete, 79 per cent found the IVR assessments convenient and almost half (48 per cent) indicated that the computer assessment allowed them to express their true feelings (30 per cent had no opinion).

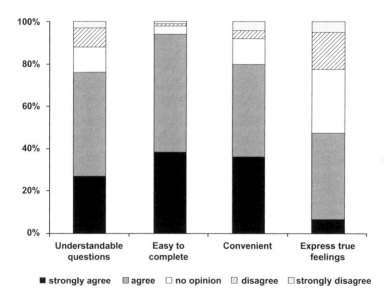

Figure 7.1   Patient acceptability ratings using IVR HAM-D in 74 depressed patients (Ewing et al., 1998)

Source: Reproduced, with permission from The Thomson Corporation and Bill Byrom and James C Mundt: The value of computer-administered self-report data in central nervous system clinical trials. *Current Opinion in Drug Discovery and Development* (2005) 8(3): 365–373. Copyright 2005, The Thomson Corporation.

Using Computerised Assessments to Prevent Rater-bias

One potential issue with the use of clinician-assessed subjective rating scales is the potential to introduce bias into the measurements. Most studies, for example, employ subjective ratings to assess a patient's eligibility to participate. Depression studies using the HAM-D endpoint commonly require a baseline HAM-D ≥ 20 as an inclusion criterion. Pressure to enrol subjects, and the fact that compensation is normally contingent upon randomisation, may lead to conscious or subconscious bias being introduced into baseline ratings in order to satisfy inclusion criteria. Inflation of scores at baseline creates treatment-independent improvements post-baseline, which contribute to the placebo effect and exacerbate the problem of showing treatment-related differences. In addition, subconscious bias can be introduced by knowing the duration of treatment a patient has received. A subject having maintained treatment for over four weeks may be considered more likely to show improvements from baseline than one just commencing therapy. This could influence the way in which a patient is subsequently scored.

To protect against potential bias due to knowledge of the treatment duration and previous visit assessments, Renfordt and Busch (1976) have proposed using video recordings of rating interviews that were subsequently rated in a random order at the end of the study. This approach has been evaluated comparatively by Corruble et al. (1999) who compared the assessments of recorded MADRS depression rating interviews when rated in chronological order and in random (time-independent) order. In their study of sixty patients, they concluded that the psychiatrists' assessment of depression severity was influenced by knowledge of the previous duration of treatment. Whilst using videotaped interview recordings and performing the assessments in random order at the end of a study protects against this, it does not help when assessments need to be made immediately – such as those required to determine eligibility. These baseline assessments may also be influenced by rater bias, as illustrated in the interesting study (Figure 7.2) reported by DeBrota et al. (1999).

In this study, the researchers compared clinician HAM-D ratings to computer scores collected using IVR at each of eight weekly treatment visits in a study of 291 depressed subjects. In addition, however, they also blinded the investigators to the true start of double-blind treatment by including a variable duration phase of placebo treatment after randomisation. Figure 7.2 displays the HAM-D scores measured by clinician and computer (IVR) at four study time points. At baseline (visits 1 and 2), the distribution of clinician scores

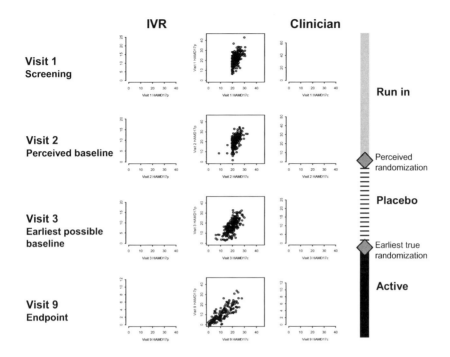

Figure 7.2   Concordance of IVR and Clinician HAM-D ratings pre- and
               post-baseline for a study requiring baseline HAM-D scores ≥
               20 (DeBrota et al., 1999)

Source: Reproduced, with permission from The Thomson Corporation and Bill Byrom
and James C Mundt: The value of computer-administered self-report data in central
nervous system clinical trials. *Current Opinion in Drug Discovery and Development* (2005)
8(3): 365–373. Copyright 2005, The Thomson Corporation.

observed was not normal and in fact truncated at the inclusion threshold score
of 20. Only four of the 291 patient assessments (1.4 per cent) made by clinicians
at visit 1 were below 20. In contrast, the distribution of IVR assessment scores
at this time point was normal with 38 per cent of patients rated below 20.
Following randomisation, the concordance between clinician and computer
ratings returned, despite the fact that all patients were initially treated with
placebo, unbeknownst to the investigators. At visit 3, a high proportion of
clinician scores had dropped below 20 – mirroring the computer assessments,
despite no patient receiving active drug. During the final four visits after
treatment assignment the correlation between methods was 0.84 (p<0.01)
and the mean clinician scores (0.31 points higher than IVR scores) were not
significantly different from the IVR-derived scores. The large differences in the
distributions of ratings at baseline and the convergence of assessment methods

following randomisation is suggestive of inflated clinician ratings of disease severity at baseline – potentially a major contributor to the large placebo effect often observed in these kinds of trials.

The review article by Byrom and Mundt (2005) presents a number of other compelling examples of baseline score inflation in studies using subjective clinician-assessed rating scales. The phenomenon observed is likely to be consistent with other subjective investigator ratings used as study endpoints and inclusion criteria, and illustrates a major benefit of the use of ePRO to deliver clinical assessment ratings as an alternative or adjunct to clinician ratings, at least in verification of study eligibility and baseline score. Petkova et al. (2000), for example, propose the simultaneous use of both patient self-ratings and clinician ratings in non-psychotic and non-demented populations so that the similarity between clinician ratings and patient self-ratings can provide a measure of bias in clinician ratings.

Computerised Assessments May Improve Study Power to Detect Treatment-related Differences

In addition to elimination of inclusion bias, computer-administered ratings have been reported to be associated with measurement of both smaller changes from baseline and larger treatment effects relative to placebo compared to those observed using clinician ratings. The smaller changes from baseline can be argued because of the elimination of baseline score inflation/deflation observed amongst clinician ratings, but the increased sensitivity to show treatment separation is a significant finding that may benefit future study design. This is perhaps consistent with one of the promises of ePRO in reducing the noise in data, and thus leading to the possibility of exposing smaller samples of patients (see Chapter 3).

A good example is the study of 307 patients with major depressive disorder reported by Rayamajhi et al. (2002). In this study, patients were treated for eight weeks with duloxetine, fluoxetine or placebo (see Figure 7.3). As shown in Figure 7.3(a), (adjusted least-squares) mean changes from baseline HAM-D scores were higher for each treatment group for the clinician rated assessments compared to the computerised assessments performed using IVR. As discussed in the previous section, the lower changes from baseline within each treatment group may be associated with clinician score inflation at baseline. Despite the smaller changes from baseline, pairwise comparisons of the difference in mean change between each active treatment and placebo indicated increased relative treatment effects and greater power to demonstrate treatment separation using the computerised assessment data. The analysis of both clinician and IVR rated data showed significant improvements in depression severity attributable to duloxetine compared to placebo (baseline adjusted least-square mean changes from baseline compared to placebo: -2.12 (p=0.008) and -2.25 (p=0.006) for clinician ratings and IVR ratings respectively). However, for fluoxetine treated patients, clinician ratings showed little evidence of improvement relative to placebo, whereas the IVR ratings indicated a much larger improvement that approached statistical significance (baseline adjusted least-square mean changes from baseline compared to placebo: -0.6 (p=0.536) and -1.8 (p=0.076) for clinician ratings and IVR ratings respectively). The fluoxetine arm was in fact underpowered in this study, having half as many subjects as duloxetine, making this finding all the more impressive.

See Byrom and Mundt (2005) for more detail and examples. Again, similar observations are likely with other subjective observer-rated assessments applied in other therapy areas.

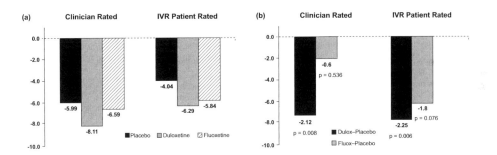

Figure 7.3   (a) Baseline adjusted least-squares mean changes from baseline HAM-D following 8 weeks treatment with placebo, duloxetine or fluoxetine, and (b) corresponding treatment related changes from placebo, in a study of 307 patients with major depressive disorder (Rayamajhi et al., 2002)

Source: Reproduced, with permission from The Thomson Corporation and Bill Byrom and James C Mundt: The value of computer-administered self-report data in central nervous system clinical trials. *Current Opinion in Drug Discovery and Development* (2005) 8(3): 365–373. Copyright 2005, The Thomson Corporation.

Conclusions

The literature and scientific meetings over the last decade have demonstrated the potential of using computerised clinical assessments in clinical trials. More significantly, they present evidence showing equivalence between computer-delivered patient interviews and ratings and the corresponding clinician-delivered versions. Examples cited in this chapter relate mainly to instruments used in depression and anxiety, and such evidence has been pivotal in FDA experts indicating that use of the IVR HAM-D would be acceptable as a primary endpoint in depression outpatient trials.

Studies reviewed in this chapter have illustrated the advantages and utility of computerised clinical assessments, in particular in elimination of inclusion bias observed when subjective clinician ratings form the basis of patient eligibility. In addition, the reduction of inter-rater variability and reduced placebo effect due to elimination of baseline score inflation gives computerised clinical assessments increased sensitivity to detect treatment-related differences from placebo.

Although much of the work to date relates to the assessment of CNS disorders such as depression and anxiety, many of the observations and findings we report would apply to any therapy area which depends upon investigators to provide subjective measures of disease severity or improvement. Some treatment effects are in fact known only to the patient and that patient perspective can be lost when it is filtered through a clinician's evaluation of the patient's response to clinical interview questions. Computerised assessments provide a step towards standardising the collection and interpretation of patient perspective data.

These techniques promise to have application beyond the clinical trial setting. Physicians treating patients in routine care may benefit from the ability to make strandardised assessments of patients to aid their assessment of optimal treatment. The use of ePRO more generally to inform patient treatment in the routine care setting is discussed in more detail in Chapter 10.

References

Byrom, B. (2006). Innovative ePRO: tapping into the potential. *Applied Clinical Trials*, June: 64–72.

Byrom, B. and Mundt, J.C. (2005). The value of computer-administered self-report data in central nervous system clinical trials. *Current Opinion in Drug Discovery and Development*, 8(3): 365–373.

Cameron, E., Sinclair, W. and Tiplady, B. (2001). Validity and sensitivity of a pen computer battery of performance tests. *Journal of Psychopharmacology*, 15: 105–110.

Coons, S.J., Gwaltney, C.J. and Hays, R.D. et al. (2009). Recommendations on evidence needed to support measurement equivalence between electronic and paper-based patient reported outcome (PRO) measures: ISPOR ePRO good research practices task force report. *Value in Health*, 12: 419–429.

Corruble, E., Duret, C. and Payan, C. et al. (1999). Agreement between time-blind and time-non-blind assessments of depressive symptomatology. *Psychiatry Research*, 86: 251–258.

Cronbach, L.J. (1951). Coefficient alpha and the internal structure of tests. *Psychometrika*, 16: 297–334.

DeBrota, D.J., Demitrack, M.A. and Landin, R. et al. (1991). A comparison between Interactive Voice Response system administered HAM-D and clinician administered HAM-D in patients with major depressive episode. *39th Annual Meeting of the New Clinical Drug Evaluation Unit Program*, Boca Raton, FL, USA.

Demitrack, M.A., Faries, D. and DeBrota, D. et al. (1997). The problem of measurement error in multisite clinical trials. *Psychopharm Bull*, 33: 513.

European Medicines Evaluation Agency. (2002). Note for guidance on clinical investigation of medicinal products in the treatment of depression. www.emea.eu.int/pdfs/human/ewp/056798en.pdf

Ewing, H., Reesal, R. and Kobak, K.A. et al. (1998). Patient satisfaction with computerized assessment in a multicenter clinical trial. *38th Annual Meeting of the New Clinical Drug Evaluation Unit Program*, Boca Raton, FL, USA.

Feiger, A., Engelhardt, N. and DeBrota, D. et al. (2003). Rating the raters: an evaluation of audio taped Hamilton Depression Rating Scale (HAMD) interviews. *43rd Annual Meeting of the New Clinical Drug Evaluation Unit Program*, Boca Raton, FL, USA.

Girdler, N.M., Fairbrother, K.J. and Lyne, J.P. et al. (2002). A randomized crossover trial of post-operative cognitive and psychomotor recovery from benzodiazepine sedation: effects of reversal with flumazenil over a prolonged recovery period. *British Dental Journal*, 192: 335–339.

Greist, J.H., Mundt, J.C. and Kobak, K. (2002). Factors contributing to failed trials of new agents: can technology prevent some problems? *J Clin Psychiatry*, 63: 8–13.

Hamilton, M. (1959). The assessment of anxiety states by rating. *Br J Med Psychol*, 32: 50–55.

Hamilton, M. (1960). A rating scale for depression. *J Neurol Neurosurg Psychiatry*, 23: 56–62.

Katzelnick, D.J., Kobak, K.A. and DeLeire, T. et al. (2001). Impact of generalized social anxiety disorder in managed care. *Am J Psychiatry*, 158: 1999–2007.

Khan, A., Leventhal, R.M. and Khan, S.R. (2002a). Severity of depression and response to antidepressants and placebo: an analysis of the Food and Drug Administration database. *J Clin Psychopharmacol*, 22: 40–55.

Khan, A., Khan, S. and Brown W.A. (2002b). Are placebo controls necessary to test new antidepressants and anxiolytics? *Int J Neuropsychopharmacol*, 5: 193–7.

Kobak, K.A., Greist, J.H. and Jefferson, J.W. et al. (2002). Validation of a computerized version of the Liebowitz Social Anxiety Scale Administered by telephone via Interactive Voice Response (IVR). *42nd Annual Meeting of the New Clinical Drug Evaluation Unit Program*, Boca Raton, FL, USA.

Kobak, K.A., Greist, J.H. and Jefferson, J.W. et al. (1998). Validation of a computerized version of the Hamilton Anxiety scale administer over the telephone using Interactive Voice response. *American Psychiatric Association 151st Annual Meeting*, Toronto, Canada.

Kobak, K.A., Mundt, J.C. and Greist, J.H. et al. (2000). Computer assessment of depression: automating the Hamilton Depression Rating Scale. *Drug Info J*, 34: 145–156.

Kobak, K.A., Reynolds, W.M. and Greist, J.H. (1993). Development and validation of a computer-administered version of the Hamilton Anxiety Scale. *Psychological Assess*, 5: 487–492.

Kobak, K.A., Taylor, L.H. and Dottl, S.L. et al. (1997a). A computer administered telephone interview to identify mental disorders. *JAMA*, 278(10): 905–910.

Kobak, K.A., Greist, J.H. and Jefferson, J.W. (1997b). Computerized assessment in clinical drug trials: a review. *37th Annual Meeting of the New Clinical Drug Evaluation Unit Program*, Boca Raton, FL, USA.

Lamond, N., Dawson, D. and Roach, G.D. (2005). Fatigue assessment in the field: validation of a hand-held electronic psychomotor vigilance task, *Aviation Space and Environmental Medicine*, 76: 486–489.

Millard, R. and Carver, J. (1999). Cross-sectional comparison of live and interactive voice recognition administration of the SF-12 health status survey. *Am J Managed Care*, 5: 153–159.

Montgomery, S.A. and Åsberg, M. (1979). A new depression scale designed to be sensitive to change. *Br J Psychiatry*, 134: 382–389.

Muller, M.J. and Szegedi, A. (2002). Effects of interrater reliability on psychopathologic assessment on power and sample size calculations in clinical trials. *J Clin Psychopharmacol*, 22: 318–325.

Mundt, J.C., Katzelnick, D.J. and Kennedy, S.H. (2006). Validation of an IVRS version of the MADRS. *Journal of Psychiatric Research*, 40: 243–246.

Petkova, E., Quitkin, F.M. and McGrath, P.J. et al. (2000). A method to quantify rater bias in antidepressant trials. *Neuropsychopharmacol*, 22: 559–565.

Rayamajhi, J., Lu, Y. and DeBrota, D. et al. (2002). A comparison between interactive voice response system and clinician administration of the Hamilton depression rating scale. 42nd Annual Meeting of the New Clinical Drug Evaluation Unit Program, Boca Raton, FL, USA.

Renfordt, E. and Busch, H. (1976). Time-blind analysis of TV-stored interviews. An objective method to study antidepressive drug-effects. *Int. Pharmacopsychiat*, 11: 129–134.

Tiplady, B. (1994). The use of personal digital assistants in performance testing in pharmacology. Demonstration, British Pharmacological Society, London, January 1994, *British Journal of Clinical Pharmacology*, 37: 523.

Tiplady, B., Barton, C. and Dudman, A. et al. (2004). Zig-zag tracking: a test of psychomotor speed and accuracy designed for repeated administration. *British Association of Psychopharmacology meeting*, Harrogate, UK.

Tiplady, B., Oshinowo, B. and Thomson, J. et al. (2009). Alcohol and cognitive function: Assessment in everyday life and laboratory settings using mobile phones. *Alcoholism: Clinical and Experimental Research*, 33: 2094–2102.

Turner, C.F., Ku, L. and Rogers, S.M. et al. (1998). Adolescent sexual behavior, drug use and violence: increased reporting with computer survey technology. *Science*, 280: 867–873.

Williams, J.B. (1989). A structured interview guide for the Hamilton Depression Rating Scale. *Arch. Gen. Psychiatry*, 46(5): 481–2.

8

Diary Design Considerations: Interface Issues and Patient Acceptability

Brian Tiplady

Introduction

In 1993, the first Personal Digital Assistants (PDAs), hand-held computers with pen interfaces appeared and a number of research groups began to use them to collect data directly from patients, either to take home to use as symptom diaries, or for collecting questionnaire data in the clinic.

We were by no means the first in the field that became known as ePRO. Others had used clamshell organisers, touch-screen computers and telephone-based systems for some years, and the earliest systems for obtaining data directly from patients using a computer go back much further (see, e.g. Lucas et al., 1976; French and Beaumont, 1987; Siegel et al., 1988; Taylor et al., 1990; Hyland et al., 1993). But the PDA had a compelling combination of portability and ease of use that greatly stimulated the growth of this type of data collection.

One of the earliest questions raised was whether patients could handle the technology. Sure, we researchers all found the devices easy to use, but what about the elderly, particularly if they had poor eyesight? What about those who had never used a computer and who might feel threatened by this type of system? So when we carried out studies evaluating the use of PDAs we included a questionnaire asking patients how they found the technology and whether they preferred electronic or paper. We were pleased to find that patients generally liked the devices, found them easy to use, and preferred the electronic method to paper (Drummond et al., 1995; Tiplady et al., 1997). This conclusion was equally valid for elderly patients and for those who were unfamiliar with computers.

This finding has been repeatedly confirmed. For example Rabin et al. (1996) compared 36 women with overactive bladder symptoms with 36 age-matched women who used computerised and written paper voiding diaries. More than 98 per cent of the patients and 80 per cent of controls preferred the computer version. The sample included women up to 84 years old. Johannes et al. (2000) compared a menstrual diary set up on a handheld PC with a paper diary in 24 women. 70 per cent of women preferred the electronic diary, compared with 9 per cent who preferred paper. Hufford et al. (2002; see also Stone et al., 2003) present data from 80 patients aged 18–70 who completed either a paper or electronic pain diary. Each patient used only one type of diary, so preference data could not be obtained, but a high level of acceptability and ease of use was found for both paper and electronic diaries. Aiello et al. (2006) studied 86 women over 50 who used a tablet-PC based breast cancer screening questionnaire. The great majority of the women preferred the PC to paper, and this was true both for those aged 60 or over (89 per cent) and those under 60 (93 per cent). Meacham et al (2008) reported greater diary compliance amongst elderly patients compared to middle aged or younger, in a meta analysis of 10 studies using Interactive Voice Response (IVR) pain dairies.

But acceptability and ease of use are not inherent properties of electronic diaries and questionnaires – they require careful design and an ability to take the user perspective into account. I will review here some of the issues that need to be addressed to develop a robust user interface that will be suitable for data collection with the wide variety of patients enrolled in clinical trials. I shall present these issues from the point of view of a system designer, but the principles I shall outline are just as important for those who select a system from a vendor or specify the details for a particular study protocol.

The design principles I shall describe apply equally when developing an ePRO system from scratch or when transferring an existing paper instrument to electronic mode. However, when migrating from paper to electronic there is an additional constraint; the electronic instrument should be equivalent to the paper original. New instruments may be developed from the start in electronic format, and doubtless this will increase, but at present the majority of instruments are migrated from paper to electronic mode, so this is an important concern.

User interface issues are important in a number of different ways, which can affect both the conduct of the study and the completeness and quality of the data obtained. I shall deal with the following:

1.   skills required to use the system;

2.   legibility of material presented;

3.   organisation of the instrument;

4.   cognitive load;

5.   taking the patient's perspective.

I shall deal in most detail with screen-based systems, as most of my experience has been with this type of data collection. The principles, and some of the details, are equally applicable to other types of system, for example telephone-based methods which Bill Byrom, Keith Wenzel and James Pierce discuss in more detail in Chapter 7 of this volume, and to web-based methods. Some of the ideas in this chapter were developed jointly with my colleague Mikael Palmblad (Palmblad and Tiplady, 2004).

Skills

It is often thought that systems based on computers will be problematic for computer-naïve or 'technophobe' users. Older patients are often assumed implicitly to belong to one or both of these groups, though the present 65 year old author wishes to dissent from this view! The numbers of people who have never used a computer is declining, but still significant. Government statistics show that 61 per cent of UK households had access to the internet in 2007 compared to 47 per cent in 2002 (National Statistics, 2007). Computer use is not identical to internet access, but these numbers give a general indication of familiarity with computers. In a study carried out in 2002, Begg et al. (2003) found that about a third of the 32 female patients recruited for a post-surgical diary study had never used a computer. All of the computer-naïve women were over 40. Thus we still need to allow for those who are unfamiliar with computers even in the developed world. And of course many clinical trials are carried out in countries where computer use is lower than this.

The answer to the skill problem is actually very simple – don't require any computer-related skills! Figure 8.1 below, gives an illustration of a screen layout that might be used with a patient. The first thing to note is that a single question is shown. With very short and simple questions it is sometimes possible to have more than one on a screen at a time, but as a general rule with the small screens of handheld computers, one question is presented to the patient at a time with the patient tapping on a 'next' button to move on to the next question.

Several things can be seen from this example. Firstly, the screen shows all the information needed by the patient to answer the question. Secondly everything is laid out within the limits of the screen size. There are no scroll bars or drop-down menus. This is important if computer-naïve users are to be able to use the system comfortably after a minimum of training, as regular computer users often under-estimate the effort required to initially master such controls. Finally, the area to be tapped is large, and explicitly defined by the border of the response box. There are no little check boxes next to the selected text. This makes it easier for the patient to understand what is required.

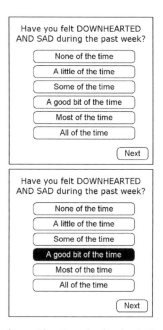

Figure 8.1   A question from the Psychological General Well-Being Index (PGWB: Dupuy et al., 1984)

Note: Patients make their responses by tapping on the screen with a stylus. The selected option is highlighted by reversing the black and white parts of the response box. The patient can change the selected option by tapping on a different box. Once the intended choice is selected, the patient taps 'Next' to move to the next question.

Legibility

I said previously that all information required by the patient should be visible on the screen, and that scroll bars should be avoided. This raises a potential problem. The example previously does not have too much text, and fits easily on the screen of a small handheld such as a Palm E2. Not all questionnaires are so modest in their requirements, and many have considerably more text per question. Up to a point this can be accommodated by making text smaller, but that point is quickly reached.

Several approaches are possible. One is to use scroll bars or drop-down option selection and accept the training load required to initiate new users to the method. This would require not only training but a demonstration that the training had been effective and that the patients are using the controls without adding sufficient extra load to affect their performance in completing the questionnaire. It would also be necessary to show that visibility effects, bias towards the options initially visible in the display, (Couper et al., 2004) are not occurring.

A second approach is to split the question and present the question on one screen and the responses on the next. This has the danger that patients will not remember all the required information at the point they are making their responses. This is a real danger, since screen splitting would only be considered if the amount of text is comparatively large. Again it would be necessary to demonstrate that patients could deal adequately with this layout in practice. One recent report suggests that screen splitting may lead to real problems in practice (Juniper et al., 2009).

The best approach is again a simple one. Use a device with an adequate screen size. This has been a problem in the past, as there was very limited availability of devices with screen size between that of the handheld and a small laptop. However there are now a wide range of devices available with varying screen sizes that are suitable for ePRO use. These are less portable than handhelds, such as the Palm, but in practice this is seldom an issue as the longer questions are generally found in quality of life or health economic questionnaires carried out at a clinic visit rather than taken home by the patient.

Organisation

Even when a large screen is used, the space available is likely to be less than that available on an A4 sheet of paper, and some changes to the way the instrument is ordered and laid out are likely to be necessary. One example has already been mentioned, the presentation of one question on the screen at a time. This is in contrast to a layout commonly used for paper as well as web-based questionnaires where questions with similar response options are grouped together with the response options in horizontal rows. See Figure 8.2, for an example of a questionnaire laid out in this way.

As well as the change from a group of questions to single questions, there is often a change from a horizontal response layout to a vertical one, and instructions that are common to a group of questions are often given at the start of the group on a separate screen. Paul Beatty discusses the implications of these changes for paper-electronic equivalence in Chapter 2 of this book. I shall concentrate here on the user interface aspects.

Placing instructions on a separate screen might seem to raise the same problems as raised above for screen splitting. This could be a problem, but there is an important difference. When the question is split from the response, the patient must remember what is involved in the current question, which is of course different from the previous one. Thus the memory load the patient must handle is constantly changing. By contrast, instructions stay the same for a group of questions, and often for the entire questionnaire, so the memory load is constant. This involves much less processing; much less cognitive load, than changing information. Nonetheless it is desirable to limit this load as far as possible by placing the most important information, such as the assessment period, on each screen and limiting the amount of information presented on the initial screen. I will discuss cognitive load in more detail below.

Presenting questions one at a time on the screen is likely to reduce the sense of linkage between adjacent questions. This may be a good or a bad thing. Where the grouping is simply based on convenience, for example, of questions which have similarly phrased responses, or what will fit on a page, then grouping itself may introduce a subtle form of bias due to the tendency of questions within a group to correlate more highly with each other than questions not in the group (see e.g. Couper et al., 2001). These effects are generally small but if anything, single item presentation should improve the psychometric properties of the scale in such a case.

In other cases, the grouping is conceptually important, for example where questions are clearly samples of a larger category. An instance of this is the Health Assessment Questionnaire, where activities are assessed in groups such as hygiene, grip or eating. Two groups from this questionnaire are shown in Figure 8.2.

In this case the grouping is an important part of the questionnaire design and contributes information to the patient that is relevant in making the response. It can be maintained in the electronic version by placing the group heading at the top of each question screen and also on the initial instruction screen where this is used. Thus the information available to the patient is as similar as possible in both electronic and paper versions.

The change from vertical to horizontal arrangements of text-based response options seems unlikely to have much impact on the user experience. Both left-right and top-down text arrangement are familiar in most societies, and both layouts are common in paper and web-based questionnaire designs. There is some evidence of effects of horizontal or vertical layout on responses to visual (line) analogue scales, but these effects appear to be small (Breivik and Skloglund, 1998; Stephenson and Herman, 2000).

Please check the response which best describes your usual abilities OVER THE PAST WEEK:				
	Without ANY difficulty	With SOME difficulty	With MUCH difficulty	UNABLE to do
DRESSING AND GROOMING				
Are you able to:				
• Dress yourself, including tying shoelaces and doing buttons?	☐	☐	☐	☐
• Shampoo your hair?	☐	☐	☐	☐
ARISING				
Are you able to:				
• Stand up from a straight chair?	☐	☐	☐	☐
• Get in and out of bed?	☐	☐	☐	☐

Figure 8.2   Two of the groups of activities assessed by the Health Assessment Questionnaire Disability Index (HAQ-DI: Fries et al., 1980)

Electronic systems allow the behaviour of the application to depend on the patient's response. Navigation will be discussed below, but another example is the way missing data are handled. In some circumstances it is appropriate to allow patients to leave a question out. Common examples are questions about personal or sensitive issues such as financial income or sexual activities. When a missing response is allowed, there should always be an explicit 'I prefer not to answer' option, so it is clear that the omission was intentional.

In other situations, missing data is undesirable. Fallowfield (1996) has identified missing data as the main quality issue with quality of life data, and electronic methods can help to ensure data completeness. The instructions for many quality of life scales encourage patients to give the best answer they can if none seems to fit exactly. An ePRO application can be programmed to give this encouragement just when it is needed, by bringing up a message box when the 'Next' button is pressed with no response option selected. A typical message might be 'If you are not sure how to answer a question, please choose the response that is closest to how you feel at the moment'. Warning messages can also appear if inconsistent response combinations are chosen.

When we set up our early ePRO applications, we were concerned about whether patients would object to a response being required. These studies invited patient feedback but no resistance to this was encountered in a series of over 800 patients. Thus ePRO applications can combine methods to ensure data completeness with patient acceptability.

Cognitive Load

The task required of the patient in answering questionnaires is often a significant one, and is easily underestimated. Apparently simple questions may actually require considerable amounts of effort to interpret. For an example see Paul Beatty, Chapter 2 in this volume. Except for the simplest here and now questions, responses are not immediately available in the patient's mind but must be constructed. These issues are discussed by Shields, Stone and Shifffman in Chapter 1 of this volume. Cognitive load refers to the processing effort required for interpretation of questions and response options, the construction of the response and any ancillary tasks required by the questionnaire (e.g. remembering or referring back to a previously given definition or instructions concerning time period).

To a considerable extent, the cognitive load is dependent on the questionnaire rather than the mode of administration, but a number of aspects of user interface design can affect the load required of the patient when completing an ePRO application. One example has already been mentioned, that of material that the patient must remember. If information given on one screen must be used by the patient to interpret material on a subsequent screen, this material must be both *held* in memory and *processed*. This combined requirement is the definition of working memory, and a classic series of studies by Baddeley and co-authors (see e.g. Baddeley, 1986) documented the degree to which such memory loads could interfere with the performance of concurrent tasks. The degree of interference is greater for changing memory loads than for constant ones. To avoid this type of interference, as far as possible all information needed by the patient should be explicitly available on the response screen. For a more detailed discussion of this (see Palmblad and Tiplady, 2004).

Interference will also occur if the patient is required to perform any sort of concurrent task. Making the response can be considered a concurrent task to formulating the response. Normally the response is so simple; ticking a box, circling yes or no, tapping on a text button on screen, that the load associated with this is trivial, but it may not always be so. I have already suggested that we should avoid requiring computer skills in order to make our systems easy for all patients to use, but computer-specific methods or conventions such as scroll bars, drop-down menus, or responding using a mouse, are likely to impose additional load on patients for whom these methods are not completely automatic.

Another task that may be required is presented by feedback. Feedback is generally considered a good thing, but any message that appears on the screen has to be read and the patient usually has to take some action, such as tapping an OK box to close the message and continue with the questionnaire. Thus there should always be a good reason for providing this sort of information. One use of feedback is to inform patients of invalid selections. For example a question that asks patients if they have experienced any of a number of symptoms may allow several of the response boxes to be selected. There may also be a 'none of the above' box. If 'none of the above' is checked as well as one or more symptoms, a message may appear warning the patient of the inconsistency. Such messages can be useful, but in many cases it is better to construct the question in such a way that only valid choices can be entered in the first place. By example, a numeric entry for the question 'How many days did you have diarrhea in the past week' could use a generic numeric entry and then warn the patient if a number greater than 7 was entered. However a neater solution is to design the response options so that only numbers from 0–7 can be entered in the first place.

Navigation that requires patients to make choices also constitutes a concurrent task. Most of us are familiar with forms, often from the taxman, with instructions like 'If YES continue with the next question, if NO, go to question 37'. At best such conditional logic increases the complexity of the user's task, at worst it can lead to errors and lost data. This is an area where electronic methods can greatly simplify the patient's task, as the branch points do not need to be seen by the patient at all. The device simply offers the next question that is appropriate to the situation, and all the patient sees is a series of questions one after the other. Thus the cognitive load can actually be decreased by using electronic methods.

Telephone-based Systems

An alternative approach to ePRO is to use the patient's own telephone as a data collection device. Patients call a toll free or free phone study number, which can even be dialed by the system, and hear a spoken script with the instructions, questions and response options. They might, for example rate symptom severity using a numeric code 'If your symptoms have been mild today, press 1. If moderate, press 2, if severe, press 3'. Readers will recognise this as similar to the automated call systems widely used by commercial organisations, and the underlying technology is the same, being referred to by the acronym IVR, for interactive voice response. While the details of constructing an IVR system are substantially different, many of the basic considerations for developing a system that is easy to use are similar to those for screen-based systems. A great advantage of IVR is that patients are already familiar with telephones and will not have to learn any new skills. IVR also mirrors the aural administration of questions as asked by a physician. IVR administration partially overcomes the issue of literacy as many patients may be functionally literate, that is they understand the spoken word but may have limited reading comprehension skills. A possible disadvantage is that many of the commercial systems currently in use are poorly thought out from a user perspective. Patients who have been frustrated by such in the past may not approach a clinical trial system with an entirely positive attitude. But good IVR systems can be developed, and again the need is for careful design and the ability to take the user perspective into account.

These are voice-based systems so the first issue is to get the voice right. Clearly patients must find it easy to understand what is said, so speed of presentation must be considered, and speakers with strong regional accents avoided. The question of accents, however, goes well beyond intelligibility of speech. Listeners respond differently to accents from different regions. Thus in a British context, speakers with accents from industrial areas of England may tend to be rated as of lower status and less pleasant than those with Received Pronunciation (Giles, 1970). The gender of the speaker does not, in general, seem to be an issue but there are situations in which it can be important. Thus in a questionnaire about sensitive sexual issues it may be preferable to use a speaker of the same sex as the respondent. Intonation is also important: the voice must be appropriately moderate in emphasis. In clinical trials you do not wish to introduce a therapeutic effect. The voice recording should neither be too 'high' or happy nor too 'low' or sad. This is something that is easily managed with instructions and standards for voice recording, but it is something of which system designers must be cognisant.

An important difference between screen-based and IVR systems is that IVR material is presented serially and must be remembered by the patient. With information on a screen or paper the patient can look back at the beginning of the text. With IVR, methods of going back must be explicitly provided, for example 'To hear these options again, press 9'. Such options should be used in a consistent way throughout the application, and careful thought given to how instructions for using them are given. It is not uncommon for IVR systems to repeat the question should the patient not respond in the expected time interval. This is a viable alternative to 'To hear these options again, press 9.'

There is a converse issue. Patients will typically use the application many times. This means that as they get familiar with it they will remember what they have heard. A common source of frustration with IVR systems is having to wait for a section of text to end before being allowed to make a response. I know – I frequently use a teleconferencing system that won't let me enter my security code until the instruction has ended. I've probably only heard it a hundred times, but it seems like much more! There is a balance here between the convenience of the respondent and being sure that she/he really does remember the options correctly. One idea to consider is to use a short definition that is presented in full, and a longer clarification that can be interrupted. There are other possibilities such as requiring that the question be uninterruptible, but permitting the response descriptions to be interruptible or having uninterruptible questions and responses the first few times, for example three, an instrument is administered and then making the questions and/or responses interruptible. The designer should balance ease-of-use with the need to ensure that the patient is taking account of all the necessary information.

One possibility in designing an IVR system is to get the patient to confirm that choices have been correctly entered. Typically the responses are read back to the patient, who keys in a Yes or No. If no, the question can be re-presented. This feature can be useful, but again can be tedious for the patient to use. If you have a few items that are critical, e.g. primary outcome measures, it could be worth confirming just these items.

Some types of question cannot be implemented directly using an IVR system, for example where graphic displays are required. Thus if your paper questionnaire has a visual analogue scale, you will have to think carefully about what you want to measure. Visual analogue scales are generally scored from 0 to 100, for example with 0 meaning 'no pain' and 100 meaning 'worst possible pain'. However the patient using the scale does not see these numbers, just a line with 'no pain' and 'worst possible pain' at the ends. Technically it is straightforward to ask the patient to enter a number between 0 and 100 into the phone keypad. But it raises two questions. Firstly, are patients comfortable doing this, do they feel they can meaningfully assign a number to their pain? We can ask the patients whether they do or not. Secondly, does it actually mean the same thing; do we get the same number, within experimental error, for the two types of rating. Damian McEntegart gives details of how to answer this question in Chapter 9 of this book.

There is an alternative approach to visual analogue scales. The current trend is towards replacing them with other scale types. The IMMPACT recommendations for pain assessment, for example, state: 'VRS (Verbal Rating Scale) and NRS (Numeric Rating Scale) measures tend to be preferred over VAS measures by patients. Furthermore, VAS measures usually demonstrate greater amounts of missing and incomplete data than NRS measures, presumably because NRS measures are less abstract and easier to understand.' (Dworkin et al., 2005). Numerical and verbal rating scales are straightforward to implement on IVR.

IVR systems should tell the patients how long the call is expected to last, and in a longer assessment it is a good idea to give feedback on progress, such as: 'You are now half way done with today's assessment.' An appropriate concluding statement should be made so the patient understands the assessment is complete, such as: 'Thank you for your call today. Today's assessment is complete. Please remember to call tomorrow for your next assessment between six and ten pm.'

Patients complete their assessments in a real world where doorbells ring at unexpected times, children wake up, and nature calls. So it is a good idea if patients can put the system 'on hold' or call back in and complete an assessment without having to go back to the very beginning.

A Patient-centred Approach

Patient Reported Outcomes aim to assess the patient's point of view of illness and treatment. It is equally important to put the patient at the centre of things when designing, specifying or selecting an ePRO solution. But the idea of 'the patient' is itself problematic. Patients vary. We have young and old, male and female, robust and frail, computer experts and those who have never used a computer, those with poor eyesight or tremor, those in pain, anxious, or fatigued by disease or its treatment.

Does this mean that we have to design or specify different applications for every target group, taking into account their abilities and limitations? In some case we may need to, and we certainly need to ensure that our target patient groups can use our ePRO systems effectively. But it is my belief that we can go a very long way with an inclusive approach to system design. As a starting point, let me go back to the beginning of the chapter and my suggestion that we get round the issue of computer skills by not requiring them. Suppose we set up a system on a handheld that is so simple that a completely computer-naïve patient can use it after a few minutes training. This is not an unreasonable expectation. I have seen it happen many times. What if we give this to someone who has been using computers for as long as they can remember? Will they have a problem? It hardly seems likely.

In general if we design an application for those who are most likely to have problems and make it easy to use for them, then the rest of us will have no difficulty. This inclusive approach can be applied to a wide range of design considerations. I'll give a few examples, but the approach is a broad one.

About 1 per cent of the male population cannot see the difference between red and green. So if you use these colours as the only way to convey important information, this minority will not get it. It is always possible for the designer to use other cues. Colour is great when used to enhance and emphasise, but is risky as the sole source of information. Yes, it may only be 1 per cent but a percent here and a percent there, and soon you have a substantial proportion of people affected. And quite a lot more people have a degree of colour anomaly, making it harder, but not impossible, to distinguish red/green differences. Why make it more difficult than it needs to be for *anyone*?

People with tremor or poor eyesight may have trouble with small tick boxes beside the response text. Tick boxes in electronic applications have always puzzled me. It is a completely paper-based way of entering choices. With pen and paper you have to make a mark somewhere, and it shouldn't be *on* the text, as this would obscure it and might be confused with crossing out the unwanted choice, so you provide a tick box. With electronic entry you have to tap or click somewhere, but there is no need for the mark to go exactly where the tap is. It's much more logical to tap anywhere in the text area and highlight the entire selected text, rather than having a box to one side, as in Figure 8.1. It also makes the area to be tapped bigger than if you have a tick box. This makes it easier if you have tremor – and no harder if you don't.

ePRO systems often have alarms to remind patients when to make their entries. Hearing loss is common in, though by no means confined to, older patients and often involves particular frequencies. A useful trick is to make alarm signals run up and down through the frequency range. Alarms can also start relatively quiet, and get steadily louder. These techniques again make using the system easier for those with a degree of hearing loss without making it harder for those with robust hearing.

This inclusive, patient-centred approach can be summed up as follows:

- Think it through from the patient's point of view.

- Design for the person who is likely to find the system most difficult to use. Then the rest of us won't have any problems.

- Do not make it harder than it needs to be for anyone.

Good user interface design has an importance that goes beyond a desire that our patients should be comfortable with the systems we ask them to use, important though that is. It is an essential part of ensuring a properly run clinical trial programme. If substantial numbers of patients are unable or unwilling to use ePRO systems, it could have an effect on clinical trial recruitment. At best this could make it more difficult to run studies but it could also introduce a source of bias, especially if those not included in the study tend to be elderly; a group who should be fully represented in most trial programmes not least because they consume a good deal more medicine than younger people and are more likely to suffer from adverse effects. Thus the clinical trial population should represent the population of those who will take the medicine once marketed, and our methods should be suitable for use with all types of patient who meet study recruitment criteria.

Fortunately, the experience from many researchers over the past decades has shown that this goal is eminently attainable. The patient's voice is becoming increasingly important in clinical research, and the approach outlined here may help to keep it centre stage.

Summary

Creating ePRO systems that are easy for patients to use requires careful design and ability to think the system through from the patient's perspective, plus an inclusive approach to design that takes into account the differences among patients. If we design systems that can be used by patients who do not use computers, or those with tremor or poor eyesight, the rest of us will have no problems. In practice this means attention to presentation, legibility and size of the area to be tapped with a screen-based system, voice type and speed for IVR; to what the user has to do, response choices and navigation, and to what the user has to remember while using the system. Systems can be complex yet simple to use. Using these principles it is possible to set up ePRO systems that can be used successfully by a wide range of patients. Many studies have shown that patients find such systems easy to use and often prefer them to paper. ePRO systems can thus be used in large scale clinical research programmes without limiting recruitment or skewing the characteristics of the patient group being studied.

References

Aiello, E.J., Taplin, S. and Reid, R. et al. (2006). In a randomized controlled trial, patients preferred electronic data collection of breast cancer risk-factor information in a mammography setting, *J Clin Epidemiol*, 59: 77–81.

Baddeley, A. (1986). *Working Memory*. Clarendon, Oxford.

Begg, A., Drummond, G. and Tiplady, B. (2003). Assessment of postsurgical recovery after discharge using a pen computer diary, *Anaesthesia*, 58: 1101–1105.

Breivik, E.K. and Skloglund, L.A. (1998). Comparison of present pain intensity assessments on horizontally and vertically oriented visual analogue scales, *Methods Find Exp Clin Pharmacol*, 20: 719.

Couper, M.P., Traugott, M.W. and Lamias, M.J. (2001). Web survey design and administration, *Public Opinion Quarterly*, 65: 230–254.

Couper, M.P., Tourangeau, R. and Conrad, F.G. et al. (2004). What they see is what we get: response options for web surveys, *Social Science Computer Review*, 22: 111–127.

Drummond, H.E., Ghosh, S. and Ferguson, A. et al. (1995). Electronic quality of life questionnaires: a comparison of pen-based electronic questionnaires with conventional paper in a gastrointestinal study, *Quality of Life Research*, 4: 21–26.

Dupuy, H.J. (1984). 'The Psychological General Well-Being (PGWB) index,' in *Assessment of Quality of Life in Clinical Trials of Cardiovascular Therapies*, N.K. Wenger et al., (eds), LeJacq Publishing, pp. 170–183.

Dworkin, R.H., Turk, D.C. and Farrar, J.T. et al. (2005). Core outcome measures for chronic pain clinical trials: IMMPACT recommendations, *Pain*, 113: 9–19.

Fallowfield, L. (1996). Quality of quality-of-life data, *The Lancet*, 348: 421–422.

French, C.C. and Beaumont, J.G. (1987). The reaction of psychiatric patients to computerized assessment, *British Journal of Clinical Psychology*, 26: 267–287.

Fries, J.F., Spitz, P. and Kraines, R.G. et al. (1980). Measurement of patient outcome in arthritis, *Arthritis Rheum*, 23: 137–145.

Giles, H. (1970). Evaluative reactions to accents, *Educational Review*, 22: 211–227.

Hufford, M.R., Stone, A.A. and Shiffman, S. et al. (2002). Paper vs. electronic diaries: compliance and subject evaluations, *Applied Clinical Trials*, 11: 38–43.

Hyland, M.E., Kenyon, C.A.P. and Allen, R. et al. (1993). Diary keeping in asthma: comparison of written and electronic records, *BMJ*, 306: 487–489.

Johannes, C., Woods, J. and Crawford, S. et al. (2000). Electronic versus paper instruments for daily data collection, *Annals of Epidemiology*, 10: 457.

Juniper, E.F., Langlands, J.M. and Juniper, B.A. (2009). Patients may respond differently to paper and electronic versions of the same questionnaires, *Respiratory Medicine*, In press, corrected proof.

Lucas, R.W., Card, W.I. and Knill-Jones, R.P. et al. (1976). Computer interrogation of patients, *British Medical Journal*, 2: 623–625.

Meacham R., McEntegart D. and O'Gorman H. (2008). Use of and compliance with electronic patient reported outcomes within clinical drug trials. Poster presented at ISPOR 11th Annual European Congress 8–11 November 2008. www.perceptive.com/files/pdf/Models%20for%20Use.pdf

Palmblad, M. and Tiplady, B. (2004). Electronic diaries and questionnaires: designing user interfaces that are easy for all patients to use, *Quality of Life Research*, 13: 1199–1207.

Rabin, J.M., McNett, J. and Badlani, G.H. (1996). 'Compu-Void II': the computerized voiding diary, *J.Med.Syst.*, 20: 19–34.

Siegel, K., Mesagno, F.P. and Chen, J.Y. et al. (1988). Computerized telephone assessment of the 'concrete' needs of chemotherapy outpatients: a feasibility study, *Journal of Clinical Oncology*, 6: 1760–1767.

Stephenson, N.L. and Herman, J. (2000). Pain measurement: a comparison using horizontal and vertical visual analogue scales, *Applied Nursing Research*, 13: 157–158.

Stone, A.A., Broderick, J.E. and Schwartz, J.E. et al. (2003). Intensive momentary reporting of pain with an electronic diary: reactivity, compliance, and patient satisfaction, *Pain*, 104: 343–351.

Taylor, C.B., Fried, L. and Kenardy, J. (1990). The use of a real-time computer diary for data acquisition and processing, *Behav.Res.Ther.*, 28: 93–97.

Tiplady, B., Crompton, G.K. and Dewar, M.H. et al. (1997). The use of electronic diaries in respiratory studies, *Drug Information Journal*, 31: 759–764.

9

Equivalence Testing: Validation and Supporting Evidence When Using Modified PRO Instruments

Damian J. McEntegart

Introduction

The background for this article is the increasing use of PRO measures both generally in health research and in pharmaceutical trials. Willke et al. (2004) noted that PROs are used in 30 per cent of product labels. Increasingly electronic versions of PROs (ePROs) are being used for the reasons discussed overleaf. ePRO versions include telephone based interactive voice response systems (IVR), handheld personal digital assistant (PDA) computers and touch screen tablets. As a result of the increasing use of PROs, in 2009 the Food and Drug Administration (FDA) in the United States issued guidance (FDA, 2009) on the use of PROs in regulatory submissions; a short summary based upon the draft of this guidance has also been published (Burke et al., 2008). This guidance included a section to the effect that further validation is needed when the mode of administration changes, usually this would be from paper PRO to ePRO.

A particular advantage of ePRO instruments is that higher quality data are obtained (Shea et al., 2004). The data are time stamped thus verifying when the patient filled out the entries; this compares to paper where the joke is that patients often complete their paper diaries in the car park before seeing the investigator. Patients can receive automated reminders, thus improving compliance. Secondary data entry errors are avoided and there are no written comments which are difficult to know how to deal with. The entries are less variable and a higher effect size has been shown in a number of studies (Lee

(2006), McKenzie (2004)). ePRO instruments are more convenient for the patient in a number of ways including the fact that questions with complicated skip patterns are automatically implemented.

So it is clear that ePRO instruments have advantages over paper. There are hundreds, if not thousands, of paper PROs that are validated to a greater or lesser extent (Emery et al., 2005); although how many of these meet the highest validation standards is another question altogether. It is natural that practitioners would want to convert some of these paper instruments into ePROs. The question is how do we validate the modified instruments? Further if the instrument is to be used in a regulatory submission, what evidence is necessary to support the use of the modified instrument?

FDA PRO Guidance

To answer the above question, our starting point is the FDA guidance. The FDA PRO Guidance states that 'when a PRO instrument is modified, sponsors generally should provide evidence to confirm the new instrument's adequacy.' (FDA, 2009)

The Guidance provides examples of changes that can alter the way that patients respond to the same set of questions, and therefore may require additional work to establish the instrument's measurement properties:

- changing an instrument from paper to electronic format;

- changing timing of or procedures for PRO instrument administration within the clinic visit;

- changing the application to a different setting, population, or condition;

- changing the order of items, item wording, response options, recall period or deleting portions of a questionnaire;

- changing the instructions or the placement of instructions within the PRO instrument.

This article concentrates on changed mode of administration which includes the cases of an interviewer-administered scale being modified for self-administration, a paper-and-pencil self-administered PRO being modified for administration by computer or other electronic device and finally where the instructions or procedures for administration differ from those used in validation studies.

The FDA Guidance is not explicit in what type of validation is required for the various degrees of modification that are possible. This question has been considered by the ePRO task force of the International Society for Pharmacoeconomics and Outcomes Research (ISPOR). The task force paper (Coons et al., 2009) provides a classification of the three types of modification that would require different extents of validation:

- A minor modification would be one that is not expected to change the content or meaning of the items and response scales. In these cases a small study involving cognitive debriefing and usability testing would be sufficient evidence.

- A moderate level of modification would be one that potentially changes the meaning of the assessment items. In this instance a small randomised study would be required for validation. Examples include changing a single item into multiple screens and altering the order of presentation or converting the paper scale into an IVR format. The latter is included as there is as yet insufficient evidence that moving from a paper-based visual experience to an auditory experience does not alter the properties of the instrument; as more evidence accumulates this type of modification may come to be regarded as minor.

- Substantial modification is the highest level, where the change modifies the content or meaning of the assessment; here full psychometric validation is required.

The methods involved with cognitive debriefing and full psychometric validation are described in other chapters of this book. Thus for the remainder of this chapter, I am going to focus on the case where a small randomized study to demonstrate equivalence to the original instrument is required as evidence of validation to regulatory standards. If such a study is carried out then by definition there is no need to address the content validity of the modified instrument and it is sufficient to rely on the properties of the original instrument.

Randomised Studies to Demonstrate Equivalence

The objectives of such a study will be to demonstrate the equivalence of the modified instrument to the original, usually paper. This sounds simple enough but the devil is in the detail. The questions I shall consider in the forthcoming sections include key design questions such as the type of study and how to perform sample size calculations. Also which equivalence measures should be used? Should we use classical or equivalence testing? Should we focus on point estimates or confidence intervals? What is the appropriate minimum threshold for us to use to determine agreement? Are large sample approximations for confidence intervals always appropriate? What factors should be included in the analysis? How do we approach various design issues such as the gap between administrations and the need for a test-retest component?

In addressing these questions, I will cite examples of good and bad practice from the literature. In a previous presentation (McEntegart, 2008) the extent of various practices was quantified with reference to 11 published equivalence studies randomly sampled from a total of 54 collated from 3 recent overviews (Burton et al. (2007), Gwaltney et al. (2008), Lane et al. (2006)). The publication years of the sampled articles ranged from 1998 to 2006. Additional articles have been published since 2006 and it is beneficial to add these to the random sample in order to get a more up to date impression; this is relevant as it appears to this author that standards of design, analysis and presentation are rising. In all, a pool of 30 references were considered.

ESSENTIAL DESIGN QUESTIONS

This section covers the major design questions that the researcher has to consider, namely type of study, sample size and primary analyses. The three topics are inherently linked.

Parallel group studies

The first question a researcher has to consider is what type of design will be employed. Assuming the design is randomised to eliminate bias, the question is whether to use a parallel group or a crossover study. This will largely depend on the sample size and we will see that generally a crossover study will be selected for efficiency reasons. But it is convenient to detail the approach for parallel group studies first.

Before performing any sample size calculations, a researcher must select the appropriate analysis suitable for demonstrating equivalence. In respect of the mean response scores, one possibility would be to perform a classical significance test against a null hypothesis of equality and to conclude the two modes are equivalent whenever they do not differ significantly. This would be a mistake on two counts. A small sample size would virtually guarantee a failure to find a significant difference. Secondly it is inherent in the logic of statistical significance that one draws a definitive conclusion only when a hypothesis is rejected, not when it fails to be rejected. For these reasons the correct approach is to determine a value δ which is in some sense clinically important. Then the hypotheses to be tested can be framed in terms of ruling out differences larger than δ i.e. non-equivalence as two one-sided null hypotheses. If both hypotheses are rejected then we would conclude equivalence. Operationally the analysis can be conducted by determining whether the 95 per cent confidence interval for the mean difference lies entirely within the interval –δ to +δ. If the confidence interval lies outside the range of –δ to +δ then the correct approach is to accept the null hypothesis of non-equivalence. If the interval includes one or both of -δ or +δ then no definitive conclusion is possible – equivalence is possible but not proven the sample size was possibly too small. P-values for the formal statistical tests of the two null hypotheses can be computed if desired but the confidence interval is sufficient. A pictorial representation of the situation is given in Figure 9.1. The value of δ would normally be chosen to be close to the accepted boundary between clinically important and unimportant differences. The ISPOR task force noted that a small effect size (difference of between 0.20 and 0.49 SD) may be meaningful and represent the minimally important difference. To be conservative, the value of δ may be smaller than the minimally important difference and be regarded as a value of undisputed clinical importance. Although aimed at therapeutic trials, guidance from European regulators (CPMP, 2000) provides a good overview of the topic.

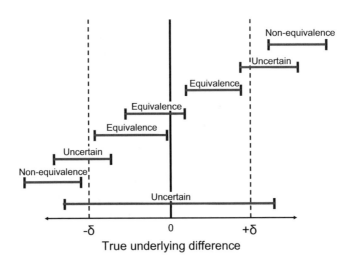

Figure 9.1   **Equivalence, non-equivalence and uncertain conclusions based upon the position of 95 per cent confidence intervals relative to the interval –δ to +δ**

For parallel group trials using equivalence methodology, the sample size formula for a parallel group study for a 100 (1-2α)% two sided interval is as follows (Jones et al., 1996):

$$n = 2(s^2/\delta^2) \, (Z_{1-\alpha} + Z_{1-\beta/2})^2$$

where

n = number per group.

s^2 = estimate of variance for observations.

δ = equivalence margin to be ruled out.

$Z_{1-\alpha}$ = 100(1-α) % point of the normal distribution with α denoting the type I error of deciding the treatments are equivalent when they are not.

$Z_{1-\beta/2}$ = 100(1- β/2) % point of the normal distribution with β denoting the Type II error of deciding the treatments are not equivalent when they in fact are.

Thus for a $2\alpha=0.05$, $Z_{1-\alpha}=Z_{0.975}=1.96$ and for 80% power $Z_{1-\beta/2}=Z_{0.90}=1.28$

Notice the definitions of α and β are reversed as compared to classical testing against a zero null.

As an example, to rule out differences of 0.30 standard deviations with 80 per cent power, 234 subjects per group would be required.

Crossover studies and analysis

An alternative to the parallel group design is the crossover design where each PRO instrument is administered in a randomised order with adequate duration between administrations. Then the comparison of the mode means can be made using equivalence methodology as before. Further points about the design and analysis of crossover studies will be made in later sections.

If a crossover design is to be performed, then the appropriate (large sample – see below) formula for the sample size calculation is as follows:

$$n = (s_d^2/\delta^2)\,(Z_{1-\alpha} + Z_{1-\beta/2})^2$$

where

n= the total sample size with each subject completing both modes.

s_d^2=the standard deviation of the difference between paired observations on the same subject. This corresponds to $2s^2(1-\varrho)$ where ϱ is an estimate of the correlation between observations.

$Z_{1-\alpha}$ and $Z_{1-\beta/2}$ are as before.

By substitution the formula can be rewritten as:

$$n = 2(1-\varrho)\,(s^2/\delta^2)\,(Z_{1-\alpha} + Z_{1-\beta/2})^2$$

Thus it can be seen that the total number of patients for a crossover study is equal to the total number required for a parallel group study multiplied by $(1-\varrho)/2$. For a typical equivalence study, a value of ϱ of 0.90 might be considered appropriate (this was the average in a meta analysis (Gwaltney et al., 2008)) which would lead to a multiplication factor of 0.05, although it would be prudent to do sensitivity analyses with more conservative values. Returning to our previous example, the number of subjects required in a crossover study would be 468 * 0.05 = 23.4 i.e. 24. This marked increase in efficiency explains why the crossover is the predominant design in equivalence studies. Forty out of the 46 studies in the meta analysis had a crossover component.

With the typical magnitude of the sample sizes in mode validation studies, use of the t-distribution will usually be more appropriate than the normal distribution (Liu and Chow, 1992). As such, once the value of n has been computed using the formula above, the calculation should be repeated with the t-distribution percentiles for n-2 degrees of freedom replacing the standard normal distribution percentiles. The calculated sample size will generally rise by 1–2 subjects; the calculation is then repeated using the updated value for n-2 until the value of n does not change.

Unfortunately equivalence methodology was rarely used in the crossover trial articles in my literature pool but there is a suggestion that it is filtering through in more recently published studies e.g. Junker (2008).

Intraclass correlation coefficient

So far our discussion has focused on means. But it is also important to focus on the shape of the distribution of the scores as mean differences can hide large individual variations. In a parallel group study the equality of the distributions can be tested by the Kolmogorov-Smirnov test (Stuart et al., 1999). In the more usual case of a crossover study, we can use a reliability measure based on the paired observations. Reliability refers to the extent to which the measure yields the same score each time it is administered, all other things being equal. Pearson's correlation coefficient should not be used as it does not consider a shift in scores between the instruments. The Intraclass Correlation Coefficient (ICC) should be used instead, as this takes into account the relative position in the distribution and the amount of deviation from the group mean. The ICC is the proportion of total variability accounted for by the variability between subjects; the higher the value (maximum of 1) the more reliable the measure. Weighted kappa is an alternative to the ICC but provided the most common weighting scheme is used, the statistic is the same as the ICC; thus there would not seem a good reason to use it as the ICC is more widely known and understood. The ISPOR task force (Coons et al., 2009) recommended examination of the ICC in addition to mode means in a crossover study. In my literature sample, Pearson's correlation was used in approximately the same proportion of instances as ICC.

To illustrate the difference between the ICC and Pearson's coefficient, consider the following exaggerated situation. Assume the two PRO mode scores are perfectly related by the straight line equation mode2=2+3*mode1 – clearly this would indicate very poor performance! The situation is depicted in Figure 9.2. The Pearson correlation will be equal to 1.0 whereas the ICC will be equal to only 0.17. The ICC will only be equal to 1.0 if there are identical observations on each subject.

In published studies the analysis generally focuses on the point estimate of the ICC (or Pearson's coefficient) but the correct procedure is to compute a one-sided 95 per cent confidence interval to ensure the reliability is above a predefined lower bound. As with the situation with means, it is also possible to compute the corresponding test statistic but again this adds little value; the test would be of the null hypothesis that the ICC equals the lower bound with the alternative that the null exceeds the lower bound.

Computation of the ICC needs some care. Six ICC coefficients were defined by Shrout and Fleiss in 1979 and McGraw and Wong added another four in 1996. PRO publications rarely state which one is used and one wonders whether they have all used the correct one. The correct coefficient is the absolute agreement of the instruments based on an Analysis of Variance (ANOVA) from a mixed effects model with subject considered as a random effect and mode as a fixed effect. Following Streiner and Norman's (2003) notation this would be denoted

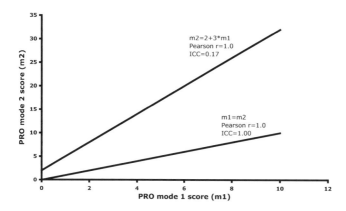

Figure 9.2   Theoretical examples of ICC and Pearson's coefficient exploring the concordance of two PRO measures

as ICC3(A,1). In the McGraw and Wong notation this is ICC(A,1) and in the Shrout and Fleiss notation this is ICC(2,1). Published papers unfortunately rarely quote the confidence interval; when they do it is always the two moment approximation detailed in McGraw and Wong. But the coverage of this estimator is poor and, as shown in the appendix, a better estimator is the Modified Large Sample estimator investigated by Cappelleri and Ting (2003). A SAS® (SAS Institute, 2001) macro to compute the ICC with this interval is detailed in their paper. None of the literature in the sample uses this superior estimator.

If one uses the ICC in a crossover study, then sample size considerations can be performed. For the case of 2 PRO modes the appropriate formula is as follows (Walter et al., 1998):

$$n = 1 + [2(Z_{1-\alpha} + Z_{1-\beta})^2 / (\ln C_0)^2]$$

where

$Z_{1-\alpha}$ and $Z_{1-\beta}$ denote % points of normal distribution as before.

$C_0 = (1 + 2[\varrho_0/(1-\varrho_0)]) / [1 + n\varrho_1/(1-\varrho_1)]$

ϱ_0 = lower bound for ICC.

ϱ_1 = estimated value of ICC in population.

Application of this formula will produce a different sample size than the calculation for the comparison of means with the difference depending on the values chosen for δ, ϱ_0 and ϱ_1. Under certain conditions, however, the values may be similar. Assume we require 80 per cent power, 5 per cent significance and a true underlying ICC of 0.85. Further assume the difference we want to rule out equates to an effect size of one quarter of a standard deviation and a lower bound for ICC of 0.70. Then using these assumptions, the required sample size is 53 for the comparison of means and 43 for the evaluation of ICC. One simply takes the higher of the two values. As these assumptions are typical values, one might also suggest that a ballpark figure for mode validation studies is around 50.

We note that the ICC should be interpreted with a degree of caution as it is dependent on the variability of the underlying population. The greater the between subjects variation, the greater the ICC will be. But perhaps the key point is that a modified PRO instrument should be tested on a sample from the relevant population and this is something the FDA make clear in their guidance.

Minimum threshold for ICC

What value should we use for the lower limit of reliability that we want to exceed? The ISPOR task force noted that 0.7 seems to be a generally accepted lower limit if the purpose is to use the modified instrument for use in clinical trial group comparisons. If the modified instrument is to be used for individual comparisons, then higher values are recommended. The ISPOR task force recommended a minimum value between 0.85 and 0.95. This is within the range of a previous recommendation of values in the range of 0.90 to 0.95 (Scientific Advisory Committee of the Medical Outcomes Trust, 2002). The rationale for this tighter limit can be explained because the confidence interval for an individual's score depends directly on the reliability. Specifically the standard error of measurement is equal to the standard deviation multiplied by the square root of 1 minus the reliability. So an ICC of 0.91 leads to a standard error of measurement that is equal to 0.3 of a standard deviation. Thus the 95 per cent confidence interval around observed scores is plus or minus 0.6 standard deviations. Half of a standard deviation is often taken as a medium sized effect. So even an ICC value of 0.9 encompasses measurement error that exceeds a medium effect albeit the probability of this actually happening is toward the outer limits of the confidence interval. Do individual assessments apply to clinical trials? The answer may be positive if PRO methods are being used to determine eligibility or decisions on dosing. The FDA guidance discusses responder analyses and defining responders would also involve consideration of individual values. If any of these individual level criteria are being used, then an ICC value higher than 0.70 may be required.

Bland and Altman method

Another method of analysis that applies to crossover studies is the method due to Bland and Altman (1995). The method involves calculating the standard deviation of the difference (SDD) of the paired observations. The limits of agreement are then calculated as the mean plus or minus 2 SDDs. These limits thus define the interval in which one would expect 95 per cnet of individual differences to lie. Two modes can be used interchangeably if the limits of agreement are not clinically important. Thus we can see the Bland and Altman method is focused on individual values and more stringent than the comparison of means. Specifically the 95 per cent confidence interval for the difference in means uses the same formula as Bland and Altman but with a root n divisor (if we ignore the period effect element of the crossover design). Thus the limits on the mean difference are obviously tighter.

A feature of the Bland and Altman method is to plot the difference between pairs against the mean of the pair to see if there is any relationship; this can be informative even if equivalence is established on the primary analysis measure. Essentially this is simply a rescaled plot of X-Y vs X+Y rotated through 45º. The plot can alert the researcher to systematic trends such as a monotonic drift in the agreement related to the value of the measurement, or an increase in error related to the value of the measurement. An example of a plot without any apparent relationship is given in Figure 9.3. Even if we are focused only on using the instrument for group comparisons, the Bland and Altman plot is a useful exploratory tool. Unfortunately plots were rarely reported in the literature sample, although there is one good example (Ring, 2008).

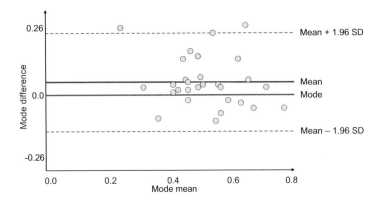

Figure 9.3   Bland-Altman plot showing no apparent relationship between paired PRO observations

OTHER DESIGN CONSIDERATIONS

Sample composition

The sample in which the instrument is validated should be relevant to the population in which it is intended to use the modified instrument. Of course it should be ascertained that the original instrument has been validated for use in this population too. Recruitment limits on patient sub-types, for example young vs. elderly, or cancer type, may be employed to ensure the sample is representative and/or to ensure representation in any sub-groups of particular interest. Kleinman (2001) restricted the sample to ensure that the split was 50 per cent young and 50 per cent elderly. Such restrictions are more easily enforced at single centre trials or by electronic central randomisation if the trial is a multicentre one.

Randomisation

One would expect allocation to mode in a parallel group study, or to order of administration of modes in a crossover study, to be randomised. Randomisation is used to ensure the approximate, long-run, comparability of treatment groups or orders on known and unknown factors that are predictive of outcome. In the context of therapeutic trials, it is also used to minimise the influence of selection bias where investigators might attempt to allocate certain treatments to particular subjects. Although the motivation for selection bias is perhaps less apparent in mode equivalence studies, the consideration remains.

Randomisation, however, does not ensure the comparability of groups within any given trial; an individual trial is subject to imbalances on prognostic factors due to chance (McEntegart, 2003). Stratification may be considered to ensure the comparability of the groups/orders on important predictive factors such as disease severity. For a parallel group study this will increase the power of the study slightly; perhaps more importantly it provides an insurance policy to ensure comparability which safeguards the credibility of the study when it is being assessed by journals or regulators. If stratification is employed, then the stratification factor should be accounted for in the analysis to preserve the correct Type I error. If the trial is conducted at more than one centre, then stratification by centre is generally recommended; this may also help with logistics as it means that allocation can be made by sealed envelopes rather than through a centralised randomisation system. For a crossover study with an expected high completion rate, there is less merit in ensuring comparability unless dropouts are potentially linked to predictive factors; each subject serves as their own control. On the other hand, stratification in a crossover can do no harm and again may contribute to credibility. A detailed explanation of the topic of randomisation is given in McEntegart (2003).

If a randomisation list is being used, the choice of block size should be less controversial than it is in blinded therapeutic trials where there is much concern to prevent intelligent guesswork on allocations by the investigator (McEntegart, 2008). Nevertheless it would seem prudent to avoid block sizes that are too small and a minimum of four would be my recommendation for a study of two modes of PRO administration. In a later section in this chapter on test-retest, one source of potential selection bias is discussed.

Within the sample of references, most studies were randomised with nothing remarkable; there were two exceptions. One study reports that their original intention was to assign patients to mode order in an alternate fashion (Agel et al., 2001) . But problems in the clinical setting meant that the alternation was done by enrolment day rather than patient. Furthermore one clinic had difficulty following the alternation and enrolled almost exclusively into one order. Dunn et al. (2007) describe an equivalence study conducted as part of a parallel group study to compare three treatments. Patients completed paper and IVR versions of the instrument on four separate days; the order was not randomised, presumably for practical reasons.

Follow-up

If the setting for at least one mode of administration is at home then there is the issue of ensuring good compliance. This is particularly the case if the ePRO administration is performed in the office and the subject is given the paper PRO to take home with instructions to return the paper version by mail or at the next clinic visit. Appropriate efforts should be taken to maximise compliance with the paper version, including stressing the importance of the research for the condition, personalised mailing with handwritten addresses, using a small incentive for completion where possible and follow-up reminders by mail or telephone. Pouwer et al. (1998) illustrate the problems that can occur in their study of paper at home vs. computer administration in the clinic. One hundred and five patients were invited to take part in the study; 13 did not complete either mode. Of the 92 who completed one mode, only 71 completed both. The relatively high non-completion rate gives rise to some concern. Ideally the missing administrations would have been repeated at the next or an unscheduled clinic visit to ascertain that the non-completers had the same equivalence properties as the completers but this may not always be possible. Similar completion rates were seen in a study of paper vs IVR administration where both were conducted at home (Lam et al., 2009). Of 157 patients enrolled, only 103 completed both administrations.

Duration between administrations

If a crossover comparison is being conducted, then the durations between administrations should be carefully considered. The duration should be short enough so that the underlying condition has not changed but long enough to avoid any carryover effects from the previous administration. For instance, if subjects are less familiar with the electronic mode, they may have to concentrate more and thus conceivably may more readily remember their response when completing the paper version; this carryover would apply only to the ePRO/ paper order and potentially less so to the paper/ePRO order. Similarly, an appropriate duration will minimise time period effects that apply equally to both orders, although as explained later, such period effects can be adjusted for in the analysis and it is carryover that is the big concern. Clearly the nature of the population being tested, the number of questions/items on the PRO scale and the number of PRO scales being evaluated in the study are relevant factors to consider in making the decision.

Within the sample of references, durations between administrations were typically between a day and a week. But there were some notably shorter durations. In a study to compare paper and electronic visual analogue scales on subjective motivation to eat, Whybrow et al. (2006) reports that the paper and ePRO versions were completed 'immediately one after the other'. Desire to eat is clearly a condition that changes rapidly but one would query the non-existent durations in this study. Similarly, one would query a duration of ten minutes (Chen et al., 2007). In some reports of scales authored by Juniper, (Caro et al. (2001), Juniper et al. (2007)) the duration of administration was two hours, but then a high ICC value (at least 0.95 point estimate) was required to establish equivalence, perhaps by way of compensation.

Test-retest reliability

The FDA PRO Guidance notes that test-retest reliability is an important property of an instrument but this is mentioned in the context of full psychometric validation of the entire instrument. Test-retest reliability measures the ability of the instrument to produce the same score if the underlying conditions are the same. Test-retest reliability is assessed by the ICC; the calculation is as before except that the fixed effect factor for mode of administration is replaced by one for the administration order (first or second).

The FDA guidance does not mention a requirement for a test-retest component in respect of showing equivalence to the original validated instrument when the mode of administration is changed. This seems reasonable – if a changed mode of administration is equivalent to the original validated instruments then one can expect it to have the same test–retest properties. Support for this position comes from the Gwaltney meta-analysis (Gwaltney et al., 2008). The authors found four studies, encompassing 44 scales (although note a collection of VAS scales would count as multiple scales if no overall summary measure was derived) that examined paper PRO vs ePRO concordance and paper-paper test – retest reliability. In these studies the average correlation between the paper and ePRO scores had a value of 0.88 which was comparable to the test-retest reliability of the paper measure (0.91). Thus the authors argue that administering an ePRO test is just like re-administering the paper test a second time.

In spite of the above argument, about 10 per cent of investigators have investigated test-retest reliability of a modified PRO instrument either as a separate study (Velikova et al., 1999) or as an add-on administration to the crossover study designed to show equivalence. In a comparison of two modes performed by crossover, there are essentially three ways of adding the additional administration:

a)   The second administration can be repeated for both crossover orders. Thus the orders would be paper/ePRO/ePRO and ePRO/paper/paper. The advantage of doing this is that it allows a direct comparison of the test-retest properties of paper and the ePRO instrument. This was the approach taken by Bushnell et al. (2006) who concluded that the paper and ePRO reliabilities were broadly comparable e.g. the overall IBS score reliability was 0.99 for paper and 0.95 for ePRO.

b)   The second administration can be repeated just for the paper/ePRO order to reduce effort and cost. This was the approach taken in two studies, although only a random subset of patients in the relevant order underwent the third administration (Kleinman (2001), Lam et al. (2009)). On each of the 6 sub-scales administered, the ICC was higher for the ePRO test-retest than the paper vs. ePRO reliability but no formal comparison was performed.

c)   A second administration of the paper scale can be added to both orders. This allows a comparison of the paper test-retest against the paper/ePRO reliability. It would seem appropriate to use only the data from the second and third periods for this comparison. This approach is answering a slightly different question from the test-retest.

If one of these approaches is followed, then the extra burden on the subjects has to be considered with conceivably a higher drop-out rate after period 1. The additional possibility of memory effects and/or changes in the underlying disease state also have to be considered. If approach b) is opted for, then there should be adequate control of the randomisation mechanism, including the ability to conduct a retrospective audit. This is to ensure that the process has not been subverted; the investigator could conceivably exercise selection bias by only placing subjects who she/he considers more reliable in the order with the third administration.

In summary, I contend there is no need to do a separate test-retest study unless there are circumstances which make the investigator consider it is particularly warranted. If it is deemed that one is desirable, then it can be performed as a separate study or as an add-on administration to an existing study. If it is felt that adding-on an additional administration is not suitable in a crossover study, then a parallel group study could be considered. A repeat administration in a parallel group study also allows a direct comparison of the paper and ePRO test-retest properties.

Other design considerations

The ideal situation is that the modified instrument is validated before it is used in a therapeutic trial or other investigative study. While this is the FDA's preference, the FDA has indicated there are cases where validation has been performed within a therapeutic study, (Burke, 2008) but this is done at the sponsor's risk. The FDA would expect such a validation to be done before the start of any Phase III trial and this would seem consistent with standard practice about the Phase III trial being of a confirmatory nature. If validation is carried out within a therapeutic study, then it has the advantage of ensuring that validation is carried out using the population in which it is intended that the instrument is used.

One way to do the validation within a therapeutic study is to perform both the paper and ePRO assessments during a screening period. In this way the actual randomised portion of the trial is not compromised. For practical reasons it may be appropriate to limit such a sub-study to a single site. Similarly there may be the possibility of simply recruiting extra patients who meet the study criteria, but just enrolling them in the validation study; this requires that recruitment is not an issue, which is seldom the case. Alternatively, the instruments may be administered within the trial, albeit with some risk to the trial interpretation if equivalence is not subsequently demonstrated. Wilson et al. (2004) report an application in which there was full crossing of two treatments and two modes of administration (paper and IVR) so that there were four treatment/mode orders.

ANALYSIS CONSIDERATIONS

Good statistical practice

The ICH (International Conference on Harmonisation) E9 regulatory requirements underlying the statistical analysis of therapeutic trials should generally be adhered to as they represent sound practice (ICH, 1998). An analysis plan containing all the primary analyses should be drawn up before the study starts with the major elements included in the study protocol, including statistical models, value for δ, and limits for decision criteria. As the analyses of ePRO mode equivalence studies are not so onerous then there would seem no reason not to write the entire analysis plan in advance of the study start. As outlined by the ICH guidance, the plan would ideally detail the approach to be taken with missing values and outliers. The guidance notes that one approach for dealing with outliers is to perform one analysis with the actual values and at least one other analysis eliminating or reducing the outlier effect. Outliers have been observed in mode comparison studies (Ring, 2008).

Another area detailed in the analysis plan should be rules for inclusion and exclusion of data in so far as these can be foreseen. In therapeutic trials, it is usual practice that separate analyses are conducted for all patients (intent-to treat) and those treated as per protocol without significant deviations or data anomalies. In therapeutic equivalence trials, the roles of these two analyses differ from trials designed to show superiority of one of the treatments (CHMP, 2000). The situation is different for mode equivalence trials and it can be argued that only a per protocol analysis is necessary as the modified instrument need only be equivalent if used as intended. But if this argument is accepted then, given the trial will not be blinded, defining the general data exclusion rules in advance of the trial conduct becomes even more important. At a minimum the general data exclusion rules should be drawn up before the analysts examine the data.

There is the possibility of performing an interim analysis with a view to ceasing recruitment early if equivalence is demonstrated. If this is the case then the details of this should be in the analysis plan including precise details of the decision criteria. The price paid for the possibility of early stopping is a small increase in the total sample size; the design would require a potential commitment to enrol the full number of subjects. The probability of early stopping depends on the characteristics of the design and the underlying unknown ICC. If an interim analysis is employed but the study continues through to its full planned size, then this should be reflected in the computation of the final confidence intervals using appropriate software e.g. EAST® (Cytel Inc., 2008). Interim analyses have to the best of my knowledge not yet featured in ePRO mode equivalence studies, but it can be expected that this will happen in the same manner as they have in the bioequivalence field (GSK Study Register (2005), Bandyopadhyay and Dragalin (2007), AstraZeneca (1999), Gould (1995)). This is because recruitment to studies where the patient derives no benefit can be slow (Bandyopadhyay and Dragalin, 2007).

Another area considered by the ICH E9 guidance (1998) is the area of multiplicity where the investigator has to consider whether any adjustments for multiple comparisons are necessary if multiple endpoints are being studied. The concern is not to have too high a Type I error for the study as whole. Often this is achieved by use of a multiple comparisons technique with the most well known being the Bonferroni. So what approach should one take if it is desired to test several ePRO scales against their paper equivalents in a mode validation study? The Bonferroni, or some similar criterion could be used but this would seem unduly conservative. It is the per error scale rate that is important as the scales being tested need not necessarily be used together in future therapeutic studies. None of the papers in my reference sample adjusted for multiplicity even though many of the papers tested several scales.

Considerations for crossover designs

If the study design is a crossover study, then one question is whether period of administration be included as a factor in the analysis model? The answer is affirmative following the usual principle that you 'analyse as you randomize' to increase precision and preserve the Type I error. For the analysis of means this would mean including the period effect in the ANOVA – this was rarely done in the literature sample with just a few exceptions (Junker (2008), Velikova (1999)). For the analysis of the ICC, this would mean estimating the period component of variance using an appropriate statistical package such as PROC MIXED in SAS® (SAS Institute, 2001) and including it as a component of the denominator for the ICC formula; subsequent computation of the confidence interval would then have to be done by the bootstrap as analytical formulae do not exist. Perhaps due to the extra effort involved, no articles in the literature sample did this. Simulation studies are required to ascertain the operating characteristics of this approach.

A related question is whether an effect for order of administration, which would equate to what is called a carryover effect, be tested for prior to pooling the data across treatment orders? In therapeutic trials practice is currently against this with the emphasis being more on having an adequate duration to avoid carryover (ICH, 1998) and not to perform such tests. In principle this also applies to the present situation. But as discussed earlier, durations are sometimes quite short and thus, if there is any doubt, I would propose testing for carryover. If a carryover effect is found then the study may not be able to provide unambiguous support for mode equivalence as the estimator of the differences between modes is biased. Within the sample of references, most pooled without any prior testing. One study (Bushnell et al., 2006) analysed the two treatment orders separately with no attempt to pool; this has problems with lack of power and multiplicity. A minority of studies pooled over orders after testing for carryover – one found a significant sequence effect but pooled anyway because it was small (Kleinman, 2001).

In passing we note one study computed the ICC using an ANOVA model adjusted for the fixed effects of patient, PRO mode and order (Ring, 2008). The rationale for this is not clear.

Considerations for visual analogue scales

If it is desired to claim equivalence of an ePRO instrument to the original paper version then no alterations should be made to the paper version at the time of administration or analysis. For instance Cook (2004) compares the paper and computer versions of Short-form McGill Pain Questionnaire. A component of this scale is a 100mm Visual Analogue Scale (VAS). But their computer system would only allow VAS entries on an 11 point (0–10) scale. Accordingly the paper entries were rounded on to the equivalent 11-point scale. This is clearly inappropriate if the objective is to demonstrate equivalence to the originally validated paper scale.

Typically, hand-held computers cannot accommodate full reproduction of 100mm VAS scales. For instance, Whybrow (2006) reports screen sizes of 66 mm and 52 mm for different hand-held versions of the VAS. In performing equivalence studies, standard practice is to convert the hand-held VAS scores to the 101 point scale by use of a simple transformation e.g. multiplying the ePRO score by 100*52. This seems reasonable as there is good evidence for the equivalence of the paper and ePRO versions of the VAS. Jamison et al. (2002) showed equivalence of the measures using a 5cm ePRO VAS in healthy volunteers; the ePRO VAS scale occupied 142 pixels and so the precision of recording is similar to that of paper. Equivalence has also been demonstrated in patients suffering from chronic pain (Junker, 2008) and panic disorder (Van Duinen et al., 2008), the former involving a handheld and the latter involving a tablet PC. Visual inspection of the six studies specifically mentioned as using VAS in a meta-analysis suggests good agreement (Gwaltney et al., 2008). But, caution is warranted. In their study of six VAS, Whybrow et al. (2006) noted negative bias for scales with mean scores less than the mid-point, and positive bias for scales with mean scores greater than the mid-point. Their explanation was that subjects tended to avoid using the extremes of the VAS when using the hand-held version. This would thus appear to be a manifestation of the well-known end aversion bias (Streiner and Norman (2003), Torrance et al. (2001)). Although this study can be criticised, the authors noted that their results were consistent with previous work on electronic versions of their scales. Thus, when conducting equivalence studies, sensitivity analyses should be conducted to ensure that a linear transformation is the most appropriate. For instance the reverse of the arc-sine transformation would have the effect of stretching out the extremes of the scales upon conversion (Snedecor and Cochran, 1989). Consideration could also be given to indenting the scale anchors by 1.5mm (Almiron-Roig et al., 2009).

Other analysis considerations

Secondary analyses that may be considered are individual item equivalence and computation of Chronbach's alpha. The first mentioned involves comparing the individual items/questions by computing the percentage of patients who gave the same response on both occasions together with the proportion showing agreement within one response category in either direction. Even if overall equivalence is established, this can be informative. An example of such an approach is given in Velikova (1999). Computing Chronbach's alpha for each scale allows an informal comparison of the measure of internal consistency; the values can also be referenced against any previous validation studies. This approach was undertaken by about one third of papers in the sample of references.

Conclusion

Within this chapter, I have tried to lay out considerations for designing, conducting and analysing PRO mode equivalence studies to the highest standards. From the various examples shown, it is clear that best practice is not always followed in the literature and, in truth, I found that the practice in published ePRO versus PRO validation papers is poor relative to the standards in therapeutic trials which have been much improved since the publication of the CONSORT guidelines (Altman et al., 2001). Consideration of more recently published studies suggests that standards are improving and hopefully this chapter will help continue this trend.

In closing it is important to note that equivalence studies need not be onerous, lengthy or expensive. They can often be conducted within a population of 50 or fewer subjects. Finally, if a PRO-based labeling claim is intended, it is critical that content validity be confirmed for the original instrument before pursuing measurement equivalence. The FDA's public statements make it very clear that content validity must be first established for the PRO instrument if the goal is to pursue a PRO-based labeling claim.

References

Agel, J. et al. (2001). Comparison of interactive voice response and written self-administered patient surveys for clinical research, *Orthopaedics*, 24: 1155–1157.

Almiron-Roig, E. et al. (in press) Validation of a new hand-held electronic appetite rating system against the pen and paper method, *Appetite*, available on line October 01 2009.

Altman, D.G. et al. (2001). The revised CONSORT statement for reporting randomised trials: explanation and elaboration, *Annals of Internal Medicine*, 134(8): 663–694.

AstraZeneca. A bioequivalence study with 40 mg H 199/18 comparing a new tablet formulation with a capsule formulation in healthy subjects. Astra hassle. 7th May 1999. www.astrazenecaclinicaltrials.com/sites/133/imagebank/typeArticleparam528367/SH-QBE-0035.pdf [Accessed Nov. 12th 2009].

Bandyopadhyay, N. and Dragalin, V. (2007). Implementation of an adaptive group sequential design in a bioequivalence study, *Pharmaceut. Statist*, 6: 115–122.

Bland J.M. and Altman, D.G. (1995). Comparing two methods of clinical measurement: a personal history, *Int J Epidemiol*, 24(3): 7–14.

Burke, L. Personal communication 24th June 2008. Laurie Burke is Director, Study Endpoints and Label Development, FDA.

Burke, L.B., Kennedy D,L. and Miskala, P.H. et al. (2008). the use of patient-reported outcome measures in the evaluation of medical products for regulatory approval, *Clinical Pharmacology & Therapeutics*, 84: 281–283.

Burton, C. et al. (2007). Are electronic diaries useful for symptoms research? A systematic review, *J Psychosom Res*, 62(5): 553–61.

Bushnell, D.M. et al. (2006). Validation of electronic data capture of the irritable bowel syndrome – quality of life measure, the work productivity and activity impairment questionnaire for irritable bowel syndrome and the euroqol, *Value in Health*, 9: 98–105.

Cappelleri, J.C. and Ting, N.A. (2003). Modified large-sample estimator approach to approximate interval estimation for a particular intraclass correlation coefficient, *Statist. Med*, 22: 1861–1877.

Caro, J.J. et al. (2001). Does implementation of questionnaires used in asthma alter responses compared to paper implementation? *Quality of Life Research*, 10: 683–691.

Chen, T-H. et al. (2007). Crossover randomized controlled trial of the electronic version of the Chinese SF-36, *J Zhejiang Univ Sci B*, 8: 604–608.

Committee for Proprietary Medicinal Products. Points to consider on switching between superiority and non-inferiority. 27 July 2000. CPMP/EWP/482/99. www.emea.europa.eu/pdfs/human/ewp/048299en.pdf [Accessed Nov. 12th 2009].

Cook, A.J. et al. (2004). Electronic pain questionnaires: a randomized, crossover comparison with paper questionnaires for chronic pain assessment, *Pain*, 110: 310–317.

Coons, S.J., Gwaltney, C.J. and Hays, R.D. et al. (2009). On behalf of the ISPOR ePRO Task Force. Recommendations on evidence needed to support measurement equivalence between electronic and paper-based patient-reported outcome (PRO) measures: ISPOR ePRO good research practices task force report, *Value Health*, 12(4): 419–429.

Cytel Inc. EAST® Proprietary Software Release v5. 2008 Cytel Inc. Cambridge MA.

Dunn, J.A, Arakawa, R., Greist, J.H. and Clayton, A.H. (2007). Assessing the onset of antidepressant-induced sexual dysfunction using interactive voice response technology, *J Clin Psychiatry*, 68: 525–532.

Emery, M-P., Perrier, L-L. and Acquadro, C. (2005). Patient-Reported Outcome and Quality of Life Instruments Database (PROQOLID): frequently asked questions, *Health and Quality of Life Outcomes*, 3:12doi:10.1186/1477-7525-3-12. http://www.hqlo.com/content/3/1/12 [Accessed Nov. 12th 2009].

Food and Drug Administration. Guidance for industry: patient-reported outcome measures: use in medical product development to support labeling claims (final), December 2009. Available at: http://www.fda.gov/downloads/Drugs/GuidanceComplianceRegulatoryInformation/Guidances/UCM193282.pdf [Accessed December 8, 2009].

Gould, A.L. (1995). Group sequential extensions of a standard bioequivalence testing procedure, *Journal of Pharmacokinetics and Biopharmaceutics*, 23: 57–86.

GSK Study Register. A single dose, group sequential, four period crossover study to demonstrate bioequivalence between 37.5 mg and 12.5 mg + 25 mg controlled release paroxetine tablets manufactured at Cidra. Glaxo Smith Kline 10 Oct 2005. www.gsk-clinicalstudyregister.com/files/pdf/2132.pdf [Accessed Nov. 12th 2009].

Gwaltney, C.J. et al. (2008). Equivalence of electronic and paper-and-pencil administration of patient-reported outcome measures: a meta-analytic review, *Value in Health*, 11(2): 322–33.

International Conference on Harmonisation, E-9 Document, 'Guidance on Statistical Principles for Clinical Trials,' Federal Register 63 (179) 49583-49598 1998. http://www.ich.org/cache/compo/475-272-1.html#E9 http://www.fda.gov/cder/guidance/91698.pdf [Accessed Nov. 12th 2009].

Jamison, R.N. et al. (2002). Comparative study of electronic vs. paper VAS ratings: a randomized, crossover trial using healthy volunteers, *Pain*, 99: 341–347.

Jones, B., Jarvis, P., Lewis, J.A. and Ebbutt, AF. (1996). Trials to assess equivalence: the importance of rigorous methods, *BMJ*, 313:36–9; 62(9): 1091–1093.

Juniper, E.F., Riis, B. and Juniper, B.A. (2007). Development and validation of an electronic version of the Rhinoconjunctivitis Quality of Life Questionnaire, *Allergy*.

Junker, U. (2008). Paper versus electronic rating scales for pain assessment: a prospective, randomised, cross-over validation study with 200 chronic pain patients, *Current Medical Research and Opinion*, 24: 1797–1806.

Kleinman, L.A. (2001). Comparative trial of paper-and-pencil versus computer administration of the Quality of Life in Reflux and Dyspepsia (QOLRAD) Questionnaire, *Medical Care*, 39: 181–189.

Lam, M.Y. et al. (2009). Validation of interactive voice response system administration of the short inflammatory bowel disease questionnaire, *Inflamm Bowel Dis*, 15: 599–607.

Lane, S.J. et al. (2006). A review of randomized controlled trials comparing the effectiveness of hand held computers with paper methods for data collection, *BMC Med Inform Decis Mak*, 31; 6: 23. http://www.biomedcentral.com/1472-6947/6/23 [Accessed Nov. 12th 2009].

Lee, P. (2006). Why Go ePRO? *European Pharmaceutical Contractor*. Spring.

Liu, J-P. and Chow, S.C. (1992). Sample Size Determination for the Two One-Sided Tests Procedure in Bioequivalence, *Journal of Pharmacokinetics and Biopharmaceutics*, 20: 101–104.

McEntegart, D. (2008). Blocked Randomization. In *Wiley Encyclopedia of Clinical Trials*, (eds) D'Agostino, R., Sullivan, L. and Massaro, J., Hoboken: John Wiley & Sons, Inc. doi 10.1002/9780471462422.eoct301.

McEntegart, D. (2008). Validation of Modified PRO Instruments: The State of the Statistical Science. Presentation at Drug Information Association Annual Meeting in Boston U.S. June 25th 2008.

McEntegart, D.J. (2003). The pursuit of balance using stratified and dynamic randomisation techniques. *Drug Inf. J*, 37: 293–308.

McGraw, K.O. and Wong, S.P. (1996). Forming Inferences about some intraclass correlation coefficients. *Psychological Methods*, 1: 30–46 (erratum *Psychological Methods*, 1: 390).

McKenzie, S. (2004). Proving the eDiary dividend. *Applied Clinical Trials*, 13: 54–68. http://appliedclinicaltrialsonline.findpharma.com/appliedclinicaltrials/Feature+Article/Proving-the-eDiary-Dividend/ArticleStandard/Article/detail/98374 [Accessed Nov. 12th 2009].

Pouwer, F. et al. (1988). A comparison of the standard and the computerized versions of the Well-being Questionnaire (WBQ) and the Diabetes Treatment Satisfaction Questionnaire (DTSQ). *Quality of Life Research*, 7: 33–38.

Ring, A.E. (2008). a randomized study of electronic diary versus paper and pencil collection of patient-reported outcomes in patients with non-small cell lung cancer. *Patient*, 1: 105–113.

SAS Institute. (2001). SAS® Proprietary Software Release 8.2 (for Windows) Cary, NC, SAS Institute Inc.

Scientific Advisory Committee of the Medical Outcomes Trust. (2002). Assessing health status and quality-of-life instruments: Attributes and review criteria. *Qual Life Res*, 11: 193–205.

Shea, H.E. et al. (2004). Electronic Patient Diaries in a Clinical Trial – the Holistic Approach. *Drug Inf. Journal*, 38: 225–238.

Shrout, P.E. and Fleiss, J.L. (1979). Intraclass correlations: uses in assessing rater reliability. *Psychol Bull*, 86: 420–8.

Snedecor, G.W. and Cochran, W.G. (1989). *Statistical Methods* (8th edition). Oxford: Blackwell Publishing, 289–290.

Streiner, D.L. and Norman G.R. (2003). *Health Measurement Scales: A Practical Guide to Their Development and Use* (3rd edition). New York: Oxford University Press.

Stuart, A., Ord, K. and Arnold, S. (1999). *Kendall's Advanced Theory of Statistics* 2A. London: Arnold, a member of the Hodder Headline Group, 25.37–25.43.

Tian, L. and Cappelleri, J.C. (2004). A new approach for interval estimation and hypothesis testing of a certain intraclass correlation coefficient: the generalized variable method. *Statist. Med*, 23: 2125–2135.

Torrance, G.W., Feeny, D.H., Furlong, W.J. (2001). Visual analog scales. Do they have a role in the measurement of preferences for health states? *Med Decis Making*, 21: 329–334.

Van Duinen, M. and Rickelt, G.E. (2008). Validation of the electronic Visual Analogue Scale of Anxiety. *Prog Neuropsychopharmacol Biol Psychiatry*, 32: 1045–7.

Velikova, G. et al. (1999). Automated collection of quality-of-life data: a comparison of paper and computer touch-screen questionnaires. *J Clin Oncol*, 17(3): 998–1007.

Walter, S.D., Eliasziw, M. and Donner, A. (1998). Sample size and optimal designs for reliability studies. *Statistics in Medicine*, 17: 101–110.

Whybrow, S., Stephen, J.R. and Stubbs, R.J. (2006). The evaluation of an electronic visual analogue scale system for appetite and mood. *Eur J Clin Nutr*, 60: 558–60.

Willke, R.J., Burke, L.B. and Erickson, P. (2004). Measuring treatment impact: a review of patient-reported outcomes and other efficacy endpoints in approved product labels. *Controlled Clinical Trials*, 25: 535–552.

Wilson, S.J. et al. (2004). Evaluation of actigraphy and automated telephoned questionnaires to assess hypnotic effects in insomnia. *Int Clin Psychopharmacol*, 19: 77–84.

Yan, L. (2008). The Use of the Bootstrap Methods in Crossover Designs. M.Sc Project, Nottingham University, August 2008.

Appendix

Cappelleri and Ting (2003) considered the performance of three different estimators of the ICC for a two way random effects model with effects for rater (mode) and subject. In the case of only one factor in addition to subject, the random effects model is equivalent to the mixed effects model and all computational formulae are the same. They generated three chi-squared values representing the mean squares between subjects, between raters (modes) and error. Thirty-six parameter sets reflecting different values of the mean squares (and hence different underlying values of the ICC) were considered. For each of the 36 parameter sets, 25,000 simulated values were generated. The simulated values for the mean squares were substituted into the appropriate formulae and confidence intervals were calculated. In each of the 36 parameter sets, the true underlying ICC is known. Thus the coverage of the interval was determined by calculating the number of intervals that contained the true underlying value of ICC and then dividing by 25,000. The median coverage over the 36 datasets was then determined, thus representing the coverage over a range of ICC values.

We restrict ourselves to the case of two modes and a one-sided 95 per cent lower confidence bound. The results are presented in Table 9.1. It can be seen that the coverage of the standard two moment estimator is quite poor with, for example, 88 per cent coverage for a sample size of 50. The modified three moments estimator is a little less conservative with a value of 91.9 per cent, the modified large sample (MLS) estimator was too liberal with a value of 97.9 per cent. Note that an increase in the number of subjects resulted in a shorter width for each of the intervals.

The above results are unfortunately not presented by underlying values of the ICC. This was however done for coefficients 0.60, 0.75 and 0.90 under three different values for true rater/mode to error variability 0.5, 1.0 and 4.0; this exercise was performed only for the situations of three and five raters/modes. Looking at this particular subset does not seem to suggest that coverage of the estimated intervals is particularly improved for higher values of ICC. But focusing on the MLS estimator for three modes, sample size 50 and higher ICC values of 0.75 and 0.90, the median of the six coverages presented is 95.85 per cent. Thus it would seem the MLS estimator is adequate for our purposes.

The authors also recommend the MLS estimator as having the best performance of the three methods. In the sense that it is liberal and thus more likely to reject equivalence against a pre-specified lower bound than it should, then this estimator can be recommended for equivalence studies. In a later paper (Tian and Cappelleri, 2004), one of the authors compared the MLS approach to a generalised confidence interval approach and found the latter to be closer to the correct nominal coverage for two-sided intervals. But as the MLS tended to perform slightly better for one-sided intervals, which are our usual focus, then this does not alter our conclusion.

The authors mention that bootstrapping methodology is a viable alternative. This has been confirmed in preliminary simulations of 2,000 datasets (Yan, 2008). For the two-way fixed effects model and the scenario most typical of an ePRO validation study (sample size 50, true ICC=0.80), the 2 moment estimator had a coverage of 89.9 per cent compared to the percentile bootstrap coverage of 91.6 per cent for normal data. The percentile bootstrap also did better for non-normal data.

Table 9.1   Median per cent coverage of approximate 95 per cent lower confidence bounds for ICC across 36 parameter sets (based on 25,000 simulations) for case of 2 modes

Number of subjects	2 moment estimator	Modified 3 moments	Modified large sample
10	95.5	96.2	98.7
25	92.3	94.4	98.5
50	88.0	91.9	97.9
100	82.0	89.1	97.2

10

ePRO Applications and Personal Mobile Phone Use: Compliance Documentation and Patient Support

Breffni Martin

Introduction

Most of this book is concerned with the use of ePRO in the context of clinical research. This is a highly regulated environment in which it is not sufficient to have good data but is necessary to demonstrate that this is the case. This places a high premium on the ability of electronic systems to provide documentation around compliance and to support the patient in the context of a complex protocol.

Electronic methods are potentially also of great value in the regular provision of health care to patients. The model is often a bit different when ePRO is used in this way. Data are not averaged over a large sample to support the efficacy of a treatment, but are used either directly by the patient or by the practitioner responsible for adjusting the patient's treatment. Either way the individual patient becomes even more central to the process.

Obesity is an example of a condition where involvement of the patient is crucial. Arguably it is the number one healthcare problem in the developed world (Wang and Beydoun, 2007). Its incidence is increasing and is now also significantly affecting the developing world (Prentice, 2006; Caballero, 2007). Efforts to date to treat the disease both at patient and at a public health level have for the most part failed. Obese patients present a number of unique and difficult problems in terms of health data capture. To understand these problems it is necessary to understand the context of the disease from the point of view of the patients, their families, their physicians, the healthcare system and society at large. To this end we will examine the nature and cause of the disease and epidemic, review attitudes to obesity, examine problems in traditional paper-based data capture, and outline how ePRO solutions can address these problems. Stemming from those solutions, we will review how the concepts in regard to data capture in the context of obesity may be extended to other conditions.

Figure 10.1   The Venus of Willendorf, 22,000–24,000 B.C., in the collection of the Natural History Museum, Vienna

Origins and Etiology of Obesity

Obesity is unknown in free-living wild animals. In human society it has been present at low levels as far back as 22,000 years ago as shown by Stone Age artefacts of obese women, often called Venus figures (see Figure 10.1). It is likely that obesity became possible at the advent of agriculture, which gave rise to the combination of extended leisure time and surplus food. In times of famine or natural disaster, obesity probably conferred a significant survival advantage so that human populations that were forced through famine-driven genetic bottlenecks were selected for genetic traits for obesity. The genetics of obesity are beyond the scope of this paper but to summarise, famine bottlenecks have been shown to select out 'satiety' genes. Once the biological mechanism that switches off hunger when the subject has eaten enough fails, the possibility of extreme weight gain becomes a reality.

An instructive example can be seen amongst the population of certain Polynesian islands. Before the Second World War the islands were relatively isolated from the modern world. Life on the islands was characterised by long periods of relative prosperity interrupted by occasional disastrous tropical storms. In normal times food was obtained principally by fishing and by harvesting and preparing breadfruit and other vegetables and fruits, both activities requiring considerable physical effort. Periodically a tropical storm would wipe out all fruit and vegetables, as well as boats for fishing, meaning that the local population would starve until food could re-grow and fishing boats could be replaced. During this period only those individuals who had a high body weight would survive; those who were thin would die of starvation and their 'satiety' genes would be lost to the population. In recent decades, cheap western food has become available so that exercise in harvesting and preparing food is no longer necessary and traditional foods are eschewed in favour of fatty, sugary, western foods. Because of the lack of a biological mechanism for limiting food intake, these islands now have the highest rates of obesity on the planet (McGarvey, 1991; Keighley et al., 2006).

It is important to note that the Polynesian obesity epidemic is reinforced by Polynesian cultural mores because, in the past, obesity was valued as a survival mechanism. This positive view of obesity, emblematic of beauty, strength and power, is common in many other traditional societies (Kumanyika, 1993; Bindon et al., 2007).

Obesity may also be exacerbated by repeat dieting, where it is postulated that dieting causes a lowering of Basal Metabolic Rate resulting in the modification of food-intake set points. This may cause the well-documented phenomenon of weight gain rebound after dieting. These issues are still controversial: Hill (2004) provides a short and very readable introduction to this area.

A Global Epidemic

Over one third of the population of the USA is obese and a further third is overweight. Globally about 1.6 billion adults are overweight or almost a quarter of the world's population. On current trends about 700 million adults will be obese by 2015 (Huang and Glass, 2008).

The statistics are of particular concern when it comes to children. We now have a situation where up to a quarter of those under the age of 5 in the UK are overweight. In the EU, 22 million school children are overweight and of these 1.2 million are obese and their number is rising by at least 300,000 each year (Dehghan et al., 2005).

Furthermore we are now seeing data to suggest that obesity is becoming a significant problem in developing countries, particularly with the new urban middle classes. In one study in India it was shown that among this group 30 per cent of schoolchildren were overweight – similar to the situation in Europe. And the problem is increasing, tracking economic growth in these countries. Even in China, around 14.7 per cent of the population is overweight, and 2.6 per cent obese. Most worrying was data regarding school children that showed the prevalence of overweight and obesity in children aged 7–18 years increased 28 times and actual obesity increased four times between 1985 and 2000 (Raj et al., 2007; Wu, 2006).

Health Consequences of Obesity

Obesity is not just a question of aesthetics but a very real danger to life and health. Obesity related-diseases include:

- 80 per cent of type II diabetes is related to obesity;

- 70 per cent of Cardiovascular disease is related to obesity;

- 42 per cent of breast and colon cancer is diagnosed among obese individuals;

- 30 per cent of gall bladder surgery is related to obesity;

- 26 per cent of obese people have high blood pressure (see Guh et al., 2009).

Childhood obesity presents particular risks with one in four overweight children showing early signs of type II diabetes (impaired glucose tolerance) and 60 per cent already having one risk factor for heart disease (Spiotta and Luma, 2008).

Social and Cultural Factors in Obesity

Obesity is caused by two main factors: over-eating and under-exercising. Generally it is the effect of these two factors in childhood that leads to obesity in adulthood. The reason for the recent epidemic growth in obesity can be tracked to the increased availability of high fat, high sugar fast food and the recent growth of sedentary forms of entertainment and leisure activities. In effect, unlike past generations, modern children eat more food and much of it is the wrong kind; they also take less exercise because of the time they spend on the internet, watching TV or playing video games.

The US fast food industry has grown from $6 billion in 1970 to $110 billion in 2000. The usage of video games, TV, DVD and Internet have grown exponentially over the same period, with children being specifically targeted for unhealthy food products. Eight to 18-year-olds average 44.5 hours per week in front of a TV, video game or computer.

To summarise, the lack of exercise and too much fatty, sugary food in childhood adversely impacts the individual's ability to control food intake and breaks down the normal control mechanisms. This may be exacerbated by a genetic predisposition to obesity discussed above. Obese children will generally spend their entire lives combating the condition, usually to little avail. Despite the fact that being overweight or obese has very negative connotations in our culture, both for cosmetic' and for health reasons, the problem continues to grow (Turner 1978, Olstad and McCargar, 2009).

Attitudes to Obesity

Unlike most other diseases, obesity does not provoke an automatically sympathetic response and this is important in the context of data capture.

THE GENERAL PUBLIC

Attitudes to obesity vary with the cultural context, going from positive in less economically developed regions or periods, to negative in the economically developed West. As societies grow economically, the obese population also increases, tracking changing attitudes. In societies where there is a significant obese/overweight population, this population tends generally to be viewed negatively and this is particularly reflected not just in the media, advertising, and the like, but directly in its impact on overall success in life. The obese are viewed not as victims of a disease but rather as 'lazy and greedy' individuals who are the authors of their own problems. Obese children are often bullied at school and adults are less successful than the general population in terms of earnings and career. Eating may become a rare source of comfort for such children. This reinforces the tendency to conceal, invent or 'forget' how much they eat (Larkin and Pines, 1979; Greenleaf et al., 2006).

PHYSICIANS AND HEALTHCARE PROFESSIONALS

A major survey of over 5000 physicians, of which 620 responded, found that the obese are generally viewed in a negative light by physicians. In one key finding 'More than 50 per cent of physicians viewed obese patients as awkward, unattractive, ugly, and noncompliant', reflecting the opinion of much of the public (Foster et al., 2003). The overall conclusions of this survey suggest that for many physicians, it is a hopeless situation where obese patients present with a range of illnesses, all of which are attributable to the central problem of obesity that itself cannot be resolved. Again, understandably, this tends to make obese patients evasive and non-compliant.

VIEW OF SELF

As a result of this the obese often have a very negative view of themselves, judging themselves to be 'failures' because they cannot control their weight. Participation in dieting and weight-loss activities rarely produces sustained results and this leads to defeatism – 'I've tried dieting and it doesn't work for me' – and low self-esteem. As a result, the obese often conceal or delude themselves regarding their eating and exercise habits. Another reaction may be obstinacy, where the patient refuses to accept there is a serious problem because they feel 'normal' (Myers and Rosen, 1999; Wang et al., 2009)

This has a major impact on the success of data capture from obese study subjects in that subjects will tend to under-report food consumption and over-report exercise. Anecdotally, this has led to situations where reported food consumption was not enough to maintain basal metabolic rate, which, if true, would imply that the patient in question was dead.

Treatment of Obesity

Treatment of obesity depends on the correct diagnosis of the problem. Obesity can be a symptom of several diseases unrelated to eating and these must be excluded. It is then necessary to gather and track information about eating and exercise habits. On the basis of this, the treating healthcare professional, whether a nutritionist, dietician, physician or other, undertakes nutritional counselling and recommends an exercise regimen. Conventional dieting may not be recommended as it may lead to learned helplessness, as well as weight-gain rebound, as discussed previously. In some instances drug therapy may be recommended, though the current arsenal of drugs is of limited usefulness. In some instances mental health counselling and support is required and in extreme circumstances surgical intervention such as bariatric surgery may be indicated, although this carries an inherent 1 per cent mortality risk. For a review of treatment modalities, see Hainer et al. (2008).

The key to treating obesity or to supporting research on obesity-reducing drugs, is the collection of accurate information on food consumption and exercise. To achieve this, the physical, psychological, familial and societal factors must be taken into account.

Traditional Methods of Data Capture from Obese Patients

The traditional methods of gathering data about energy consumption and expenditure involve the following methods:

DIET HISTORIES

These are questionnaires, sometimes self-administered, that ask pre-set, open-ended questions regarding food consumption. An example is the Diet History Questionnaire published by the National Cancer Institute (NCI, 2007).

24-HOUR DIET RECALL

These involve determining the total amount of food consumed in the previous 24 hours and are often conducted by an interviewer or may be computer-assisted (Slimani et al., 2000). They may form part of a diet history questionnaire.

FOOD DIARIES

These are prospective diaries, typically recorded for seven days, where subjects record everything they eat in a timely way. They may involve the use of food models, weighing scales and measuring cups to ensure that data is as accurate as possible (see, e.g. Biltoft-Jensen et al., 2009 for a discussion of diary methodology).

FOOD FREQUENCY QUESTIONNAIRE (FFQ)

These are self-administered questionnaires about usual food consumption over a specified time period of up to one year. They often involve lists of foods and ask the subject to indicate the frequency of consumption of these foods, often including food categories and portion sizes (Yarnell et al., 1983).

FOOD LISTS

These questionnaires target types or groups of foods, often to identify deficiencies in vitamins or minerals (see e.g. Rohrman and Klein, 2003).

MEASURING EXERCISE OR ENERGY EXPENDITURE

Self-reported activity methods include the following methods:

- seven-day physical activity recall interview;

- self-administered physical activity checklist;

- Minnesota leisure time activity questionnaire;

- modifiable activity questionnaire;

- physical activity scale for the elderly;

- Zutphen physical activity questionnaire.

Examples of the use of such measures are given by Craig et al. (2003) and by Richardson et al. (1994, 2001).

And there are several objective methods including:

- use of a pedometer;

- use of an accelerometer device (1 to 3 plane);

- video monitoring;

- direct observation.

Some recent work in this area is described by Harris et al. (2009) and by Yang and Hsu (2009).

If used in conjunction with ePRO, the data collected by the pedometer or accelerometer (discreet strap-on devices) may be manually entered into the electronic system or electronically transferred, either by cable or wirelessly.

Validation

Studies have been undertaken comparing reported food intake against various biomarkers such as the nitrogen content of 24-hour urine. These have produced only moderate agreement between reported consumption and excreted nitrogen and total energy expenditure. The bias is particularly significant with obese subjects. Obese subjects are often private in regard to their eating habits and may not wish to disclose them or to write them down in a diary where they may be read by others. There is no means of checking the contemporaneousness of data entry in paper-based methods – it is well known that the longer after the event, the more positive a spin the subject will report on it (memory bias). Other problems may exist in regard to the attributability and legibility of data. With self-reporting methods how can the investigator be certain the study subjects reported the data themselves; and is the writing legible in open text diaries? For a review of validation work on food questionnaires, see Cade et al. (2004).

In regard to physical activity, obese subjects have been shown to over-report exercise. This can be overcome relatively easily through the use of pedometers or accelerometers, which can electronically estimate most physical activity with a few exceptions such as stationary cycling. Note that techniques such as direct observation and video monitoring, as well as interviewing, produce significant observer effects and can also be influenced by bias on the part of the observer.

Paper-based methods are also heavily resource intensive, involving deployment of an interviewer in the domestic setting, and heavy use of paper that has to be distributed, collected and electronically transcribed.

Potential Role of ePRO for Tracking Food and Exercise in Obesity Research and Treatment

When working with obese study subjects in a clinical context it is often important to have an accurate method of estimating their calorific intake and expenditure. Typically, this would include situations such as:

- clinical research on obesity-reducing drugs;

- clinical research on drugs used on obese patients;

- establishment of baseline data on diet and exercise for the purpose of comparison;

- to gain an understanding of the public health epidemic.

As discussed previously, traditional paper-based methods of deriving these data present several problems:

- bias due to the attitudes of obese study subjects, healthcare professionals and society;

- memory bias where data is reported too long after the event;

- concerns about confidentiality on the part of obese study subjects;

- illegibility of data, particularly in open text diaries;

- uncertainty about the attributability of data. Was the instrument completed by the carer or the subject?

ePRO solutions involving the use of personal handheld devices, mobile phones or IVR systems also present a number of advantages in relation to paper-based methods:

- data are more likely to be reported contemporaneously because the device is 'always on' and carried on the person.

- time of data entry and time of food consumption are both recorded – cramming data entry at the end of the day can be detected.

- the device is password-protected so data entered are confidential and attributable.

- data are de facto legible.

Other significant advantages include the possibility of real-time communication of data to a server for analysis or even for feedback and remedial action if required. The ePRO solution can also be an information delivery system, capable of providing detailed data about food composition and calorific content, and of monitoring performance against preset targets. In this instance, it can potentially act as a cybernetic bio-control system providing feedback to the study subject and alerting him/her when calorific balance is off. (see e.g. Glanz et al. (2003) who report subject acceptance of an IVR obesity management system that provides nutrition and exercise counselling based on patient reported data and responses).

People develop interesting attachments to their personal mobile phone. Studies have shown that people often touch their phone for reassurance even when they do not plan to use it; sales people who use mobile phones in their work can be observed touching and even fondling their phone even when not using it. People arguably develop a relationship with their phone, almost as though it were some sort of religious artefact, and indeed feel lost without it! (Vincent, 2006)

There are about four billion mobile phones connected, roughly one for every two people in the world (www.gsmworld.com, accessed 11/Nov/2009). These numbers give some idea of the potential market for an ePRO type solution using mobile phones.

In summary, personal mobile phones have not only the advantages of attributability, contemporaneity, accuracy, legibility and originality versus paper-based methods, they also have the advantage over dedicated devices that they are specific to the user, ubiquitous, always switched on and always carried on the user's person. Furthermore, the fact that the data is in electronic format means immediate cost gains in terms of transcription, data entry and the logistics of managing huge amounts of paper. Finally people have a distinct comfort factor when using their own phone.

Case Study

An Irish company, Wirefile Ltd., developed an ePRO application called V-Clinic, aimed at the obese/ overweight market.

INITIAL DESIGN

This ePRO product started as a simple calorie-counting JAVA application downloadable to a personal mobile phone. The application enabled the user to enter calories consumed and calories expended with the aim of enabling the user to keep both in balance. A subsequent version of the product added the typical calorific value of various commonly used foodstuffs, as well as standardised values for various types of physical activity. Thus the user could enter 'hamburger', 'coke' and 'walking for 5km' and the application would calculate the calories consumed and expended as a result.

Following testing of this application it was concluded that users would be interested in not only the calories consumed but also in other elements of food composition such as fat, protein and carbohydrate content and subsequently up to 30 food components, including vitamins, minerals, oligo-elements etc., were added. This meant that the system was capable of tracking up to 30 different food components indefinitely by cumulating each element as food was consumed. Similarly, every conceivable type of exercise was added so that an accurate real-time user recorded picture of food consumption and exercise was available in a single package accessible from a personal mobile phone (Figure 10.2).

ON-LINE DATA CAPTURE

To complement the mobile phone data-capture system, an online system was developed. This system included all the features of the phone based system as well as a simpler interface for entering data and sending data to the mobile phone and an administration tool (Figure 10.3). This tool made it possible for an administrator, such as a healthcare dietician or a clinical trial investigator, to monitor and manage several patients.

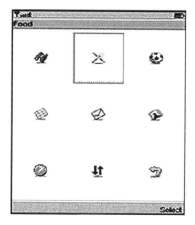 

Figure 10.2   Mobile phone interface

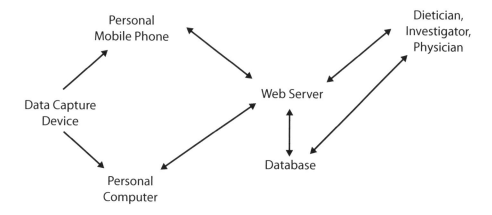

Figure 10.3   Architecture of the obesity application

Other features of the online system include the facility to post photographs of patients and provide the facility for communication and feedback to the patient via text messages, either pre-programmed as alerts or generated manually as ad hoc messages at any time. In particular the online system made it possible for a healthcare professional to keep track of a patient remotely by way of a simple user-friendly interface (Figures 10.4–10.6).

The dietician or clinician can access the accounts of any user, client or study subject. Opening a user account shows a summary of the status of the user to date (Figure 10.5).

This is also the view the users get of their own account. To input food consumption data, the user clicks on the 'Nutrition Diary' and opens the following screen as depicted in Figure 10.6.

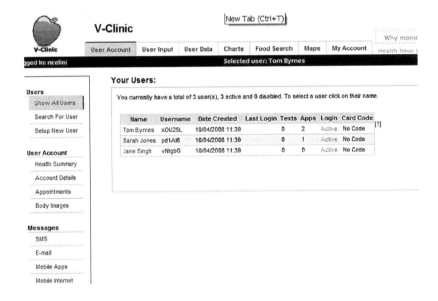

Figure 10.4   **Interface used by the healthcare professional to track a number of patients in the obesity application**

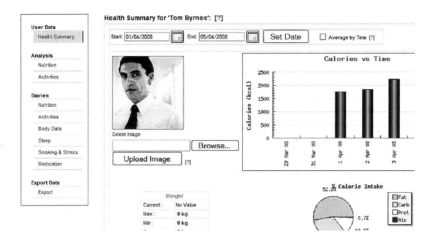

Figure 10.5   Summary details of a single patient in the obesity application

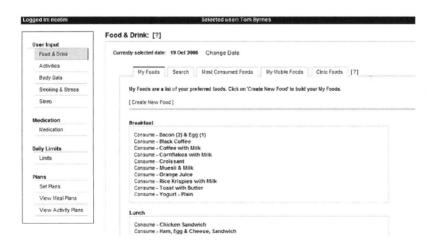

Figure 10.6   Interface used to select foods that will be tracked in the diary of the obesity application

The user pre-selects food options, as many people eat much the same food over the longer term, so that repeat items may be quickly and easily input. To input a new food or to check the nutritional value of food, a search function may be invoked. For example, Figure 10.7 illustrates some of the data presented relating to the nutritional composition of a steak sandwich. This gives an idea of the detail that it is possible to provide with such a system. The data are derived from either the USDA database or from the McCance and Widdowson composition of food database (FSA, 2002) which tracks more than 54 food components, presenting amounts and units, cumulating them but also recording each individual meal. With the screen sizes of modern mobile phones, it is entirely possible to present this detail in an easy to view format. It should be pointed out that the end user does not have to deal with this much detail unless he or she chooses to!

Exercise data can be entered as easily, particularly when the system is combined with a pedometer. A feature of the system of particular interest is the ability of users and administrators to set limits, alarm levels and targets of particular foods or food components and to provide the user with feedback if targets are exceeded.

To summarise, the obesity solution is designed as a one-stop-shop for the administration of a dietician or nutritionist practice, and for health care professionals or investigators studying nutrition and exercise, whether in a clinical or a public health context. In terms of the benefit to users, it is theorised that applications such as V-Clinic may be useful as a cybernetic biofeedback system for people whose normal biological food intake control system has failed for the reasons described above. However specific research would be needed to confirm this proposition.

The model for the obesity solution is based on a complex online application that can generate a small application that is sent to the user's mobile phone and which is tailored to the needs of that particular patient. In this way users benefit from all the power of the full application, with its listings of over 30,000 types of food online, while downloading to their phone only data on the kinds of food they are likely to eat or exercise they are likely to take. Furthermore, because the user's mobile phone is used, the patient is spared from carrying around dedicated devices. Use of the patient's personal mobile phone means that generally speaking the phone will always be with the patient, always on, confidential (accessed by a password), discreet, familiar and low cost. The same devices can also be used as tools for the delivery of advice, remedial action, diet/exercise plans, information on the composition of food and the calorific impact of exercise, as well as the fundamental information balancing calorific intake with output. All of this has implications for other ePRO tools.

1.	Carbohydrate, by difference	25.47	g
2.	Cholesterol	36	mg
3.	Energy kcal	225	kcal
4.	Energy kj	941	kj
5.	Fatty acids, total monounsaturated	2.62	g
6.	Fatty acids, total polyunsaturated	1.64	g
7.	Fatty acids, total saturated	1.87	g
8.	Protein	14.87	g
9.	Total lipid (fat)	6.9	g
10.	Water	51.07	g
11.	Calcium, Ca	45	mg
12.	Copper, Cu	0.108	mg
13.	Iron, Fe	2.53	mg
14.	Magnesium, Mg	24	mg
15.	Manganese, Mn	0.18	mg
16.	Phosphorus, P	146	mg
17.	Potassium, K	257	mg
18.	Selenium, Se	20.6	µg
19.	Sodium, Na	391	mg
20.	Zinc, Zn	2.22	mg
21.	Folate, total	44	µg
22.	Niacin	3.58	mg
23.	Retinol	1	µg
24.	Riboflavin	0.18	mg
25.	Thiamin	0.2	mg
26.	Tryptophan	181	mg
27.	Vitamin B-12	0.77	µg
28.	Vitamin B-6	0.18	mg
29.	Vitamin C, total ascorbic acid	2.7	mg
30.	Alanine	0.887	g
31.	Arginine	0.928	g
32.	Ash	1.7	g
33.	Aspartic acid	1.263	g
34.	Cystine	0.164	g
36.	Folate, DFE	63	µg
37.	Folate, food	17	µg
38.	Folic acid	27	µg
39.	Glutamic acid	2.76	g
40.	Glycine	1.003	g
41.	Histidine	0.443	g
42.	Isoleucine	0.631	g
43.	Leucine	1.157	g
44.	Lysine	1.087	g
45.	Methionine	0.325	g
46.	Pantothenic acid	0.45	mg
47.	Phenylalanine	0.593	g
48.	Proline	0.894	g
49.	Serine	0.607	g
50.	Threonine	0.59	g

Figure 10.7   Typical screenshot showing the first 50 components of a steak sandwich

Applicability of the Model

One of the key features of the obesity case study is the combination of a comprehensive and necessarily complex model of eating behaviour with a relatively simple user interface using a subset of the model tailored to the patient's specific situation. This approach could be used in a number of other circumstances.

DISABILITY AND LIMITATIONS

Patients with disability or conditions that limit their activities often find it is the inability to do specific things that bothers them most. Thus a patient who has been in the habit of walking 20 miles in a day might be very distressed by only being able to walk 12 miles, while another patient might never have walked 12 miles in a day. Some assessments have attempted to address this by personalising questioning. For example, the original Asthma Quality of Life scale (Juniper et al., 1993), a clinic-based instrument, initially asks about specific activities in which the patient is limited, and then asks about these specific activities on subsequent visits. The degree of customisation that can be achieved in this setting is limited, and administration of the customised instrument on paper can be problematic. Electronic implementation of this type of paradigm would be much more satisfactory.

FEEDBACK

Another way in which applications can be customised to individual patient needs is in the provision of feedback, as is done in the obesity application. A further example is in the area of stopping smoking. For example, Whittaker et al. (2008) have developed a multimedia mobile phone programme aimed at young smokers. Individually tailored feedback is also valuable in conditions such as diabetes, where a mobile phone application has been shown to lead to improved metabolic control (Kollman et al., 2007). Clearly diet is also an important aspect of diabetic control, and many of the features of the obesity application are also directly relevant.

TRANSMITTING PICTURES

Wound healing is a topic that is not amenable to conventional PRO assessment. Designing diaries or questionnaires to assess specific symptoms such as pain or tenderness is straightforward, but a clinical assessment collects much more information than this. Mobile phones, though, have cameras, and a patient could take a photo of the wound at regular intervals and transmit this to the clinic, making a great deal of useful information available without the need for the patient to visit. This approach has been described by Chanussot-Deprez and Contreras-Ruiz (2008) and by Martinez-Ramos et al. (2009), see Figure 10.8.

HEALTH SURVEYS

Public health authorities are often interested in conducting research on issues in public health, in particular on health-related phenomena that may pass under the radar of the existing public health system. These include surveys on quality of life, general health, availability of health services or diseases which are not normally reported such as common colds, coughs, headaches etc, particularly in children. These topics are often too detailed to be covered by such large scale surveys as the annual Health Survey for England, and the continuous Scottish Health Survey. Such surveys could identify respondents with conditions of interest and target them for more detailed, focused questionnaires. These could take the form of one-off questionnaires, or more interestingly, as diaries to follow the trajectory of a condition over time. Using the respondent's own phone for such continuing assessments could be extremely cost effective. Mobile phones record their location when connected to the network and this could provide additional valuable information, for example in tracking the epidemiology of allergic conditions or of infectious diseases such as influenza.

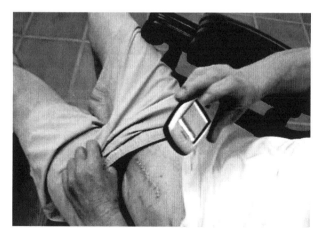

Figure 10.8   Patient photographing a surgical wound, as part of a telecare programme

Source: Photograph from Martinez-Ramos et al. (2009), courtesy of the authors and publisher.

In an all-encompassing model including elements of all of the above, we could imagine a scenario where an obese patient who suffers from allergy gets an alert on the phone that a particular allergen is in the air. He/she could then visit a doctor to get a prescription. The prescription could be delivered directly to the phone from the doctor's surgery either by Bluetooth or through a web service. The patient then visits a pharmacy to collect the prescription which is read electronically from the patient's mobile phone, thereby reducing transcription errors. The pharmacist transfers the current Product Information to the phone again by Bluetooth or similar. The patient now gets a reminder from the phone on when to take the drug and can consult product information at any time on the phone screen should there be any concerns about side-effects. If patients suffer a mild adverse event, in the form of a rash for example, they can use an additional screen on the phone which enables them to enter the ADR data and send it with a photo of the rash to their treating physician, the relevant regulatory agency and the manufacturer. In this way patients can receive immediate advice on what to do which could again be sent directly to their phone and the agency obtains better and timelier pharmacovigilence information. Meanwhile the phone is also being used to follow a recommended eating regimen, record it, capture exercise and provide remedial advice as and when necessary.

Conclusion

The potential of mobile phones as data capture devices increases as they become more widely available, more technically sophisticated and more connected to the internet and other devices. Add to this the fact that they bring all the advantages of eClinical methods in terms of attributability to patient, legibility of data, contemporaneous data entry, accuracy and originality of data, and also confidentiality, privacy, personalisation, familiarity, and comfort to the patient. To this, add again the new, ever more sophisticated, native functions and the ability to access the internet and other services, we can see that the humble mobile phone may soon be the central tool in health data capture (Figure 10.9) in the context of everything from personal medicine, to public health, to pharmacovigilance, to the most sophisticated clinical study.

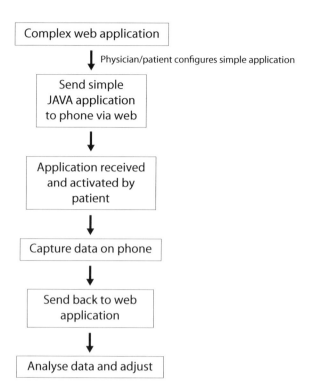

Figure 10.9   Flow Chart for ePRO system using mobile phone with web application

References

Biltoft-Jensen, A., Matthiessen, J. and Rasmussen, L.B. et al. (2009). Validation of the Danish 7-day pre-coded food diary among adults: energy intake v. energy expenditure and recording length, *Br.J Nutr*, 1–9.

Bindon, J., Dressler, W.W. and Gilliland, M.J. et al. (2007). A cross-cultural perspective on obesity and health in three groups of women: the Mississippi Choctaw, American Samoans, and African Americans, *Coll.Antropol*, 31(1): 47–54.

Caballero, B. (2007). The global epidemic of obesity: an overview, *Epidemiol. Rev*, 29: 1–5.

Cade, J.E., Burley, V.J. and Warm, D.L. et al. (2004). Food-frequency questionnaires: a review of their design, validation and utilisation, *Nutr Res Rev*, 17(1): 5–22.

Chanussot-Deprez, C. and Contreras-Ruiz, J. (2008). Telemedicine in wound care, *Int Wound.J*, 5(5): 651–654.

Craig, C.L., Marshall, A.L., Sjostrom, M., Bauman, A. E., Booth, M. L. et al. (2003). International physical activity questionnaire: 12-country reliability and validity, *Med Sci Sports Exerc*, 35(8): 1381–1395.

Dehghan, M., Khtar-Danesh, N. and Merchant, A.T. (2005). Childhood obesity, prevalence and prevention, *Nutr J*, 4: 24.

Food Standards Agency. (2002). McCance and Widdowson's The Composition of Foods integrated dataset (CoF IDS). http://www.food.gov.uk/science/dietarysurveys/dietsurveys/

Foster, G.D., Wadden, T.A., Makris, A.P., Davidson, D., Sanderson, R. S. et al. (2003). Primary care physicians' attitudes about obesity and its treatment, *Obes.Res*, 11(10): 1168–1177.

Glanz, K., Shigaki, D., Farzanfar, R., Pinto, B., Kaplan, B., Friedman, R.H. (2003). Participant reactions to a computerized telephone system for nutrition and exercise counseling, *Patient Education and Counseling*, 49(2): 157–163.

Greenleaf, C., Chambliss, H., Rhea, D.J., Martin, S.B. and Morrow Jr, J.R. (2006). Weight stereotypes and behavioral intentions toward thin and fat peers among white and hispanic adolescents, *Journal of Adolescent Health*, 39(4): 546–552.

Guh, D.P., Zhang, W., Bansback, N., Amarsi, Z., Birmingham, C. L. and Anis, A.H. (2009). The incidence of co-morbidities related to obesity and overweight: a systematic review and meta-analysis, *BMC.Public Health*, 9: 88.

Hainer, V., Toplak, H. and Mitrakou, A. (2008). Treatment modalities of obesity: what fits whom? *Diabetes Care*, 31(2): S269–S277.

Harris, T.J., Owen, C.G., Victor, C.R., Adams, R., Ekelund, U. and Cook, D.G. (2009). A comparison of questionnaire, accelerometer, and pedometer: measures in older people [Miscellaneous Article], *Medicine & Science in Sports & Exercise*, 41(7): 1392–1402.

Hill, A.J. (2004). Does dieting make you fat? *Br.J Nutr*, 92(1): S15–S18.

Huang, T.T.K. and Glass, T.A. (2008). Transforming research strategies for understanding and preventing obesity, *JAMA: The Journal of the American Medical Association*, 300(15): 1811–1813.

Juniper, E.F., Guyatt, G.H., Ferrie, P.J. and Griffith, L.E. (1993). Measuring quality of life in asthma, *Am.Rev.Respir Dis*, 147(4): 832–838.

Keighley, E.D., McGarvey, S.T., Turituri, P. and Viali, S. (2006). Farming and adiposity in Samoan adults, *Am J Hum.Biol*, 18(1): 112–122.

Kollmann, A., Riedl, M., Kastner, P., Schreier, G. and Ludvik, B. (2007). Feasibility of a mobile phone-based data service for functional insulin treatment of type 1 diabetes mellitus patients, *J Med Internet Res*, 9(5): e36.

Kumanyika, S.K. (1993). Special issues regarding obesity in minority populations, *Annals of Internal Medicine*, 119(7) Part 2: 650–654.

Larkin, J.C. and Pines, H.A. (1979). No fat persons need apply: experimental studies of the overweight stereotype and hiring preference, *Work and Occupations*, 6(3): 312–327.

Martinez-Ramos, C., Cerdan, M.T. and Lopez, R.S. (2009). Mobile phone-based telemedicine system for the home follow-up of patients undergoing ambulatory surgery, *Telemedicine and e-Health*, 15: 531–537.

McGarvey, S.T. (1991). Obesity in Samoans and a perspective on its etiology in Polynesians, *American Journal of Clinical Nutrition*, 53(6): 1586S–1594.

Myers, A. and Rosen, J.C. (1999). Obesity stigmatization and coping: relation to mental health symptoms, body image, and self-esteem, *Int J Obes.Relat Metab Disord*, 23(3): 221–230.

National Cancer Institute. Diet History Questionnaire. http://www.riskfactor. cancer.gov/DHQ/forms/2007

Olstad, D.L. and McCargar, L. (2009). Prevention of overweight and obesity in children under the age of 6 years, *Appl.Physiol Nutr Metab*, 34(4): 551–570.

Prentice, A.M. (2006). The emerging epidemic of obesity in developing countries, *International Journal of Epidemiology*, 35(1): 93–99.

Raj, M., Sundaram, K.R. and Paul, M. et al. (2007). Obesity in Indian children: time trends and relationship with hypertension, *Natl Med J India*, 20(6): 288–293.

Richardson, M.T., Leon, A.S. and Jacobs, D.R. et al. (1994). Comprehensive evaluation of the Minnesota leisure time physical activity questionnaire, *Journal of Clinical Epidemiology*, 47(3): 271–281.

Richardson, M.T., Ainsworth, B.E. and Jacobs, D.R. et al. (2001). Validation of the stanford 7-day recall to assess habitual physical activity, *Annals of Epidemiology*, 11(2): 145–153.

Rohrmann, S. and Klein, G. (2003). Development and validation of a short food list to assess the intake of total fat, saturated, mono-unsaturated, polyunsaturated fatty acids and cholesterol, *Eur J Public Health*, 13(3): 262–268.

Slimani, N., Ferrari, P. and Ocke, M. et al. (2000). Standardization of the 24-hour diet recall calibration method used in the European prospective investigation into cancer and nutrition (EPIC): general concepts and preliminary results, *Eur J Clin Nutr*, 54(12): 900–917.

Spiotta, R.T. and Luma, G.B. (2008). Evaluating obesity and cardiovascular risk factors in children and adolescents, *Am Fam Physician*, 78(9): 1052–1058.

Turner, R.W. (1978). Perspectives in coronary prevention, *Postgrad.Med J*, 54(629): 141–148.

Vincent, J. (2006). Emotional attachment and mobile phones, *Knowledge, Technology & Policy*, 19: 39–44.

Wang, Y. and Beydoun, M.A. (2007). The obesity epidemic in the United States – gender, age, socioeconomic, racial/ethnic and geographic characteristics: a systematic review and meta-regression analysis, *Epidemiological Reviews*, 29: 6–28.

Wang, F., Wild, T.C. and Kipp, W. et al. (2009). The influence of childhood obesity on the development of self-esteem, *Health Rep*, 20(2): 21–27.

Whittaker, R., Maddison, R. and McRobbie, H. et al. (2008). A multimedia mobile phone-based youth smoking cessation intervention: findings from content development and piloting studies, *J Med Internet Res*, 10(5): e49.

Wu, Y. (2006). Overweight and obesity in China, *BMJ*, 333(7564): 362–363.

Yarnell, J.W., Fehily, A.M. and Milbank, J.E. et al. (1983). A short dietary questionnaire for use in an epidemiological survey: comparison with weighed dietary records, *Hum.Nutr Appl.Nutr*, 37(2): 103–112.

Yang, C.C. and Hsu, Y.L. (2009) Development of a wearable motion detector for telemonitoring and real time identification of physical activity, *Telemedicine and e-Health*, 15: 62–72.

11

Future Developments and Applications: Emerging Technologies and New Approaches to Patients

Brian Tiplady and Bill Byrom

Amid all the hype about new computer technology it is easy to lose sight of the fact that paper is technology, the result of a long and diverse development which probably started with pictures scratched in the sand with a stick and continued though tree bark, tablets of wax and clay, sheets of crushed reed and scraped animal skins before it arrived at the plastic-wrapped ream of white A4. Like all important innovations, it is part of a web of associated technologies, including pens of various kinds, movable type, the printing press, book-binding, and photography.

Paper has many advantages. It is flexible, inexpensive and easy to use. It is readily available and requires nothing except a pen or pencil and enough light. For some purposes, however, its very flexibility becomes a problem. In many situations, including the recording of research results, it is necessary to structure the use of paper. This structuring takes two forms. Firstly, the paper itself may be modified, by printing as forms, by binding as notebooks, or a combination of the two, as with NCR paper, where several copies are produced when the form is filled in. The second aspect is structuring the process by setting up procedures to be followed and documented. Thus laboratory notebooks are bound but not spirally, as pages could be removed without leaving a trace, and have printed fields for entering date, project number, and signatures of the researcher and a witness. The process requires that changes should always be made by addition, not deletion. Whole books have been written on this process (see for example, Kanare 1985).

In an experimental setting, which includes clinical trials, such methods can work well with paper, provided there is an adequate level of supervision and monitoring. This is usually the case when a clinical researcher enters data into a Case Report Form in a clinic. However, when patients enter data, for example using a daily symptom diary, things are very different. In this unsupervised setting it is impossible to be sure patients are entering their data at the scheduled time. In the first chapter of this book Alan Shields and colleagues have explored the implications of this situation and presented evidence of the extent of the problem with unsupervised paper data collection.

The majority of this book has concerned the ways in which electronic methods of data collection can be used to provide valid patient reported data in clinical research. In nearly all the cases discussed, the electronic system replaces a paper method that is already in use. In many cases there is considerable experience with the paper system and a corresponding volume of validation data to support its use. This has two consequences. Firstly the electronic solution must be compared to the paper system and shown to produce equivalent data. The methods for this have been discussed by Paul Beatty and Damian McEntegart in Chapters 2 and 9. The second consequence is that the electronic solution is likely to be limited to matching what can be done with paper. The advantages of avoiding invalid entries, automatic navigation, time-stamping, compliance monitoring and so on described in earlier chapters, are of vital importance, of course, but the actual capture of data from the patient is likely to be modelled more or less precisely on that of the paper instrument.

This is changing. The systems used for ePRO are not just automated pieces of paper or scripts, they are active technologies that can go far beyond the ancient technology of paper. This chapter will look at what may be in store in the field of data collection directly from patients. We will start by looking at some of the areas other than clinical trials where this type of method is already in use. Areas such as telemedicine and monitoring aids offered directly to the public do not have the weight of established convention behind them, and so are more open to innovation. One might say they start with a blank slate, but that might be considered too backward-looking a metaphor in the circumstances! Breffni Martin (Chapter 10) has already introduced some of the ideas we will be developing in this chapter.

The practice of medicine generally uses a mixture of information reported by the patient (symptoms), information observed by the physician (signs), and objective measures such as exercise tolerance, laboratory tests and, lung function tests. In clinical trials, patients may record the results of objective tests they carry out themselves, for example peak flow or blood glucose measurements carried out at home and recorded in the symptom diary.

A simple example of the benefits of self-monitoring is the use of home blood pressure monitoring as a component of routine care for patients suffering from hypertension. Cappaccio et al. (2004) showed that more patients achieved clinic-recorded blood-pressure targets when using home blood pressure monitoring. The reason for these improved outcomes with self-monitoring is likely to be due to improved awareness of their condition and associated improvements due to drug treatment. This may result in increased motivation to maintain therapy and comply with a dosing regimen, thus improving overall effective health management. Where possible the involvement of patients in managing their own blood pressures is highly motivating and provides a greater feeling of sharing in the treatment and management of their condition (Byrom and Stein, 2007).

When electronic devices are used for these measurements they can transfer the data to a mobile phone or PDA for transmission along with ePRO data. This type of device integration has been available for some time, but its use is not yet widespread. The availability of relatively inexpensive devices which use Bluetooth wireless data transmission will likely lead to this technology becoming much more widely used. The rest of this chapter will review some of the trends which are emerging, both within the ePRO environment and in related areas of health provision and informatics.

Telemedicine has a long history. The term appears in Medline from 1974, but the first application which we would now think of as telemedicine was reported over half a century ago, with facsimile transmission of X-ray images from a rural hospital in Pennsylvania for expert evaluation in Philadelphia (Gershon-Cohen, 1950).

The initial aim of telemedicine was to improve health care in areas remote from specialist services by transmitting medical information rather than moving people. In the early applications, the patient was not alone – a nurse or physician would attend the patient, and the purpose of the telemedicine component was to bring specialist consultation into the diagnostic process.

However, as technology has changed, more general monitoring functions have become routine, and these can often be carried out by the patient, or, to an increasing extent, automated. In parallel, telemedicine has expanded to cover not just geographically remote areas, but to improve provision of healthcare to patients in their homes.

One of the powerful benefits of this approach is not only the collection of outcomes data by which the patient and physician can monitor progress, but also in the provision of targeted health-related feedback to patients based upon their recordings or observations. This is the concept of disease management programmes, which have been used successfully in many areas such as nutrition and exercise, smoking cessation and diabetes, in addition to delivery via a variety of modalities including IVR, mobile phones, PDAs and the internet.

For example, Friedman et al. (1996) report the evaluation of a disease management system for patients with hypertension that used regular scheduled IVR calls to interact with the patient. In their study, 267 hypertensive patients, aged 60 years and over (mean 76 years), entered the study which compared usual medical care with and without an IVR monitoring system. The IVR programme required subjects to call in on a weekly basis over a six-month treatment period. In addition to collection of outcomes (systolic and diastolic blood pressures), the IVR system also delivered questions regarding their understanding of their medication regimen (medication names, dosages and frequency of administration), their adherence to the regimen and whether they were experiencing any known side effects. The questioning delivered by the system was intended to ensure the correct dose was being taken, provide motivation to continue therapy, and provide positive feedback and encouragement for improvements seen along with advice on maintaining them. The concept was that the system would emulate the monitoring and counselling strategies and conversational style of a clinician. Each interaction with the IVR system typically took around 4 minutes per call. The study showed great value in this simple approach. Overall, medication adherence increased more amongst the patients receiving IVR monitoring, especially amongst the subgroup of patients that were non-adherent before the programme. In addition to this, the management programme was associated with greater improvements in blood pressure. For example, amongst patients defined non-adherent at baseline, systolic blood pressure was reduced by an average of 12.8 mm Hg with IVR compared to 0.9 mm Hg with routine care, and diastolic blood pressure reduced by an average of 6.0 mm Hg compared to an increase of 2.8 m Hg observed under routine care.

With the availability of more technology options comes the capability to deliver more sophisticated approaches in telemedicine. A good example of this is the support of patients with diabetes. Shea et al. (2009) describe the use of a monitoring system (IDEATel) in patients living in areas of New York State classified as underserved by medical services. Patients were supplied with a home telemedicine unit. This used a PC as its core as well as two monitors, for blood glucose and blood pressure, which were connected to the unit by cables. The PC transmitted data from the monitoring devices to the centre and also had a camera for videoconferences. This system has been evaluated over a five-year period, and showed an improvement in the control of diabetic patients compared to normal treatment.

The system is quite bulky (Figure 11.1a), and shows its age – the IDEATel project was set up in 2000. Nowadays most of the functions of a telemedicine system can be carried out by a mobile phone or wireless device, as shown in Figure 11.1b, using, for example, Bluetooth® to provide connectivity with other peripheral devices.

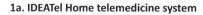

1a. IDEATel Home telemedicine system

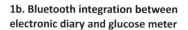

1b. Bluetooth integration between electronic diary and glucose meter

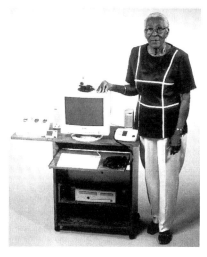

Figure 11.1   Early (1a) and more modern (1b) home telemedicine systems

As monitors get smaller and better connected, the possibilities increase. Not only does the use of several monitors become realistic; they can be carried around and so used more frequently, or they can be worn, with readings being taken continuously or automatically, so that apart from putting the device on, the user need do nothing. This is a very good way of improving compliance!

Wearable monitors may simply be strap-on devices. Figure 11.2 shows an example.

Wearable is becoming increasingly literal, with sensors being built in to garments such as shirts. There is now a category of e-textiles. For the disco-minded, this may refer to clothes which glow or change colour, but in the medical area it refers to fabrics which monitor body function with sensors built into the fibres (Paradiso and De Rossi, 2008).

Some monitors don't even need to be connected to the patient. A recently developed sleep monitor sits on the patient's bedside and uses a Doppler radar system to log the sleeper's movements and breathing. This allows the stages of sleep to be classified and recorded (de Chazal et al., 2008).

Some of this technology is already being used in the clinical trial area. Integration of devices such as glucose monitors and spirometers with diaries using phones or PDAs has been around for some while, though most of the published work so far has been in the area of service provision, not clinical research. This is likely to change before long.

Figure 11.2.   Example of a wearable ePRO devices: the Beurer Heart Rate Monitor Glove

Clinical research traditionally sees data flow as mostly a one way affair, with data flowing from the patient, via the investigator, to the research centre, where it is analysed. This has never been the case with telemedicine, which has used telephone and more recently video conferencing for exchange of communication between doctor and patient, and is increasingly using other methods such as the web and text messaging on mobile phones. Again these trends are reflected in research applications and this will continue. The communication from research site to patient thus far has mostly been around compliance. With ePRO, site staff can see in near real time which patients are filling in their diaries well and which are missing entries or completing them late. They can then contact patients in the latter group and offer help and encouragement. This has been shown to improve study compliance.

Two-way communication allows data that is appropriate to the situation to be provided to a patient. Patients often use the web to obtain information about their condition and the treatment they are taking, and this type of data can also be made available on a PDA or mobile phone.

The Cancer Care Research Centre at Stirling University has pioneered an approach of this kind for managing outpatients receiving chemotherapy. The symptoms of chemotherapy are often distressing, and sometimes serious. Blood dyscrasia, for example, can be fatal. It is therefore important to monitor such patients so that problems are dealt with promptly and effectively. Prof. Nora Kearney and her colleagues (Kearney et al., 2009) have set up a mobile phone system for this purpose.

The initial stage of this is a straightforward ePRO application. Patients fill in a symptom questionnaire on the phone twice a day, or at any time if their symptoms change. Data are sent to a central server by GPRS as soon as the entry is complete. The clever bit is what happens next. Firstly patients automatically receive self-care advice on the phone, tailored to the symptom pattern they are experiencing. This kind of approach has become increasingly practicable in recent years as the processing power available on small devices and phones has increased. We do not normally think of mobile phones as computers, but they are. A mid-range phone such as the Nokia 6300 has at least as much computing power as a Windows 95 PC from the mid 90s. Obviously it is a far better communications device. So it doesn't just have to be a data relay but can carry out real time analysis of data and give feedback or other information that is tailored to the needs of the specific patient.

The second action that can be taken on receipt of patient data is raising alerts whenever the pattern or severity of symptoms suggest more serious problems. These alerts, sent out through a pager system, have two levels of urgency. Amber alerts indicate an increasing symptom burden. Red alerts suggest more serious toxicity, and patients should be contacted within 1 hour in such cases. In this way potentially serious complications can be dealt with before they become really problematic.

Evaluation studies have shown that the system is practicable and generally well-accepted by patients and health professionals. There was concern in the Cancer Care group that the level of surveillance involved would be seen as intrusive or intimidating. Interviews with patients, however, did not indicate a problem of this sort. Patients felt the system gave them easier access to cancer specialists and were reassured, not threatened, by the monitoring and feedback process. One patient is worth quoting (Forbat et al., 2009).

> *just the whole experience is reassurance… because, you know, it's a big thing and, and the mind plays tricks, and left in the house on my own and all the rest of it for a while. But no, they were very, very good and, eh, and the fact that they were able to respond so quickly, as I say, was, was really great.*

Nursing staff also like the system, though some expressed concern about the workload generated by the amber alerts, especially in cases where they felt they could not add much to the advice already given. Clearly we need more evaluation, and it will be especially important to see the impact of such monitoring on the occurrence and outcomes of serious complications. These events are relatively uncommon, so larger studies will be needed to get reliable information, but this combination of monitoring, automated feedback and intervention seems a very powerful one.

In addition to enhancing the quality and integrity of data collected, the use of ePRO technology can provide additional features that enable us to take new and enhanced measurements from patients. EPRO provides us with the potential to do far more than we ever could using pencil and paper.

Electronic solutions can not only record the response or entry made by a patient, but also information about the nature of how that response was obtained. One example is in the delivery of cognitive function tests that can be administered to patients remotely and measuring, for example, the speed at which subjects respond to a stimulus. Such test batteries have been successfully delivered using IVR systems, mobile phone application and PDAs (see for example: Wesnes et al., 1999; Girdler et al., 2002; Tiplady, 1996; Tiplady et al., 2009). Because cognitive testing in clinical trials is normally performed using dedicated hardware and software at specialist centres, this new approach facilitates the measurement of cognition in large samples in a cost-effective way. It also affords the opportunity to provide such measures within primary and secondary care, simply and efficiently.

Electronic solutions have other additional features that can be useful in assessing patient reported outcomes. PDAs and IVR systems have the ability to record the voice of the patient, and such voice files have proved useful in a number of ways, two of which are described below and reviewed by Byrom (2006).

MEASUREMENT OF IMPROVEMENT FROM BASELINE

As described elsewhere in this book, particularly in Chapter 1, PRO instruments that require patients to rely upon memory, especially recall over a period of time, may threaten the accuracy of the data collected. Try to remember what you ate for dinner 7 days ago. Unless it was a special occasion you are unlikely to be able to. However, in clinical trials we often ask patients to rate their improvement or worsening in condition relative to a pre-treatment baseline which occurred a number of weeks previously. This is the basis of the commonly-used patient global impression of improvement (PGI-I) score in which patients rate themselves on a seven-point scale from 1 – very much better, to 7 – very much worse.

Voice recordings made by the patient have been successful in providing a memory anchor for a baseline state. One instrument, MERET (Memory Enhanced Retrospective Evaluation of Treatment, Healthcare Technology Systems) has shown promise in clinical trials, particularly in depression, where patients are asked to rate their improvement over time. At baseline, patients describe their feelings and experiences related to their condition in their own voice and words. Using the MERET instrument this is captured using an IVR system, but could also be done using a PDA. At further time points, this baseline recording can be played back to patients enabling accurate recall of their pre-treatment condition and rating of themselves relative to it using the same seven-point scale as the conventional PGI-I.

In therapy areas such as depression, it is interesting that not only the content of the recorded message helps the patient to anchor recall of their baseline status, but also the emotion, intonation, choice of words and hesitation provide additional cues to their condition at baseline. In depression, aspects of voice such as pitch variability and speaking rate relate to the severity of depression and so these additional measures can provide a rich quantity of additional information that is sub-consciously interpreted by the patient when listening to the pre-treatment recording providing enhanced insight into his/her baseline condition.

Proof of concept studies using MERET have provided encouraging results. One study in 74 depressed patients (Mundt et al., 2005) indicated that MERET was more sensitive to detecting treatment-related improvements than the standard PGI-I. In this study, depressed patients received up to four weeks treatment with duloxetine or placebo. MERET recordings were made prior to entering the double-blind phase, and patients were asked to provide improvement ratings four weeks later. Patients self-rated changes on the PGI-I first, then listened to baseline MERET recordings before providing a second rating. Although in this study both PGI-I and MERET ratings showed significant improvements on active treatment compared to placebo, MERET scores showed greater separation and effect size compared to the conventional PGI-I. Using pre-treatment experiential anchors in this way appears to enhance patients' ability to perceive the magnitude of their change in clinical condition.

VOICE ACOUSTICS ANALYSIS

Related to MERET and the auditory cues a voice recording can provide, there are more formal methods that can be used to analyse and interpret voice recordings. Voice acoustic measures have been developed that provide sensitive indicators of disease severity and therapeutic response in many CNS disorders, including Parkinson's disease, depression and schizophrenia. This is well illustrated by Cannizzaro et al. (2004) who report a study that investigated the relationship between voice metrics and depression severity. In this study, researchers captured and digitised voice samples from seven depression rating interview videos, selecting patients across a range of depression severity. The videos used were those routinely available for use in investigator training events for depression clinical trials to enable investigators to standardise the way they rate patients using the Hamilton Depression Rating Scale (HAM-D). Voice samples comprised the first 10 seconds of uninterrupted speech, and voice acoustic measures were made on the middle 5 second interval starting at the onset of a word, using commercially available software. The measures investigated were speaking rate (number of syllables spoken in the 5 second interval), per cent pause time (sum duration of pauses over 250 ms in duration expressed as a percentage of the 5 second interval) and pitch variation (a measure of how highly intonated or monotonic the voice is). Their results confirmed what is normally observed amongst depression patients that speech slows and becomes more monotonic with increasing severity of depression. Their formal analysis showed strong correlations between the HAM-D score and both speaking rate and pitch variation measured in the voice acoustics analysis.

Normally, these kinds of voice acoustics measures are made in a specialist voice laboratory but a follow-up study by Cannizzaro et al. (2005) showed that voice samples suitable for voice acoustics analysis could be reliably captured remotely via the telephone using an IVR system, and we propose that the same would be true of other ePRO modalities. In future it may therefore be possible to make these measurements from patients in a simple and cost-effective manner in large clinical studies or in routine care. However, much more work needs to be completed in validating and understanding these endpoints for use in future clinical trials.

The evolution of ePRO depends to a large extent on the development of technology in the areas of portable computing, telecommunications, and information science. The ePRO market is so far too small to lead to important technological developments just for patient data collection. So we must make use of the devices and systems that have become available primarily for consumer or corporate use. An example of this type of opportunity is the inclusion of accelerometers in recent smartphones. These can be used to continuously monitor the activity of the person carrying the phone, allowing, for example, monitoring of the amount of exercise a patient takes without the need for an additional device. Other types of technology can also be used for this purpose, for example the infrared motion detector. We are most familiar with these as security devices, for example to detect intruders, but they are increasingly being used to detect movements by the occupant of a room.

One use for this is to make a house more efficient and comfortable. For example if no one is in a particular room an IR sensor can detect this and turn down the heating and lighting. But there are major healthcare possibilities. As long ago as the 1980s, Edinburgh sheltered housing had pressure mats and infrared sensors in its rooms, to reduce both the workload and the intrusiveness of its wardens' monitoring of patients' activity (McLuckie, 1984).

Dealing with the healthcare implications of an ageing population has become a major preoccupation of planners in the last few years. As people age, the demands they place on the health system increase. Maintaining the independence of older people with health problems becomes a priority, both because people wish to live in their own homes whenever possible, and because residential care is expensive. The telemedicine approach can provide ways of supporting this independence. The aim is to provide a 'health smart home'

The smart home provides an integrated environment combining monitoring and communication. Sensors distributed around the home build up a picture of the normal behaviour of the inhabitants, and any deviations from this that could indicate deterioration in health are noted. This aspect of the monitoring is passive – the person does not have to wear anything, the sensors are part of the house. In addition, there can be active monitoring of specific aspects of health, which can include the types of physiological and ePRO methods discussed above. What makes this approach different, however, is integration. All the different types of sensor communicate using a standard protocol, and all the types of information are combined to form an overall picture of the person's activity and well-being.

An example will help an understanding of the importance of communications protocols. Once upon a time, when a telephone company provided a service to a customer, it not only brought the line into the house but provided and installed the telephone as well. Replacing this with another phone of your choice was not allowed. These days are long gone, and nowadays when it installs the line the service provider has no idea what manufacturer's phone you will choose, whether you will have one or several phones, whether they will be cordless or corded, and so on. Nevertheless, phones still work pretty well. Looking at the system from the other end, when you make a call you have no idea whether it is going along copper wires, fibre, microwave links or by satellite. This kind of inter-operability is achieved by setting standards that apply to the interfaces between the different components of the system. The computer term for this is 'Plug and Play'. Such standards are vital, not just for a phone network, but for the networks used in everything from a smart home to an intensive care unit (Wallin and Weintraub, 2004; Martinez et al., 2007).

When ePRO vendors set up patient diaries and questionnaires for a clinical trial, they still generally behave like the old-style telecom companies and provide all the components of the system in a fixed package. However, suppose they designed their systems as a specification rather than as an application to run on a specific device? Such a specification could be supplied to different devices each of which could then present the questionnaire and collect responses according to its own characteristics. The technology to do this already exists. The specification would probably be written in XML, a definition language related to html. The application to run the specification could be a browser, or a more specialised system geared to the needs of standardised questionnaire presentation.

This is not a new idea – Mikael Palmblad and one of us (Brian Tiplady) set up a system of this sort in the mid-90s, with a single specification being used to generate questionnaires on an Apple Newton, on a Macintosh computer, or on paper. We later added Windows CE (which was the core of what later became Windows Mobile).

Ideally such a specification would be used from day one of development of a new questionnaire, and tested in parallel on different platforms as the questionnaire was refined. In this way, each mode of presentation would be equally valid – the issue of showing equivalence between a new form and the 'gold standard' original paper form would disappear. So if we want to use a PDA in our early clinical trials, and IVR in the later large-scale trials, we can do so knowing that data from the two modes are interchangeable. At present we have to do quite a lot of work to document this.

A major initiative is under way to develop item banks for PRO use – the PROMIS programme, funded by the National Institutes of Health in the USA. In this programme, development is aimed at both paper and electronic administration of items from the very beginning and one of the initial validation studies used large scale internet administration of outcomes questionnaires (www.nihpromis.org).

Perhaps we could also offer patients choice. Some patients might prefer to fill in diaries on the web, some on a phone, some on a PDA. Some may also wish to use their own mobile phone rather than one provided by the study, and in this case the instrument would be delivered across a variety of different mobile phone displays and screen sizes. Usability and validation testing may need to be performed across a range of units for researchers to be comfortable with this approach, but in routine healthcare where it is only the individual's response and their changes that count, this is not a barrier.

The methods used in clinical research are connected to the broader world in two main ways. Firstly to the practice of medicine itself, and secondly to the technology available to the consumer and corporate users in other fields. It hardly needs emphasising that both these fields are developing rapidly. The connections between them are also becoming increasingly important. In this chapter we have tried to show some of the ways in which these developments will affect ePRO, and more generally the way in which the patients' involvement in clinical trials will change as patient reported outcomes move beyond what can be done with paper, and indeed moves beyond the collection of outcomes to become a two-way (or multi-way) communication system. We have, of course, only scratched the surface of this topic. In the words of the sage 'You ain't seen nuthin' yet'.

References

Byrom, B. (2006). Innovative ePRO: tapping into the potential, *Applied Clinical Trials*, 15(6): 64–75.

Byrom, B. and Stein, D. (2007). The use of interactive communications technology in disease management and compliance/persistence programmes, in *Patient Compliance and Sweetening the Pill*, M. Davies and F. Kermani, (eds), Gower.

Cannizzaro, M., Harel, B. and Reilly, N. et al. (2004). Voice acoustical measurement of the severity of major depression, *Brain and Cognition*, 56(1): 30–35.

Cannizzaro, M.S., Reilly, N. and Mundt, J.C. et al. (2005). Remote capture of human voice acoustical data by telephone: a methods study, *Clin Linguist Phon*, 19(8): 649–658.

Cappuccio, F.P., Kerry, S.M. and Forbes, L. et al. (2004). Blood pressure control by home monitoring: meta-analysis of randomised trials, *BMJ*, 329(7458): 145.

De Chazal, P., O'Hare, E. and Fox, N. et al. (2008). Assessment of sleep/wake patterns using a non-contact biomotion sensor. *Conf Proc IEEE Eng Med Biol Soc*, 514–7.

Forbat, L., Maguire, R. and McCann, L. et al. (2009). The use of technology in cancer care: applying Foucault's ideas to explore the changing dynamics of power in health care, *J Adv.Nurs*, 65(2): 306–315.

Friedman, R.H., Kazis, L.E. and Jette, A. et al. (1996). A telecommunications system for monitoring and counseling patients with hypertension. Impact on medication adherence and blood pressure control, *Am.J Hypertens*, 9(4) Pt 1: 285–292.

Gershon-Cohen, J. and Cooley, A.G. (1950). Telognosis, *Radiology*, 55(4): 582–587.

Girdler, N.M., Lyne, J.P. and Wallace, R. et al. (2002). A randomised, controlled trial of cognitive and psychomotor recovery from midazolam sedation following reversal with oral flumazenil, *Anaesthesia*, 57(9): 868–876.

Kanare, H.M. (1985). *Writing the Laboratory Notebook*. Wiley.

Kearney, N., McCann, L. and Norrie, J. et al. (2009). Evaluation of a mobile phone-based, advanced symptom management system (ASyMS) in the management of chemotherapy-related toxicity, *Supportive Care in Cancer*, 17(4): 437–444.

Martinez, I., Fernandez, J. and Galarraga, M. et al. (2007). Implementation experience of a patient monitoring solution based on end-to-end standards, *Conf.Proc.IEEE Eng Med Biol.Soc*, 6426–6429.

McLuckie, I. (1984). Advanced communications for sheltered housing, *Electronics and Power*, 374–378.

Mundt, J.C., De Brota, D.J. and Moore, H.K. et al. (2005). Memory Enhanced Retrospective Evaluation of Treatment (MERET): Anchoring patients' perceptions of clinical change in the past. 45th Annual Meeting of the New Clinical Drug Evaluation Unit Program, Boca Raton, FL, USA, Abstract 1–30.

Paradiso, R. and De Rossi, R.D. (2008). Advances in textile sensing and actuation for e-textile applications, *Conf.Proc.IEEE Eng Med Biol.Soc*, 3629.

Shea, S., Weinstock, R.S. and Teresi, J.A. et al. (2009). A randomized trial comparing telemedicine case management with usual care in older, ethnically diverse, medically underserved patients with diabetes mellitus: 5 year results of the ideatel study, *Journal of the American Medical Informatics Association*, 16(4): 446–456.

Tiplady, B. (1996). Use of a personal digital assistant to administer a visual search task, *Journal of Psychopharmacology*, 10(3): A27.

Tiplady, B., Oshinowo, B., Thomson, J. and Drummond, G.B. (2009). Alcohol and cognitive function: assessment in everyday life and laboratory settings using mobile phones, *Alcoholism Clinical and Experimental Research*, 33: 2094–2102.

Wallin, M.K.E.B. and Weintraub, S. (2004). Evaluation of bluetooth as a replacement for cables in intensive care and surgery, *Anesthesia Analgesia*, 98: 763–767.

Wesnes, K.A., Ward, T. and Ayre, G. et al. (1999). Development and validation of a system for evaluating cognitive functioning over the telephone for use in late phase drug development, *European Neuropsychopharmacology*, 9(5): 368.

Index